George Meléndez Wright

George Meléndez Wright

The Fight for Wildlife and Wilderness in the National Parks

JERRY EMORY

The University of Chicago Press
Chicago and London

The University of Chicago Press, Chicago 60637
The University of Chicago Press, Ltd., London
© 2023 by Jerry Emory
Foreword © 2023 by Jonathan Jarvis
Published 2023
Printed in the United States of America

32 31 30 29 28 27 26 25 24 23   2 3 4 5

ISBN-13: 978-0-226-82494-9 (cloth)
ISBN-13: 978-0-226-82495-6 (e-book)
DOI: https://doi.org/10.7208/chicago/9780226824956.001.0001

Library of Congress Cataloging-in-Publication Data

Names: Emory, Jerry, author.
Title: George Melendez Wright : the fight for wildlife and wilderness in the
    national parks / Jerry Emory.
Description: Chicago : The University of Chicago Press, 2023. |
    Includes bibliographical references and index.
Identifiers: LCCN 2022028845 | ISBN 9780226824949 (cloth) |
    ISBN 9780226824956 (ebook)
Subjects: LCSH: Wright, George M. (George Melendez), 1904–1936. |
    National parks and reserves—United States. | Wildlife conservation—United States.
Classification: LCC QH76 .E46 2023 | DDC 333.720973 23/eng/20220—dc03
LC record available at https://lccn.loc.gov/2022028845

♾ This paper meets the requirements of ANSI/NISO Z39.48-1992
(Permanence of Paper).

This book is dedicated to
Pamela Meléndez Wright Lloyd
who has kept her father's life and legacy
alive so others could learn.

But it is the birds of the water, beautifully wild birds by the thousand, that are encouragement and inspiration to the man who prays for conviction that the wilderness still lives, will always live. . . . Sometimes while I am watching these birds on the water, the illusion of the untouchability of this wilderness becomes so strong that it is stronger than reality, and the polished roadway becomes the illusion, the mirage that has no substance.

GEORGE WRIGHT, "The Primitive Persists in Bird Life
of Yellowstone Park," 1935

Contents

Foreword

JONATHAN B. JARVIS

In 1982, I was selected by the National Park Service (NPS) to participate in its first Natural Resources Management Trainee Program. I was pulled from a district ranger position at Guadalupe Mountains National Park in Texas and sent to Crater Lake National Park in Oregon as the park biologist. My trainee colleagues, twenty of us in total, were reclassified as biologists and sent to other national parks such as Mount Rainier, Olympic, and Yosemite. Over the course of the next two years, we were trained to build a natural resources program based on science in each of our parks. For guidance and inspiration, we turned to the life, legacy, vision, and writings of George Meléndez Wright.

The issues that the parks faced in the 1980s were essentially the same as Wright saw them in the 1930s, captured in his pioneering publication *Fauna No. 1*, the first wildlife survey of its kind. The lack of basic science to inform management decisions had enormous consequences for park resources—and conservation across America. Crater Lake National Park was a perfect example: the NPS basically knew nothing about Crater Lake itself other than that it was deep, cold, and blue. When an independent scientist noted that the famous clarity of the lake was declining, the NPS was caught flat-footed and defensive. The NPS had never seriously invested in monitoring the lake's water quality since the park was established in 1902. As the new park biologist, it became my responsibility to build a program of both research and monitoring for this magnificent and challenging lake. It was also my intent to embed the program so that monitoring the lake was as much a part of the park operation as putting up the US flag each day and greeting the visitors. Just as Wright worked with scientists from the University of California, Berkeley, I reached out to scientists at Oregon State University to apply rigor to the research and to design the monitoring program. My colleagues were doing the same with their parks, taking on complex issues and building programs that would last. Our resource specialists joined the newly established George Wright Society en masse and gathered every few years at conferences to share our successes and failures and to recognize those who embodied the spirit of Wright.

For those of us committed to changing the trajectory of conservation in the National Park system, Wright's legacy was an inspiration but also carried a warning. With his untimely death, investment in science-informed decisions died with him, for five decades. This time, we needed to not only pick up where he left off but also to institutionalize a comprehensive natural resources program at all levels. Our cadre, just like Wright, faced internal resistance from an entrenched NPS culture, more focused on the visitor and facilities than on the resource. In Wright's time, park wildlife was viewed as entertainment for the visitor—exemplified by the bear-feeding platforms in Yellowstone—and he saw these activities as inappropriate for national parks. In our time, while many of these inappropriate activities had been phased out, the attitude persisted that if we just left the wildlife and other resources alone, everything would be fine. Wright knew this approach was also wrong, and it was still wrong fifty years later. The new band of natural resource specialists began to grow with successive training programs, and the NPS made many new hires with advanced science degrees. As parks faced increasingly complex issues such as acid rain, invasive species, wildfire, air and water pollution, or human and wildlife conflicts, NPS leadership turned to these specialists to help craft solutions. For better or worse, depending on your perspective, park rangers began to focus more on law enforcement and, due to a peculiarity of federal job classification, became eligible to retire with only twenty years of service. Their early exits created a vacuum in top positions that this more scientifically trained group began to fill. These new national park leaders, now more attuned to the needs of the resource, began the slow and complex process of restoring park ecosystems such as returning wolves to Yellowstone, removing the dams on the Elwha River of Olympic, and restoring water flows into the Everglades. Now, almost a century beyond the pioneering work of Wright, the NPS has a long-term monitoring program that provides usable scientific knowledge for decision makers facing the challenges of climate change.

As Jerry Emory so eloquently details in the following book, George Meléndez Wright was ahead of his time, a visionary blessed with a warm and friendly demeanor that won him many friends and fueled his influence. His impact on the conservation of our national parks, though stalled for a period but picked up by my NPS generation, is immeasurable. There is another generation on the rise within the NPS, one that is more representative of the diversity of the nation, more attuned to the conservation challenges of the world, and more respectful of indigenous stewardship. They want to make a difference and there can be no better inspiration than the life of George Meléndez Wright.

Jonathan B. Jarvis served as a natural resource specialist in the National Park Service from 1982 to 1991, followed by several assignments as a park superintendent and later a regional director. From 2009 through 2017 he was the eighteenth director of the National Park Service.

Preface
Field Notes and Family

George Meléndez Wright's career has been described as stellar; his ideas regarding wildlife, wilderness, ecosystem management (before the term "ecosystem" was even coined), predator control, and conservation, as visionary. When he first arrived in Yosemite National Park in 1927 to work as a ranger naturalist—the first Hispanic to occupy a professional position in the National Park Service (NPS), at the young age of twenty-three—he had already visited every national park in the western United States, including Alaska, and knew more about the parks than most employees of the relatively new agency. In short order, he would go on to organize the first wildlife survey of western national parks, forever changing how the National Park Service would manage wildlife and natural resources. Before his revolutionary ideas began to influence NPS policy, however, Wright faced persistent pushback by an entrenched park service culture that disregarded wildlife except for the role fauna played as spectacle for tourists. Nonetheless, he prevailed.

I was first introduced to Wright because I fell in love with, and eventually married, one of his granddaughters: Jeannie Lloyd. In the early 1980s, Jeannie and I met on the University of California, Berkeley campus. Her mother, Pamela Meléndez Wright Lloyd, is one of Wright's daughters, and in Pam's possession were some incredible materials detailing her father's life and career: personal papers; numerous black-and-white photographs of Wright in the field and with his wife Bernice "Bee" Ray (Pam's mother); National Park Service documents; and, carefully tucked away in a box at the Lloyd house, three small blue canvas binders packed with some five hundred pages of intriguing field notes neatly written by Wright. The notes spanned 1930 to 1933—during which, I would learn, Wright and two colleagues conducted their groundbreaking scientific survey of wildlife in the western national parks.

The moment I opened the first binder, I instantly knew an irrefutable fact: Wright had been a student of Professor Joseph Grinnell at Berkeley's Museum of Vertebrate Zoology. The dimensions of the binder, the 6" × 9½" three-hole paper, and the precise note taking were the system taught by Grinnell to all of his students. I was certain of this because I had taken a field zoology class at Berkeley and had learned the exact same system of recording field notes, sixty years after the young Wright. My single blue canvas binder of field notes rests on a shelf behind me as I write this.

In the top right-hand corner of the first page of Wright's notebooks, the number "77" was written. According to Grinnell's strict method, notes were kept sequentially over your entire career. This meant: There must be more notes. Thus began the pursuit of Wright's entire collection of notes, and of the stories they would reveal about this remarkable young man from San Francisco.

Jeannie and I eventually found pages 1 through 76 of Wright's notes, not at the museum but in Yosemite National Park's old library—secure in a dusty box on a top shelf. Later, at the museum on the Berkeley campus, we discovered yet another notebook. The latter was from the summer of 1926, when Wright, then twenty-two, accompanied legendary field biologist Joseph Dixon to Alaska's Mount McKinley National Park, now Denali, on a collecting trip. In total, we gathered almost seven hundred pages of field notes—encompassing Wright's entire career as a field biologist, including his observations and thoughts as he traveled throughout the West and Alaska. Spellings, punctuation, and emphasis (underlining or italics) from these notebooks and other documents have been reproduced per the originals throughout this book.

Many years later, I met Pam's aunt, Mathilda Jane Ray (called Jane, and Bee's sister), and Jane's husband, Ben Thompson. For some ten years, Ben was Wright's best friend and thought partner. Together, he and Wright, along with Dixon, made up the trio of Park Service biologists that conducted that pioneering wildlife survey. In the late 1980s Jeannie and I were fortunate to spend a handful of days with the Thompsons, then in their eighties. Over the course of several days, I talked with Ben about the early years of the wildlife survey, and about Wright. It was because of those conversations that my resolve to pursue this biography was solidified.

This book, which draws on hundreds of letters, field notes, interviews, and other primary documents, is both a biography of Wright and a historical account of his time and of the colleagues with whom he worked. It explores and celebrates what was so special about this young man, his unique upbringing and dynamic personality, his vision for science-based wildlife management in our parks, his place of honor in the pantheon of American conservationists, and how his life and legacy are relevant to this day—even, or especially, because of the tragically short span of his career.

Wright was only thirty-one years old when he died in a car accident, leaving behind a wife, two young daughters, and a résumé of remarkable accomplishments and writings one might expect from a biologist twice his age. To this day, wildlife experts and park managers reference Wright's work, and yet surprisingly little is known about him by most natural and cultural resource professionals, academics, conservationists, and the public. Hopefully, this book is a step in the right direction to correct that.

Almost forty years after I met Jeannie and held that first notebook, I present, on the following pages, the story of George Meléndez Wright and his relentless effort to save the wildlife, and wilderness, in the national parks.

Jerry Emory
Mill Valley, California

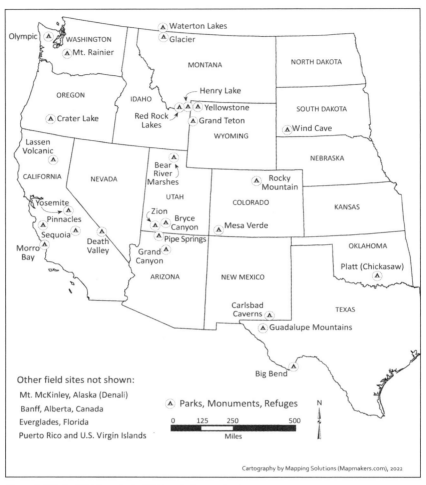

Other field sites not shown:

Mt. McKinley, Alaska (Denali)

Banff, Alberta, Canada

Everglades, Florida

Puerto Rico and U.S. Virgin Islands

Parks, Monuments, Refuges

0   125   250   500
Miles

N

Cartography by Mapping Solutions (Mapmakers.com), 2022

George Meléndez Wright, principal fieldwork sites, 1926–36.

Serendipity

Benjamin Hunter Thompson had a stellar thirty-five-year career with the National Park Service (NPS). While studying for a master's degree in 1929 at the University of California, Berkeley's Museum of Vertebrate Zoology (MVZ), Thompson began working part-time for the Park Service's newly formed wildlife team, based out of a small office near campus. For the next several years, until he completed his master's degree in 1932 and became a full-time Park Service employee, Ben spent every free moment he had crisscrossing the western United States as part of a select trio of biologists studying wildlife management issues in national parks. Ben and his colleagues were on the road for months at a time, rain or shine (or snow), living out of a converted Buick, sleeping on the ground for the most part, occasionally bunking in unoccupied Park Service cabins, and hiking into the backcountry to assess wildlife conditions.

All three were well-trained biologists, but one—whom Ben met by chance—was the undisputed leader, a charismatic champion of science-based wildlife management and conservation in an era when that was rare. Although the three were from very different backgrounds and possessed very different temperaments, together they pursued innovative work that fundamentally changed the way America's national parks are managed. This trio of field scientists were gently forged into a team by a remarkable young man, far too little known today: George Meléndez Wright.

Thompson had an exemplary career indeed—mostly in a management position, inside the Park Service's Washington, DC, office. But in 1987, when Jeannie and I were visiting Ben and his wife Jane at their home in Glenwood, New Mexico, and we sat down to talk in their living room, it was the fieldwork and the wildlife studies of the early 1930s that lived most vividly in Ben's mind. Thompson had graduated from Stanford University in the spring of 1928 with a degree in philosophy. He was planning on returning to pursue a PhD but had decided to take a break from his studies. "My brother Web and I had worked in Yosemite every summer since 1925," he recalled to me. "I took off the winter of 1928 to work there to make some extra money, and that's where I met George."[1] Ben worked as a "hasher" (waiter) at the newly opened Ahwahnee Hotel in Yosemite Valley—back then, a remote and extremely small community and yet already a world-renowned destination.

George Wright had joined the Park Service during the fall of 1927 as an assistant naturalist in Yosemite National Park. Every morning he walked from the rangers' quarters to the Ahwahnee, with the quiet, gray face of Half Dome looming straight ahead, and North Point and Glacier Point rising to the north and south respectively. He undertook this early constitutional in order to bring coffee to the room of the woman that raised him, his great-aunt, Cordelia Ward Wright. She had followed Wright to Yosemite when he was hired, and she took up residence in the newly completed hotel. He would repeat the trek most evenings to have dinner with his "Auntie," as he called her. Thompson began encountering Wright almost daily.

In his free time, Thompson visited the park's museum and library, where Wright worked, to read and study. He also participated in nature hikes that Wright and his colleagues conducted for the public. Thompson and Wright soon became good friends. "After that winter," Thompson told me, "I asked myself, do I really want to return for a doctorate in philosophy?" Thompson began to learn about the animals and plants around him. Within a few months, Wright had convinced his new friend to forgo his philosophy studies and instead enroll at the University of California in Berkeley, where Wright had studied. Wright wanted Thompson to train under Joseph Grinnell at the Museum of Vertebrate Zoology, as he had done, and then join him in the National Park Service.

Thompson, the philosopher and nascent biologist, did just that.

Just as Wright saw a sharp and inquisitive mind, and new friend, in Thompson, so too Thompson was impressed with the gregarious and persuasive young biologist. After all, it only took a few short months for Thompson to decide to place his future in Wright's hands. "George was only five feet four inches tall, with a dark complexion," Ben remembered with a smile. "He was a jovial person, always a ready wit with humor. Not only was he very perceptive of people, he was good with people, outgoing, honest, motivated. People sensed that, and they reacted to it."

During the early months of 1929, Wright began sharing an idea with Thompson that he had been formulating for over a year. He wanted to do something that had never been done before in the National Park Service: pursue wide-ranging field studies focusing on the status of wildlife species in the western national parks, and then use this information to create science-based wildlife management practices for the parks. Wright had been developing this wildlife survey concept while he worked in and explored Yosemite. He had also been discussing it with several of his mentors, but mostly with a fellow Grinnell student from Berkeley's Museum of Vertebrate Zoology—a bespectacled, taciturn yet consummate field zoologist named Joseph Scattergood Dixon, twenty years Wright's senior.

By June of 1929, the wildlife survey was a reality. Wright and Dixon opened a Park Service office in the American Trust Building next to the Berkeley campus and Thompson was enrolled at the university and studying under Joseph Grinnell. In the spring of 1930, Wright, Dixon, and Thompson started their first season of fieldwork in the national parks. George Wright was twenty-five years old.

1

The Magic Window

This is a story of many years ago, of things that were told by the magic kitchen window in an old home on Laguna Street in San Francisco. A very magic window this, for grown-ups could rub and rub its glass without ever seeing more than a very indifferent backyard, while children had merely to press their adaptable little noses against its cool surface to find themselves in an enchanted world full of the most exciting adventures.[1]

This idyllic introduction to a short recollection, "The Magic Window," about two young brothers staring out to their small backyard from the safety of their kitchen, was written by Wright at the age of thirty, reflecting back on his childhood in San Francisco's Pacific Heights neighborhood. The five-year-old in the story is Wright himself; the four-year-old his younger brother Charles.[2] The story begins with tragedy—they watch as their pet guinea pig is snatched up and carried away by a "marauding Scotch terrier"—but the narrative quickly refocuses on the world of birds as viewed through that pane of glass, foretelling how those experiences would prepare the author for a life spent in pursuit of wildlife and wild places.

The story continues on to explain how Wright installed a birdbath in the small backyard and how, with time, more and more birds discovered this well-protected spot behind the Wrights' Laguna Street Victorian to have a drink and take prolonged baths. Soon after, a feeding tray was added, and the budding young ornithologist quickly busied himself with adding new species to his list.[3]

Wright learned a lot through that cool, kitchen window. It was an opportunity for the young naturalist to read, observe, and record—to set the tenor and passion for his life to come.

On June 20, 1904, George Meléndez Wright was born into the two dynamic families whose names he bore. His parents were John Tennant Wright and Mercedes Meléndez Ramírez. John Wright was born in 1856 in San Francisco to a wealthy steamship captain, George Sutton Wright, and his wife Louise Ward. Two of John Wright's uncles and his paternal grandfather were also captains, all of whom traveled west from New York City between 1849 and 1850 and formed the Wright Line of steamships in San Francisco.[4] Their steamers carried passengers and merchandise up and down the West Coast of the Americas during the height of the gold rush and through the end of the nineteenth century—from British Columbia to Peru. Along with a few other individuals and families, the Wrights were shipping pioneers and hard-nosed businessmen during a time of phenomenal expansion in San Francisco and in California as a whole.[5]

Images of San Francisco's shoreline and its long line of docks—the Embarcadero—during the gold rush years show such a multitude of clipper ships and steamboats as to appear preposterous. Between April 1847 and April 1848 only eleven ships dropped anchor off San Francisco. After James Marshall discovered gold in January 1848, on California's South Fork of the American River at Sutter's Mill, however, word spread around the world. By early 1849, an estimated six hundred and fifty vessels crammed the waterfront and dropped off some ninety thousand fortune seekers and merchants. In just two years the city's population surged from one thousand to an estimated forty thousand, and the total number of anchored vessels increased to around a thousand. And, except for the commercial steamboats, practically none of these ships left the port. Most vessels were abandoned—the owners and crews having fled east to the Sierra Nevada and the gold fields—while others were converted to warehouses, stores, hotels, offices, and other uses.[6]

The coastal shipping industry was so fierce in the early 1850s that some steamship lines merged to form the California Steam Navigation Company in 1854, in order to suppress competition and stabilize pricing. The Wrights and their steamers, however, held out. And soon their stubbornness paid off: the newly formed company decided to pay the Wrights $5,000 a month to *not* sail their ships, adding to the family's growing assets.[7]

Mercedes Meléndez was born in 1865 in San Salvador, El Salvador. She was the second of ten children of Rafael Meléndez and Mercedes Ramírez. Her father died in 1880, but Doña Meléndez, twenty years his junior, took over the family businesses from her husband and thrived until the age of eighty-eight.

The Meléndez family was among the most powerful, and largest, families in the country. They owned plantations across El Salvador and produced principally coffee and sugar for export. Between 1913 and 1927, two of Mercedes Meléndez's brothers and one brother-in-law were presidents of El Salvador, passing the office back and forth to each other like a fraternal baton: Carlos and Jorge Meléndez and Alfonso Quiñónez (married to Mercedes's sister Leonor Meléndez).[8]

It was, at the time, common for wealthy Salvadoran families to send their children to either the United States or Europe for schooling, and this was exactly what the Meléndez family did. Several of the daughters were sent to San Francisco for education, while some of the sons sailed to Europe. It is not clear, however, where Mercedes pursued her education.

Meanwhile, John Wright was following the tradition of his family's shipping business, on the commerce side. With the help of his father and uncles, he created the San Francisco–based John T. Wright & Company in 1877, importing and exporting goods on the Pacific coast. The company maintained additional offices, or representatives, out of Guatemala, El Salvador, Panama, and South America. They exported fertilizers, lumber, typewriters, flour, iron tanks, and machinery. On the import side it was a bit simpler: mostly sugar and hardwoods, but Wright also imported coffee from El Salvador.[9]

How John Wright and Mercedes Meléndez met is uncertain. It could be that they met in San Francisco while she was attending Catholic school, or perhaps they were introduced during one of Wright's coffee-buying trips to El Salvador. What is known is that they married in San Salvador, El Salvador, in January 1892.[10] Wright was thirty-eight and Meléndez was twenty-nine. They settled in San Francisco, and Wright's company flourished. The gold rush might have faded, but at the close of the nineteenth century, San Francisco was the most important port on the West Coast.[11]

The Wrights had an active social life and a full house, filled with both English and Spanish. They also traveled back and forth between San Francisco and San Salvador for business and family. By 1894, two of Mercedes's sisters—Elena and Carmen—were in San Francisco attending Miss Lake's School and, most likely, living with the Wrights.[12] On December 21, 1896, the Wrights welcomed their first son into the family. He was also named John Tennant Wright. In 1900, they purchased their new house on Laguna Street. George was born on June 20, 1904, and Charles followed right on the heels of his brother and was born on June 19, 1905, just one day shy of George's first birthday.[13] Life was full in the Wright household.

The Magic Window's tragic beginning reflects, in a small way, the early heartbreaks of George's young life and the lives of his brothers. On April 11, 1906, Mercedes Meléndez Wright died suddenly of acute appendicitis. Her body was eventually transported back to El Salvador and buried in the family plot. Charles was only ten months old and George wasn't even two; John was ten. A week later, the great San Francisco fire and earthquake consumed a large portion of the city. The fire stopped at Van Ness Avenue, just four blocks short of the Wright residence, which still stands to this day.

The boys' father kept the household together as best he could with the help of his stepmother—Cordelia Ward Wright, or Auntie—who moved into the Laguna Street home after her husband passed away in 1905.[14] By 1910, at least four additional people lived with the Wrights, most likely relatives, all with Spanish surnames, including one Meléndez. That same year John Wright took all three of his boys to El Salvador to visit family. The youngest boy, Charles (also called Carlos), was left in the care of the extended Meléndez family to be raised there.[15]

By 1912, another tragedy struck: the boys' father was dying from a terrible cancer. In March, and then again in May, he wrote two significant letters to his sister-in-law, Carmen Meléndez de Letona (living in Paris), that give some rare insight into household activities and the status of the young Wright brothers.[16] He informed her that he had just finished incorporating his business so the boys could inherit it equally and "continue my business without interruption." And George, he wrote, was always with Auntie, who "teaches him every day for several hours." The distraught father, who was in great pain, also confirmed that he had to leave Carlos in San Salvador. "I have nobody to look after him. Auntie is so busy with George it is almost impossible to speak to her."

John Wright died a few months later. He was fifty-six. Afterward, George's brother John (also known as Juan), then sixteen, moved to El Salvador to join Carlos and live with his family there. Although he traveled back and forth to San Francisco over the years, John would make El Salvador his home. From the fall of 1912 forward, Auntie and George's obvious bond was cemented. All they had were each other. They were family. Auntie was seventy-two and George was eight.

A month after his father's death, Wright started school at the nearby Pacific Heights Grammar, walking the four or five blocks every morning and afternoon. A few years later, with a bird book in hand, he began adventuring around a San Francisco that looked very different from today's crowded, urban landscape. Wright wasn't content to sit at his kitchen window anymore. He wanted to get outside, explore, and learn.

> Recreation or "re-creation" for one man may consist in occupying 3 square feet while reading a book, while for another it may require thousands of acres of wilderness.
> NATIONAL RESOURCES BOARD[17]

There were three parks in Wright's immediate neighborhood, and the wildlands around Fort Mason and the Presidio could also be readily accessed. While a portion of today's Sunset District had street names on paper, it remained mostly sand dunes, rolling out to the windblown Pacific shore-line. Young George explored Lake Merced and Golden Gate Park (completed in 1871); Twin Peaks offered up a large open area in the middle of the city and, and on the city's bay-side shoreline, Islais Creek in China Basin—though dotted with manufacturing sites—was a marsh-lined meandering waterway.

And, as if that wasn't already enough new ground for the young naturalist to investigate, in 1915 the Panama-Pacific International Exhibition opened its gates just eight blocks down the street from the Wrights' home. The year-long extravaganza spread out across six hundred acres of today's Marina District. This massive fair, celebrating the completion of the Panama Canal, drew exhibitors from all over the Americas and the world. It was a stunning, almost unbelievable collection of pavilions, cultures, demonstrations, and technology—all connected by wide boulevards and public transportation for visitors.

Two of the most spectacular exhibits reproduced national parks in impres-sive detail. The Union Pacific Railroad, with service to Yellowstone National Park at that time, built an immense attraction that featured a thousand-seat "Geyserland Spectorium" from which visitors could watch as a re-creation of Old Faithful shot up a column of hot water every twenty minutes. Not to be outdone, the Atchison, Topeka & Santa Fe Railway, with connections to Grand Canyon National Monument, constructed a six-acre "Grand Canyon of Arizona" facility. Part of the park's El Tovar Hotel was reproduced as well as a facsimile of the canyon itself painted on thirty thousand square feet of canvas. This realistic re-creation was adorned with sand, rocks, shrubs, and trees transported by twenty-six freight cars from Arizona to San Francisco.[18]

Wright's freedom, and the encouragement to explore, were both made pos-sible by Auntie, who officially adopted Wright when he was thirteen. This inde-pendence was further enabled by the fact that Cordelia Wright had inherited her husband's estate, and George Wright, though still underage, had received a third of his father's assets when John T. Wright died. Auntie cheered her young ward to get outside and learn—to feed his passion for birds and bi-ology in general. Family lore maintains that during his teen years, Wright shouldered a rucksack one summer, took a ferry to the North Bay, and hiked alone to the Oregon border.[19]

In 1916, he began attending Lowell High School at its location then on Hayes Street, near the Panhandle of Golden Gate Park. Soon he became a reporter for *The Lowell* newspaper and wasted no time in establishing the Lowell High Audubon Society, serving as its president. The club met every Thursday and advertised that "many field trips will be made. The purpose of the Audubon Club," Wright wrote in *The Lowell*, "is to study animal life, particularly birds. The work is very interesting."[20]

Wright was a good student and took the typical cross-section of classes for the time, but his heart was in his nature studies, away from the formal classroom. And in the fall of 1917, he received a letter from an individual who would be very important to him years down the road—Harold C. Bryant, from the University of California, Berkeley—informing him of the details for what would become Wright's first official field trip.[21]

A few weeks previous, Wright had mailed in his application and payment for a series of field trips organized by the University of California Extension called "Six Trips Afield." Their purpose was to encourage citizens to study the birds, mammals, reptiles, and the botany of California. "The fact that these field trips take place on alternate Saturday afternoons," explained Bryant in an Extension Division publication at the time, "makes them possible for teachers and professional and business men and women."[22] Wright wasn't quite an average participant: he was a thirteen-year-old high school student.

Through his teenage years, Wright was also very active in Boy Scouts. During the summers of 1918 and 1919, he was an instructor at the scouts' newly established Camp Dimond in Oakland, located in what was then an undeveloped canyon and meadow.[23] He was responsible for teaching his fellow Boy Scouts about trees, plants, birds, and mammals at the camp and during field trips.[24]

Years later Wright wrote about coming across a cougar on one of these scout field trips, an outing to Mount Hamilton in July 1919.[25] (Mount Hamilton, south of Oakland, part of the Diablo Range, was wild country a century ago, and much of it remains so today.) In the article, he notes the importance of recording a cougar sighting, as scientific observations of the big cats were few and far between at the time. During the early twentieth century cougars were first shot, then observed.

He describes the intense heat of the day as he and his companions bushwhacked down a steep-walled canyon, the pungent aroma of crushed pennyroyal underfoot:

> We rounded a point of rock and were instantly thrown into a frozen surprise by the sudden rush of a very large animal up from the waterside. Then it disappeared in the protecting brush. A search of the ground revealed nothing, so that we concluded that the heat of the day had brought the predator to the stream for refreshment. We started to walk away when my boot came in contact with a small hoof protruding like a mushroom from the dead leaf bed. This belonged to a deer fawn, and not three feet away we uncovered another fawn that had been completely buried from sight.[26]

Already a keen naturalist and budding scientist, Wright returned to the site, alone, three days later to record more findings. He concluded that the cougar had lingered there for several days because the remains had been neatly consumed and not strewn about by coyotes or other scavengers.

During his last year at Lowell High School, Wright kept very busy with the Audubon Club and with writing for *The Lowell*. He was also elected class president. In "The Magic Window," Wright ends the story in the fall of 1920: "The boy who had been born in the old house moved away, and with him went the secret of the magic window."[27] That year, 1920, Auntie purchased a Mediterranean-style house across the bay on Thousand Oaks Boulevard, just north of Berkeley's campus. In January 1921, Wright started his college studies at Berkeley at the young age of sixteen and, with that, a new chapter in his life began.

University of California, Berkeley

Shortly after George Wright arrived at Berkeley, he decided upon two things that would shape his years on campus and beyond: He declared forestry as his major, and he rushed the Delta Upsilon fraternity, or DU.

The fact that Wright joined a fraternity is not surprising. After all, while he might have been young compared to most freshmen, he was raised by Auntie with all the social graces of the time. By numerous accounts he loved group field trips. He also liked to entertain, and he was good at it—all interests and traits that would ensure a nice fit with fraternity life.[1]

During most of his time at Berkeley, however, Wright appears to have lived with Auntie at their house on Thousand Oaks, about two and a half miles north of campus. But that didn't curtail his DU involvement. Leaning on his high school years as a reporter for *The Lowell* in San Francisco, he was soon contributing Berkeley DU chapter updates for the national *Delta Upsilon Quarterly*. In one piece about chapter and alumni news at Berkeley, he announced, among other items, his appointment as junior manager of Berkeley's crew team, evidence that he wasn't *always* thinking about birds and field trips.[2]

The Wrights' home on Thousand Oaks Boulevard was also the site for DU gatherings and many other events. Auntie was always part of the scene, holding court and making sure everything ran smoothly. She didn't impose any Victorian restrictions on the house guests, as one might assume considering her age, nor did she let events get out of control.

In a letter of June 10, 1926, a young man named Gareth Kellam wrote to his father about a dance he went to the previous Friday in Berkeley:

> I think the best dance I have ever been to. It was given by a boy named George Wright who lives with his grandmother. The old lady was charming and her

philosophy on youth so much broader than the average middle-aged parent. It was amazing. When I left to go down & dance after about 10 minutes of chatting, her remark was "I think you'd better let Hanan (the butler) give you a high-ball. I can see you haven't had any and the girls don't want a stupid slow one to dance with." As a result of her ideas, I didn't see one gin bottle or one drunk which is amazing. She surely has the right idea.[3]

At one DU party, Wright received a nickname that would stick with him for years to come: Togo. The origins of this name have become a little foggy across the decades, but there is one possible explanation, involving Japan's most famous admiral at the time, Heihachiro Togo, and an "American Hero" Siberian Husky named after the admiral. Togo, the husky, was a lead sled dog for the team that raced serum to Nome, Alaska, to help prevent a diphtheria outbreak in 1925.[4] Both the Japanese admiral and the husky were small and tough. Wright's close college friends rarely called him George from that point forward. It was either Togo or Toe. And he often signed personal notes "Togo," a habit that would even appear a few times in his official National Park Service correspondence years later.

The fraternity served as Wright's social anchor during his college years, and he remained an avid booster and supporter of the DUs well after his time at Berkeley, as did Auntie. He also developed many friendships with his fellow DU brothers, several of whom would play important roles in his life.

It is not clear why this dedicated birder and naturalist decided to declare forestry as his major, instead of zoology. However, the reason could lie in the fact that American forestry in the early twentieth century was seen as a dynamic and exciting field. James G. Lewis of the Forest History Society explains, "Forestry was part of the conservation movement, which itself was part of the larger Progressive Movement, which strived to apply scientific methods and reasoning to society's ills in order to solve them."[5]

Forestry in the United States experienced rapid growth from the 1890s through the early part of the twentieth century—partially due to the championing of two men: Theodore Roosevelt and Gifford Pinchot. Pinchot, a Yale-educated and German-trained forester, had served as chief of the federal Division of Forestry from 1898 until 1905. Roosevelt, president from 1901 to 1909, found an energetic and kindred spirit in Pinchot. They succeeded in transferring all US Forest Reserves from the Department of the Interior to the Department of Agriculture in 1905, thereby creating a new agency, the Forest Service, that unsurprisingly Pinchot would be the first to direct.

UC Berkeley Forestry class studying stunted bishop pine trees, Inverness, California, 1925. Wright, bottom left, writing field notes. Photograph by Woodbridge Metcalf. Courtesy of the Bioscience, Natural Resources and Public Health Library, University of California, Berkeley, and Jennifer Malone.

Together, Roosevelt and Pinchot set aside millions of acres of forest lands—almost all in the West—as buffers against the logging industry's aggressive clear-cut-and-move-on business model (evident east of the Mississippi River), to minimize land frauds, and to protect watersheds for the increasing number of farmers and ranchers in the arid West. The duo popularized the term "conservation" as it applied to their approach to forestry. Yes, use the resources for the benefit of the nation, they argued, but adopt "scientific forestry" along the way: namely, manage lands and better utilize all logged materials more purposefully.[6] But make no mistake, Pinchot did not believe in permanently setting aside forests as preserves, nor was he a fan of the national park model, which excluded all of the uses encouraged on Forest Service lands: logging, grazing, mining, and hunting. He was, as many have described him, a "utilitarian conservationist."[7]

William B. Greeley took over from Chief of Forestry Henry S. Graves (who succeeded Pinchot) and led the service from 1920 to 1928, the period during which Wright attended Berkeley. Under the Graves and Greeley tenures, the service grew and matured to focus on applied research, timber management, and, eventually, recreation opportunities for the public.

These were the Roaring Twenties, when the US postwar economy was flour-ishing and the country was becoming increasingly urbanized. The decade began with both the eighteenth and nineteenth amendments becoming the law of the land. The first instituted Prohibition (lasting until 1933), and, al-though women could already vote in most of the northern and western states, the second granted universal suffrage to women across the country. Cultural norms were also changing on many different fronts, coupled with major ad-vances in radio, music, television, architecture, aviation, and literature.

Car production and automobile use were rapidly increasing as well. Conse-quently, Americans were far more mobile than ever before, and many of them wanted to visit and camp inside national parks and in national forests. The growing, resource-dependent economy also meant that logging on private lands intensified in order to provide lumber to a nation hungry for raw materi-als. Tensions between private, state, and federal lands were coming to a head.[8]

Forest Service Director Greeley won several legislative victories during the 1920s that would shape forestry for years to come. Through these suc-cesses, Greeley and the service were able, in part, to codify a federal-public cooperation agreement as the centerpiece of Forest Service policy. They also secured federal-state collaboration regarding fire control, created the agency's research program, and aided in reforestation programs while also providing technical assistance to logging operations on private land through a forestry extension program.[9] "I want to make the national forests of greater national service," Greeley stated in 1920. "for if the Nation fails to call a halt on forest devastation, it will pay a terrible price!"[10]

Even though Wright would end up working for a federal agency whose mission was very different from that of the Forest Service, in this general con-text it makes sense why Wright was attracted to forestry: These were dynamic times for public lands, specifically in the West, and the Forest Service was a leading force in the sound use of natural resources and in the fledgling field of wildlife management. One can only assume that his decision was helped by the fact that Berkeley's forestry program at the time was overseen by one of the nation's leading foresters, Walter Mulford.

In addition to declaring a forestry major and joining the DUs, Wright encoun-tered three people at Berkeley who would have an outsized influence on his thinking, future trajectory, and professional behavior. They were, unquestion-ably, Wright's trio of mentors: Mulford, Joseph Grinnell, and Joseph Dixon.

Walter Mulford was one of the earliest foresters and forestry teachers to receive a formal education in the United States. Historically, forestry students in the late nineteenth century traveled to Europe for their education, because of the long tradition of forest management overseas; even Mulford spent time in Switzerland and Germany.[11] Berkeley recruited Mulford to create a new Division of Forestry in its College of Agriculture. He arrived in 1914, and for the next thirty-three years, he taught hundreds of students while furthering the profession of forestry at Berkeley and throughout the United States.

Mulford was a renowned and much-loved teacher. He was remembered for his keen intellect, dedication to his students, and his interest in public service and conservation.[12] He also emphasized field observation and note taking through required attendance at the Berkeley Forestry Field Camp in the Sierra Nevada of California.[13]

But what is perhaps most notable about Mulford (and his influence on Wright) are his personality traits and comportment. "He was imbued with an unconquerable idealism, transparent sincerity, and complete faith in the high mission of forestry," noted a Mulford obituary in 1955.[14] He was a great communicator, kind, organized, disciplined, and yet he possessed "a bulldog persistence in attainment of carefully considered goals, and the ability to differ with others without the bitterness of dissension."[15]

Joseph Grinnell was born in 1877, on the lands of the Kiowa, Comanche, and Wichita Indian Agency in Oklahoma where his father was a physician. Three years later they moved to the Pine Ridge Agency in the Dakotas. According Joseph's wife, Hilda, the young Grinnell "was a favorite with Chief Red Cloud and when, in later years, he dictated letters to the Grinnells . . . there was always an especial greeting for 'my little friend Joe.'" Little Joe found camaraderie among the Oglala Lakota children across the sprawling agency lands. Hilda Grinnell believed that this early exposure to the outdoors with his young companions "quickened" his senses and that perhaps, in later years, proved to be early informal training for Grinnell's uncanny ability to quickly identify species, especially birds, by sight and sound.[16]

From an early age, Grinnell was obsessed with birds and natural history, and he quickly became an exceedingly organized and enthusiastic field expert.[17] The family eventually moved to Pasadena, California, and by the time Grinnell graduated from high school in 1893, he had already collected more birds in the state than anyone else. After graduation, Grinnell enrolled in the Throop Polytechnic Institute in Pasadena—what would later become the California Institute of Technology—to study biology and botany. In the spring of Grinnell's junior year, he was invited to travel to Alaska, and the budding scientist jumped at the chance to expand his collection of birds and mammals. This would prove to be the first of several extended Alaskan trips that Grinnell would participate in throughout his early twenties.

He earned his PhD from Stanford University, but at one point he returned to Throop to teach. It was there that Grinnell met a young and very talented student named Joseph Dixon as well as his future benefactor: Annie Montague Alexander. Alexander was an incredibly adventurous woman. She convinced Grinnell to accept the directorship at the new Museum of Vertebrate Zoology (MVZ) at Berkeley that she was creating—and endowing. He started work at the museum in 1908, and eventually he persuaded Joseph Dixon to follow him north to study and work.[18]

Grinnell shaped the museum for decades to come. According to James Patton, curator and professor emeritus at the MVZ, "In vertebrate biology, he is probably the most important person from an academic institution in the early twentieth century. There is hardly a mammalogist or ornithologist in this country that doesn't trace his academic lineage to Grinnell."[19]

Just like Mulford, Grinnell was also an excellent teacher, both in the classroom and in the field. He was self-effacing, focused, fair, patient, and deferential (to a degree); encouraging of others, especially his students; and he respected differing opinions, though his position typically came out on top. And Grinnell's students, and the students of those students—his academic lineage—not only spread out across universities in the United States and abroad, but they also populated the Park Service and many other state and federal agencies.

He also created a system for taking field notes that is known, today, simply as the Grinnellian System. He was a prolific note-taker in the field and he developed a technique to clearly record his observations, so that he, or anyone, could readily refer back to them in subsequent years. He was precise about the style of notebook, the type of paper and ink used, and all the repetitive details written on each page. It took dedication and discipline to record on-the-go as well as perform the nightly ritual of writing more back at camp, regardless of weather conditions or personal comfort. It was a routine that became a strict requirement for all Grinnell students.[20]

George's observations were intense, but always with pleasure. At night, he was very self-disciplined about writing his notes. You know, when you're by a campfire, and maybe you're tired, and maybe it's cold, and damp and so on. It takes self-discipline to make yourself write those notes. He was very conscientious about that.
BEN THOMPSON[21]

In 1908, Grinnell wrote to Annie Alexander stating, with great foresight, "Our field-records will be perhaps the most valuable of all our results."[22] The Grinnellian System is still in use to this day by field scientists around the world, with some modifications and adaptations that have evolved over the decades.[23]

Joseph Scattergood Dixon was raised in Southern California, just north and inland from San Diego. He graduated from Escondido High School and went straight to Throop Polytechnic Institute, where he studied biology under a young teacher named Joseph Grinnell. That was the beginning of a relationship that lasted over thirty years. In 1907, Annie Alexander came knocking on Grinnell's door to ask about Dixon as a possible addition to an Alaskan collecting trip she was organizing.[24] Grinnell enthusiastically supported the idea, and Dixon accepted.

As with Grinnell, the 1907 trip to Alaska was the first of many for Dixon to the far north. In the spring of 1913, a wealthy East Coast naturalist, John E. Thayer, who was associated with Harvard's Museum of Comparative Zoology, paid for another collecting trip to the far north, by Point Barrow in the Arctic Ocean. He invited Dixon, who at the age of twenty-nine was already a well-known field biologist. Dixon didn't hesitate to accept.

The crew of the expedition's ship, the *Polar Bear*, had intended to leave arctic waters for home by early September, but the sea ice hadn't melted sufficiently that summer. In his field notes from September 4, 1913, Dixon wrote that after vainly attempting to dynamite a passage, they were stuck.[25] The local Inupiaq people showed the crew how to build igloos and hunt seals and other arctic wildlife.[26] As Dixon recalled years later, "Without adequate food and being forced to devise our own clothing, it was questionable at times whether we would survive the Arctic winter, but fortune favored us and all thirteen of us came through without a loss of a man."[27] Dixon eventually reveled in the extreme conditions, and he collected some one thousand specimens and recorded two hundred pages of field notes. A year later, after they freed their boat, Dixon wrote that they eventually arrived in California, "just thirteen months late for my own wedding."[28]

He was tough as nails, dedicated to the task at hand, and incredibly resourceful. He was most comfortable in the field, regardless of whether he was dealing with minus-thirty-degree weather in the arctic, stinging hail and wind in the mountains of central Alaska, or scorching conditions in Death Valley with the mercury soaring past the century mark. Alongside Grinnell, he was acknowledged as a pioneering field zoologist and a prodigious collector. The two would also become leading voices for wildlife protection and conservation in their writings and presentations.[29] Grinnell, Dixon, and eventually Wright and Thompson were truly the forerunners—early theorists and actual practitioners—of what is known today as conservation biology.[30]

Dixon was a productive writer throughout his career, publishing primarily in scientific journals but also in some popular magazines.[31] He was also a dedicated photographer during his years at the MVZ and eventually with the Park Service. He regarded photography as an essential part of his fieldwork and field notes—another way to augment and memorialize locations and species. His photographs number in the thousands and are distributed between the MVZ, Yosemite National Park, the NPS, and the National Archives.[32]

As with Mulford and Grinnell, Dixon was modest, focused, and quiet at times. He was also an excellent teacher and widely admired for his extensive, firsthand knowledge of animal and plant species, ecosystems, and even tracking. And he was very serious about the job of grooming future field biologists and naturalists, and instilling in them the value of fieldwork.

The Quaker Connection

While Mulford, Grinnell, and Dixon had many characteristics that were strikingly similar, one of the most remarkable is the fact that all three men were Quakers. Not only were they Quakers, but the trio were birthright Quakers, meaning they came from a long line of Quakers on both sides of their families.[33]

The Quaker connection is significant because, although the three men might not have been practicing Quakers while at Berkeley, they were nonetheless *raised* as Quakers. That means that the Quaker Testimonies—integrity, equality, simplicity, community—were the basic tenets that guided their lives. Not only did the Testimonies guide how they worshipped (if they did), but they also shaped how the three interacted with fellow Quakers and people in general, personally and professionally. Respect for others, and listening, are extremely important in the Society of Friends. Additionally, family and community are vital, and Wright's mentors were, in keeping, dedicated family men, all the while creating communities around them both academically and in the field.

A deep connection between Quakers and nature also began with the group's founder, George Fox, in mid-seventeenth-century England. "This tradition of careful observation of the Book of Nature," writes Laurel Kearns, who teaches ecology and religion, "can be seen in the preponderance of Quaker naturalists and botanists in our history."[34] Late nineteenth- and early twentieth-century Quakers in the United States made a clear connection between being in nature and "listening for God's words." Over time, this link evolved into a wish to understand nature and to become involved in conservation.

Wright was not a Quaker. However, it is clear that he came to Berkeley with a Quaker-like predisposition. He had excellent manners; he treated people equally; he was self-effacing; he was focused and a hard worker; he was a good listener; and the natural world was his life. As Mary Dixon Rhyne, Joseph Dixon's youngest daughter, remembered in 2000, "My mother, my sister Barbara, and I all fell in love with George. He was like no other man that we knew. Very sensitive, considerate, loving and generous."[35]

During his professional life, many colleagues and observers noted Wright's uncanny ability to get along with just about anyone, and how he created and managed a tight team of biologists. His three teachers were truly mentors, and for a young man raised without his parents—particularly, without a father—this trio of men served as role models for both Wright's life and his work.

3

Summers:
Alaska and the West

George Wright was an excellent student. This is clear based on his Scholarship Record card from Lowell High School in San Francisco. Berkeley's Division of Forestry no longer has Wright's student transcripts, but we do have a record of how Wright built on his formal classroom lessons during his summers.[1]

Wright had a craving for firsthand experiences in national parks: he wanted to see wildlife, and he gravitated to wild landscapes. His outings over a handful of summers were essential to his understanding of what it entailed to travel throughout the lightly developed West in the 1920s and, in a few years, what might be required in order to conduct serious fieldwork. These summertime excursions also revealed to him some of the issues simmering for the still-fledgling National Park Service. Combined, these trips—some fun, some serious—would serve him well in his professional life.

Alaska, Summer 1921

The first summer after entering Berkeley, the compass pointed north for Wright. In June 1921, just before his seventeenth birthday, he traveled to Seattle with an unknown female companion, likely a Salvadoran cousin. In Seattle, they boarded the SS *Princess Alice* to explore Alaska's Inside Passage—that sinuous fertile waterway renowned for its countless islands, dense temperate rainforests, dark, slate-blue inlets, massive glaciers, and abundant wildlife that extends down to coastal British Columbia, ending just north of Prince Rupert. This was a perfect blend, or confluence, of his family's steamship legacy along the Pacific coast and his newfound academic pursuits, with a dash of teenage wanderlust thrown in.

Years before Wright ventured north, Grinnell and Dixon had done the exact same thing, though with a specific focus on collecting specimens. It's as if it was a prerequisite for the era's future biologists to venture north to experience the wild Pacific shoreline and the rugged unknown interior of mystique-drenched Alaska. Wright, too, explored much of this territory, going as far north as Skagway, roughly ninety miles north of Juneau. It isn't clear what motivated the young man to head out on his first big trip. However, it is plausible that Wright had already met Grinnell in the spring of 1921, during one of Grinnell's guest lectures in Mulford's classroom, and that Grinnell had suggested such a trip to the inquisitive and enthusiastic young student.

By the time of Wright's first trip to Alaska, the region was known as the Alaskan Territory. It was also more developed and populated than it had been during Grinnell's and Dixon's early visits—though this was relative.[2] Wright's travel program varied a bit from the *Alice's* printed schedule—a detail gleaned from fifteen 3" × 5" black-and-white photographs, taken by Wright and featuring his handwritten notes on the back of seven of them.[3]

His first photograph, taken on June 19, was from Alert Bay, Canada, just north of Vancouver—as *Alice's* schedule states. The next day they stopped over in Ketchikan, Alaska, for a few hours. Wright's photograph of Ketchikan features the downtown, replete with wooden plank sidewalks and streets, a few shops with their shingles hanging out front, and a Model T Ford in the foreground (engine hand-crank protruding from the front grill). He scribbled a funny reference to Henry Ford on the back of the image.

Other images include Wrangell Bay and the Wrangell Narrows, culminating in an image north of Juneau. Wright's companion stands in the distance, resplendent in jodhpurs, tall laced boots, and a jaunty chapeau. The Mendenhall Glacier looms in the background—massive and awesome as it sculpts its way through the mountain range toward the sea. It is watched over by 4,232-foot Mount McGinnis to the north, with Mount Stroller White off to the side, both covered with snow. There is no descriptor on this image, only the glacier's name.

Adventures on the High Trail, 1922

In the summer of 1922, Wright participated in the Sierra Club's annual outing into California's famed Sierra Nevada—the High Country Trip—one of many he would join over the years. Gathering in Sequoia National Park, club members were greeted by park superintendent Colonel John R. White at a large encampment he set aside for them in Crescent Meadows.[4] Winding their way

Wright crossing a stream in California's Sierra Nevada on a Sierra Club High Country trip, early 1920s. Courtesy of Pamela Meléndez Wright Lloyd.

up and east through Kings Canyon, the impressive outing was composed of approximately three hundred participants: members, packers, and cooks.

Some highlights of the 270-mile hike included over two hundred members climbing 14,505-foot Mount Whitney, the tallest peak in the lower forty-eight states.

The sheer logistics and statistics of the trip are hard to fathom, particularly the vision of over two hundred hikers ascending Mount Whitney at once. It was one of the largest outings the club ever organized. Writer Antoinette Gurney, whose pen name was Allen Chaffee, was on the 1922 trip.[5] In her book *Adventures on the High Trail, Norma Blaisdell in the High Sierras* (a series of romance-adventure short stories set in the Sierra Nevada), she includes an appendix with an excellent hand-drawn map and details from the 1922 trip. Prior to the small village of hikers heading into the Sierra, she reports, packers made four trips into the backcountry with a ninety-mule pack train to deposit large caches of supplies, weighing over 10,000 pounds. The items included, in part: 250 pounds of fresh and dried fruit; 2,000 pounds of ham; 1,500 pounds of flour and an equal amount of sugar; 500 pounds of hardtack;[6] 400 pounds of sweet chocolate; 450 pounds of cheese; the meat of 3 steers; 50 pounds of bacon per breakfast (when used); and trout, when caught

by members.[7] Wright, an avid fly fisher, no doubt helped out with the supply
of trout when he could.

The Perils of Ponderous Peter, 1924

Though we have no diary or photographs to document Wright's summer of
1923, we can deduce some of what he did based on his trip in the summer of
1924, when Wright and two DU fraternity brothers—Bob Shuman and Carleton
Rose—hopped into "Peter," Wright's beat-up Model T Ford, and set off to tour
as many of the western national parks as they could. Wright's diary from the
trip was titled "The Perils of Ponderous Peter."[8] Although the writing is mostly
tongue-in-cheek, Wright does make some keen observations of the parks, and
numerous excellent black-and-white photographs illustrate the booklet.

Wright took to photography early. In Alaska, he might have been using
a point-and-shoot Kodak Brownie—the handheld box cameras popular at
the time. However, the images from the 1924 road trip are crisper, even when
large landscapes are captured. Perhaps he had graduated to a model possess-
ing a more powerful lens and the ability to focus shots. It is feasible that by
1924, Wright had met Dixon at Berkeley. Perhaps Dixon had emphasized to
him the importance of photography and encouraged the undergraduate to
keep pursuing it. (In later years, Wright and Dixon frequently collaborated
when taking images, with Dixon always acting as instructor.)

Intriguingly, the route the three students decided on foretells the itinerary that Wright and his Park Service colleagues—Dixon and Thompson—
would choose six years later during their wildlife survey. It's as if Wright was
practicing for his future: an informal dry run with two frat brothers. There
is no doubt this trip was all Wright's—from conception, to funding, to route.
During a seven-week period, they covered over two thousand miles—most of
those on rough dirt roads.

In the rural West, paved roads in the early 1920s were few and far between.
And since Model T Fords were basically small cars with large bicycle tires,
Peter inevitably suffered a string of blowouts on the trip: seventy-two, to be
exact. Changing tires was a frequent activity. Peter was also in and out of
shops about a half a dozen times throughout the summer. On several occasions, on exceptionally high, snow-covered passes, the trio got stuck and had
to wait for larger vehicles, or people on horseback, to tow them out.

Mechanical issues aside, the trio toughed it out in the Mojave Desert and
what is today's Joshua Tree National Park (preserved in 1936). From there they
continued to Zion National Park in Utah, then northeast to Rocky Mountain

National Park in Colorado, north to Wyoming's Yellowstone National Park, back south to Salt Lake City, north to Idaho, and on to Glacier National Park in Montana. From Glacier, "With great regret," Wright penned, "we turn towards the coast."

> I arrived at Cracker Lake shortly after ten. Over the west wall great shafts of sunlight from the breaking clouds shot downward through the purple haze. Some angles of the rocks reflected the light dazzlingly. Some goats posing on rocky prominences were illuminated from behind by these beams so that they looked twice natural size. Radiant pagan gods framed in silver halos they gazed at lower earth from their high thrones.
>
> GEORGE WRIGHT, GLACIER NATIONAL PARK[9]

They made it through Idaho and Washington, finally stopping for a few days at Crater Lake National Park in Oregon, after a treacherous last sixty miles leading up to the park. "It is wonderful to see Crater Lake once more," chronicled Wright, referring to a visit he'd made to the park the previous summer. "I hope that Carl and Bob find it worth the risk."

Throughout his diary, Wright records his thoughts on the different landscapes and parks they visited—shades of his prodigious note taking and gentle prose in years to come. He felt, for instance, "transported to another world" by the beauty of Estes Park, Colorado, at the foot of Rocky Mountain National Park. At Yellowstone, he was awed by the wild elk—although he also took note of the pens and corrals used for the elk and bison seasonally (serious management issues for years). And, waking up alongside Silver Creek in Utah, he was "gladdened by the site[10] of a beautiful Lewis woodpecker with its rose breast and glossy green back wings." He celebrated his twentieth birthday, June 20, in Missoula, Montana (with "*distant greetings from Auntie*") and the next night, camping at Flathead Lake south of Glacier National Park, he asked, "Is there anything on this earth that approaches the heavenly state more closely than a night spent at the foot of a noble pine beside a beautiful lake? So endeth the longest day of the year."

In Salt Lake City, meanwhile, Wright commented on a quite different scene: the public auto camp they were staying in—something the three travelers did on several occasions. "During the morning we laundered with the lady tourists in the public auto camp. The public auto camp is fast becoming one of America's great and peculiarly distinctive institutions."

After World War I and before the Great Depression—particularly during the Roaring Twenties—these camps, constructed specifically for car campers, were very popular. Not surprisingly, the Ford Motor Company pushed the concept of exploring and camping with a car—what it simply termed "autocamping."

Magazines and newspapers began featuring the excitement of the carefree and "gypsy" lifestyle this mode of travel afforded. Companies started manufacturing gear specifically for autocamping: special all-weather rubberized car covers, lean-to tents that attached to the side of cars, and much more. Rural western towns, initially weary of this phenomenon, soon realized that if they attracted these travelers, it could be a boon for their local economies. After all, the autocampers needed gas, supplies, and mechanics. Towns throughout the West began to build public auto camps, some with free amenities, such as bathrooms and showers, to attract these motorized vacationers.[11] Wright was observing the beginnings of an activity that would dramatically increase in subsequent years in the rural West and in national parks.

Several times in "The *Perils of Ponderous Peter*," Wright notes specific parks and locations he had visited the summer before: Yellowstone, for instance, and Crater Lake. While in Zion National Park, he compared and contrasted the cliffs and coloring to the Grand Canyon, in clear reference to a visit to this other landmark the previous summer:

> Chugging our way up the box canyon with its many-hued, almost perpendicular walls we were no longer doubters but silent devotees at one of Nature's most glorious shrines. They describe it aptly as a Yosemite with Grand Canyon colorings. Yet it is even more impressive than Yosemite because of the towering closeness of the East and West walls while the colorings of the rock are to my mind deeper and richer than in the Grand Canyon.

And when stopping over in Salt Lake City to listen to an organ recital at the Mormon Tabernacle, Wright's diary makes it clear he had also been there in 1923. "It is just a year since Bob Sibley and I attended one of these recitals."[12] Several years Wright's senior, Robert (Bob) Sibley was another DU and went on to manage Berkeley's Office of Alumni Affairs for many years. A trained engineer, Sibley was a keen naturalist and hiking enthusiast. He would eventually be a cofounder of the renowned East Bay Regional Park District in California and would have a park named after him. Sibley and Wright were good friends for many years, sharing many a hike together in the East Bay Hills during their time at Berkeley—and, apparently, a glorious summer on the road in 1923.

The Surfbird's Secret, 1926

In April of 1926, Wright wrote Joseph Dixon a letter accepting an offer to accompany Dixon on a three-month collecting expedition to Mount McKinley

Park Station, in today's Denali National Park. Wright was to pay his own way, though the Museum of Vertebrate Zoology provided all of their field-work supplies. "In return for my assistance," wrote Wright, "I may glean such knowledge and wisdom as I can."[13]

The MVZ's 1926 expedition to Alaska all started with a wealthy East Coast amateur ornithologist from Lancaster, Massachusetts, named John E. Thayer: the same benefactor who hired Dixon to go to Alaska in 1913 (when he got stuck and had to overwinter, missing his wedding). Thayer was an enthusi-astic collector of birds, bird eggs, and bird nests. However, he was more than a passionate amateur. Thayer employed his own hunter and sponsored many collecting expeditions throughout the Americas. For him, specimen acquisi-tion was critical to the scientific discovery process.[14] His personal museum in Lancaster, built specifically for this private collection, was massive.

Thayer knew Grinnell and Dixon, or, more precisely, he knew of their reputation as top-notch scientists, consummate field men, and, importantly, avid collectors. By underwriting the entire project to Alaska, he convinced Grinnell to let Dixon, who already had many collecting trips to Alaska under his belt, travel north for him. Thayer was interested in obtaining some wan-dering tattler's eggs along with a few other species, but what he really wanted was to be the first person to have a clutch of surfbird eggs in his collection.

The surfbird's secret—where it nested and what its eggs looked like—baffled Thayer, Grinnell, Dixon, and every other ornithologist in the United States. What they did know in the 1920s was that these shorebirds, which wintered somewhere in the southern hemisphere, flew north to Alaska in the spring, hugging the coastline the entire way. After their arrival from the south, these compact coastal waders disappeared inland.

Their name derives from their singular habit of foraging for mollusks and other small prey at the surf line, where they play tag with the waves be-tween grabbing quick bites. A few had been seen and collected in the interior of Alaska in the early 1920s, but never a nesting pair—the definitive proof needed to determine where their nesting grounds were located.[15]

The 1926 trip was years in the making due to a series of events that pre-vented its launch in 1924 and again in 1925. In January of 1926, Thayer penned another note to Dixon, this time in reference to Dixon suggesting he bring Wright with him as an assistant: "I think that it is an excellent idea taking someone with you and this young man that you wrote about sounds good to me. By all means take him."[16] Five days later, Grinnell reported to Thayer on Dixon's progress with his preparations. He also included a comment about Wright. "This is a young man who has been a student of mine throughout a semester," he attested. "I know him well, and have confidence in him."[17]

Graduating forestry class, UC Berkeley, May 1926. Wright is in the front row, third from right. Courtesy of the Bioscience, Natural Resources and Public Health Library, University of California, Berkeley.

A few days prior to sailing north with Dixon to the McKinley District, Wright was captured in a forestry class photograph with his fellow students and a few faculty—with slicked-back hair, in snappy suits and ties—lined up in two rows on the steps of Hilgard Hall, where the Division of Forestry was based. However, something in the image doesn't quite fit. As if they didn't get the memo about the photo shoot, Wright, with a humorous smirk on his face, and the student to his immediate right, Joe Flynn, are in the front row, looking like they just came in from a long day in the field, wearing dirty khaki pants (Wright's are particularly filthy) and work shirts under flimsy sweaters.

Dixon and Wright left Berkeley on May 3, then steamed north from Seattle on the *SS Yukon* five days later. After anchoring in Seward, Alaska, they unloaded their gear and caught an Alaska Railway train all the way to McKinley Park Station, arriving on May 18.[18] McKinley Park Station was a pioneer town in transition. It had catered to gold miners and market hunters (renowned for their excessive killing of all wildlife in order to supply mining camps and towns with meat), but increasingly it was accommodating tourists coming to experience the new national park. (Although Mount McKinley National Park was designated in 1917, it wasn't funded until the early 1920s.) A park ranger helped them load up their boxes of collecting gear and drove them out to an old cabin on the banks of the Savage River, where the snow-melt watercourse races down from the mountains.

Two days later, their first full field day, the twenty-two-year-old was in a state of constant amazement, recording a flurry of personal firsts: mountain sheep, caribou, a snow-white ptarmigan, Canada jays, and a hoary marmot, to name just a few species. Wright's field notes from this trip not only demonstrate that he was using the note-taking system taught to all Grinnell students but also that his observational and writing skills were being honed with the assistance of Dixon as they roughed it out under harsh conditions. They had a roof over their heads, but that was about it—no running water or indoor plumbing.

Wright's and Dixon's field notes detail their experiences in lively yet succinct prose. Just ten days into their stay, Wright recorded the following:

> Mr. Dixon stayed home with a strained ankle while I went prospecting for specimens in general and a hoary marmot in particular. While following the contour of the hill at approximately 4,000 feet through sheer good luck I happened to make the find of my young life. A quick movement some five or six hundred feet away attracted my attention to a grayish bird that was sneaking hurriedly along. Here was a surf bird in the nesting season. Better luck yet, when I looked down, there were the eggs, lying in a little depression. There were four of them, and they certainly looked too good to be true. When Mr. Dixon heard the good news he was inclined to think it some sort of a bum joke but was soon convinced and eager to be on the firing line.[19]

In Dixon's notes of the same day, he recounts what happened when Wright returned to fetch him, bad ankle and all:

> Wright came on to camp to tell me the good news and by 6 o'clock we packed up and left camp to investigate the nest. The surf bird was on the nest when we arrived and Mr. Wright was correct when he said 'I'm sure it is a surf bird.' To Mr. George M. Wright then belongs the credit of finding the first nest of this species on May 28, 1926 at 4 p.m.[20]

Wright and Dixon retreated to a nearby knoll in the half-light of an Alaskan summer evening to observe the surfbird overnight. They were concerned that some nearby mountain sheep might trample the precious nest. Here, Wright reveals that he could be moving and eloquent in his observations, while hunkered down against the elements.

> Shelter provided by a small rock outcropping, along with a smoky fire of alder dragged from the little creek basin some distance away, helped to make our

Male surfbird by nest, Mount McKinley National Park, Alaska, May 29, 1926. Photograph by Joseph Dixon. With the permission of the Museum of Vertebrate Zoology, University of California, Berkeley.

storm vigil more endurable. Hardly a scant half hour had passed before it commenced to rain with an accompaniment of chill wind that fairly froze.

Misty clouds would come drifting slowly up the cañon and over the rocky ridge tops in great white swirls. They moved on with a relentless sureness until finally they hung at dead level over the valley from the North mountains to the main Alaskan Range. All underneath this heavy gray mist from foothill slopes to the winding shallow river looked mysteriously unreal in the Northern twilight.

Sometimes the rain would let up as a shifting wind turned back the clouds. Then a little light filtered down to show us whole troops of mist ghosts rise right out of the tundra and go chasing away up the valley. No doubt they were on their way to join the cloud ranks again.[21]

In the morning, their intense observations completed, they collected the lone parent—a male who had been incubating the eggs—the four eggs, and the nest. "After all the pictures and observations were taken," Wright notes, "Mr. Dixon shot the parent and you may be sure it was hard to see the courageous little creature killed."[22]

Dixon wired Grinnell from McKinley Park Station about their success. Grinnell then sent a telegram to Thayer. "Dixon wires, has surf bird eggs. Congratulations."[23] A week later, after the surfbird, the eggs, and the nest had been "put up" (the bird skin prepared and the eggs cleaned out), they were carefully packaged, and Wright went to town to send them south. "Through the kindness of the truck driver for the road commission I was able to ride into McKinley Park Station with the surf bird eggs, those precious eggs."[24]

The duo had almost two more months of fieldwork ahead of them, surviving snowstorms, rain, sleet, and a questionable staple of their diet: chipped beef in a can. They maintained their base at Savage River while also exploring the Copper Mountain region, Wonder Lake, the Toklat River, Igloo Creek, and Fish Creek, collecting all the while. As Dixon would later report, they hiked approximately five hundred miles—always carrying their shotguns and knapsacks, often for fifteen or twenty miles a day—and secured "168 specimens of birds, 83 study-skins of mammals, 2 birds' nests, 4 sets of birds' eggs, 350 photographs, and 280 pages of notes."[25] During inclement weather, they would stay inside their cabin preparing specimens.

In the open, one learns the character of his companions with more rapidity and certainty than in the more conventional life of cities.

ROGER TOLL [26]

They made it back to Berkeley in early August and spent weeks unpacking their collecting materials and the specimens. Dixon wrote a long letter to Thayer and explained that he would be writing up a professional article about their discovery of the surfbird nest for the Cooper Ornithological Society's publication, *The Condor*, as previously agreed upon. "I am in hopes that Mr. Wright," Dixon noted, "who accompanied me and who was the best assistant that I have ever had, will commission Major Brooks to make a painting of the Surf Bird going on to the eggs, from a photograph which I secured in the field. Really a good deal of the success of the expedition was due to Mr. Wright." Brooks was a well-known Canadian ornithologist and bird painter. Wright agreed to commission Brooks, and Brooks's finished painting was reprinted, in color, in the article.[27] Finally, in December, Thayer enthusiastically wrote to Dixon, "The skins and eggs arrived in fine shape! A Merry Xmas and Many Happy New Years!"[28]

Prior to his death in 1933, John Thayer donated his entire collection of approximately 28,000 bird skins, 15,000 eggs and nests, and 3,500 mounted birds to Harvard's Museum of Comparative Zoology. Wright and Dixon's courageous male surfbird, its nest, and those four precious eggs reside there to this day.[29]

The Museum and Forestry Camp, 1927

Wright stayed at Berkeley for six years as an undergraduate, for unknown reasons. It could be that he took time off to be with Auntie—perhaps organizing a trip or two with her. He might have also simply loaded up his car and headed out across the western landscape one spring or fall, or hiked up into the Sierra Nevada with some Sierra Club friends. With any of these scenarios, either such adventures were not recorded or the notes and photographs were lost.

In January 1927, however, Wright started working part-time at the MVZ. It was a four-month position as assistant to the museum's economic mammalogist: Joseph Dixon. Joseph Grinnell insisted that, unless otherwise determined by Dixon, Wright should spend his time within the museum, and that he should acquaint himself with the "Schedule of Curatorial Duties for Staff Members."[30]

In April, the Cooper Ornithological Society's Northern California annual meeting was held on the Berkeley campus and across the bay at San Francisco's august scientific institution, the California Academy of Sciences. In the July issue of the society's journal, *The Condor*, Tracy Storer, an early Grinnell student who joined the MVZ staff, reported on the successful meetings as well as a dinner that Wright hosted for eighty-five people on the last night. "In the evening Mr. George M. Wright hospitably entertained the Club and its friends at his residence on Thousand Oaks Boulevard. Following a buffet supper, Mr. Joseph Dixon gave a vivid talk, accompanied by numerous lantern slides, on 'Nesting of the Alaska Willow Ptarmigan,' based on field work carried on by himself and Mr. Wright in the Mt. McKinley region during the summer of 1926."[31]

In May, Wright had just enough time to finish his job at the MVZ, pack, and drive to the Division of Forestry's Camp Califorest. Participation at the camp was a requirement of all Berkeley forestry students in order to graduate. It is probable Wright had been scheduled to attend camp the year before, in 1926, but he was busy hiking across McKinley National Park with Dixon (an arrangement no doubt agreed upon between Grinnell and Mulford). Camp Califorest was tucked into the northern Sierra Nevada foothills, just downslope from the small town of Quincy. The students, all young men, spent their days learning fundamental forestry techniques, such as surveying and creating vegetation plots. They also had guest talks from seasoned foresters, visited logging operations and mills, spent time hiking and fishing, and even took in a dance or two in Quincy.

While working at the MVZ and participating at the forestry camp, Wright was busy preparing for his next adventure. On October 17, he received a letter

from George Scott, chief of the Division of Appointments, Department of the
Interior, informing him that his application had been approved to become a
park ranger at Yosemite National Park.[32] After some preparations and plenty
of government paperwork, Wright and Auntie moved to Yosemite Valley in
November, and he officially joined the National Park Service.

4

Yosemite:
Dream Achieved, 1927–29

At the age of twenty-three, Wright achieved a goal he had been dreaming of, and striving for, his entire life: he was now working and living in a national park. He was constantly outside, surrounded by nature. This wasn't just any national park: it was Yosemite National Park, one of the most spectacular, popular, and—created in 1890—oldest parks in the system.[1]

Wright was already familiar with Yosemite, having visited on several occasions with friends. From his 1927 field notes, we know at least one of these visits was with Joseph Dixon of the MVZ, and another with a fellow Berkeley forester and future Park Service colleague, Ansel Hall. Wright was also acquainted with the small community of park staffers who worked and lived in Yosemite Valley, some of whom were Berkeley graduates. They were well aware of Wright's background and that he had recently been studying under Grinnell and Dixon. It is not surprising, then, that the park superintendent, Washington B. Lewis, and his staff were excited about Wright's hiring. In the superintendent's monthly report from November 1927, Lewis highlighted Wright's arrival to the park, adding that Wright would be "a valuable addition" to his staff.[2]

That same month, Wright settled into the rangers' living quarters, known as the Ranger's Club, and Auntie permanently moved into the newly completed Ahwahnee Hotel in order to be close to Wright. On his first day of work, November 15, 1927, Wright opened a fresh field notebook, turned to page 1, and recorded a brief, upbeat, and gently poetic entry: "The Valley is sparkling, cool and clear with an abundance of autumn coloring. About the rim there is ten inches of snow, ever so white against the blue sky."[3]

George Wright was a National Park Service Naturalist Ranger.

Despite his age, Wright entered this new position with extensive field experience, and he knew, firsthand, all of the national parks in the West, including McKinley in Alaska—a claim few people, including his new colleagues, could make. However, it is reasonable to believe he didn't fully understand, at least initially, what it meant to be working in, instead of simply visiting, a national park, particularly Yosemite. After all, Wright had very little experience with any kind of bureaucracy (except for the extensive paperwork required for his government job) or the management of people—let alone gaggles of tourists.

Wright would have no problems, for example, studying the wildlife and botany of the park and sharing that knowledge with visitors, as he had done for fellow Boy Scouts and Sierra Club members on High Country Trips. That would come instinctively to him, and he would carry out that duty with extreme joy for almost two years in Yosemite. But it is important to understand the other environment he was walking into: the human ecosystem of Yosemite National Park, both past and present, with all of its beautiful, challenging, and sometimes unpleasant idiosyncrasies. It was this other reality in the national park system, the one created by the presence of humans, which was so vividly on display in Yosemite and that Wright would, with time, focus on as his life's work. It was a challenge he would come to concisely define as "the problems caused by conflict between man and animal through joint occupancy of the park areas."[4]

In 1927, the National Park Service was only eleven years old. Prior to the creation of the service, many of the early national parks—Yellowstone, Yosemite, Sequoia, and General Grant (General Grant was incorporated into Kings Canyon National Park when the latter was created in 1940), for example—had been managed and patrolled for decades by the US Cavalry to bring order to the parks. Prior to that, under questionable civilian oversight in the late nineteenth century, poaching, logging, grazing, and general lawlessness were commonplace, including the destruction of geologic features in Yellowstone.[5]

Almost all of the national parks—numbering twenty in 1927—consisted of lands west of the hundredth meridian, that north–south longitudinal demarcation made famous by author Wallace Stegner. It emerges from Manitoba, Canada, splits the Dakotas down their middles and passes through Nebraska, Kansas, and Oklahoma before slicing through west Texas and exiting the United States through Coahuila, Mexico.[6] There were exceptions, of course, such as Lafayette (changed to Acadia in 1929), Hot Springs, Sully's Hill (redesignated as White Horse Hill National Game Preserve in 1931), and Platt (today part of Chickasaw National Recreation Area) National Parks. However, the majority of the magnificent landscape-scale parks stretched out between the hundredth meridian and the Pacific coast (and on to Hawaii). The Park Service also administered thirty-two national monuments; the Department of Agriculture oversaw fourteen national monument sites; and the War Department managed thirteen more.[7] Today there are 423 national park sites of various types.

It was a formative time for parks as the service matured under the guidance of its dynamic first director, Stephen T. Mather. Mather was one of the founding fathers of the Park Service. After helping to make the Park Service a reality as assistant to the secretary of the interior, Mather was appointed the service's first director in early 1917. He was a self-made millionaire from his time working in the borax industry, and he set about channeling his considerable business and publicity acumen into the national parks. Mather became the face of the fledgling National Park system, its primary and most passionate advocate, and the parks' supreme promoter. He was assisted the entire time by his stalwart right-hand man, Horace M. Albright, who also worked for the secretary of the interior and then became assistant director of the Park Service.

Both men were Californians, and both were graduates of the University of California, Berkeley. They were an excellent team, and with time Mather and Albright developed an unspoken, symbiotic relationship. Mather was fifty in 1917, while Albright—a newly minted lawyer—was twenty-seven. The gregarious Mather exuded confidence. With his brilliant blue eyes offset by a perpetual tan and a full head of prematurely white hair, he was the big idea guy. Albright, on the other hand, was more reserved and cautious; he knew Washington, DC, well and he was a proven administrator. Albright was the detail guy.[8]

In 1927, Mather was beginning to wind down his management of the parks, while also dealing with prolonged bouts of disabling manic depression.[9] Members of his staff had to step quietly and diplomatically into higher management roles—principally Albright, who slipped into the position of acting director—when Mather was out sick for extended periods of time. Albright revered Mather—whom he always called Mr. Mather—and he was consistently supportive and understanding of his mentor's struggles over the years.

During a period of good health, Mather assigned Albright to the service's most prized posting, at Yellowstone National Park, as its first superintendent appointed from within the Park Service, a position he held from 1919 to 1929, all the while keeping his assistant director title.[10] By the late 1920s, however, Albright was spending considerable time in the field, traveling between parks, and occasionally working out of the service's regional office in San Francisco.[11]

The economic and cultural changes of the 1920s affected the parks, particularly between 1926 and 1927, when there was a dramatic increase in tourism, chiefly due to the popularity of automobiles and autocamping. Nowhere else was this more apparent than in the large, iconic, and most popular parks: Yellowstone, Rocky Mountain, Grand Canyon, and—above all—Yosemite.

As early as November 1916, shortly after the Park Service was created, Mather, then in his position at the Interior Department, submitted a report to the secretary entitled "Progress in the Development of the National Parks." Even at that early date, he expressed amazement at the increase in automobile traffic to parks, and he suggested a concerted effort to improve roads to accommodate this growth. Mather also foreshadowed the demise of the railroads as the principal means of transport to national parks in the West as automobile numbers swelled. In the report, after he thanked no less than seventeen railroads for their financial assistance in producing a national parks promotional pamphlet, he then moved on, without hesitation, to highlighting the need to build more roads.[12]

Yellowstone's 1926 tourist numbers jumped from 187,807 to 200,825 in 1927. Yosemite's numbers, however, soared, almost doubling from 274,209 to approximately 500,000. This was nearly all the result of an increase in automobile traffic. The entire park system experienced a 21 percent increase in visitation from 1926 to 1927. In Yosemite, during the 1927 Decoration Day vacation week (today's Memorial Day), 10,000 cars entered the valley daily, and by noon on May 20, an estimated 25,000 people were in the valley. The park and concessionaires' infrastructures were overwhelmed. The existing campgrounds were overflowing, unsanctioned autocamping was rampant across the valley floor and in the meadows, and the park's scant bathrooms couldn't accommodate the wave of humanity.[13]

It was a bad situation. However, it must be remembered that although beautiful and majestic, Yosemite Valley was far from unspoiled in 1927. The area had been a state-owned reserve since 1864 when President Lincoln, in the midst of the Civil War, signed the Yosemite Valley Grant Act and ceded the valley and the Mariposa Big Tree Grove to the state of California—twenty-six years prior to it becoming a national park. The main reason the grant was approved was to help protect the area, "upon the express conditions that the premises shall be held for public use, resort, and recreation."[14] Before 1864, gold prospectors, loggers, hunters, trappers, and entrepreneurs had already severely impacted the massive and majestic valley. They were able to move in after the so-called Mariposa Battalion—a California militia formed to remove native Californians from potentially gold-rich lands—forcibly drove out the American Indians indigenous to the Yosemite area starting in 1851. Although tribal leader Chief Tenaya led a group of people to the eastern side of the Sierra to live, most of their members dispersed. Small bands and groups of the original stewards of the valley—which they called *Ahwahnee*, meaning "place like a gaping mouth"[15]—drifted back seasonally for years, while others eventually returned to live and work after Yosemite became a national park.[16] During the early years of the state reserve and well into the twentieth century, people continued to live in the valley, including many painters and early photographers. Cattle grazed everywhere, orchards thrived, and logging operations were still active.

Even in light of this history of displacement, occupation, and use, the 1927 tourist season in Yosemite was eye-opening, and startling, to park administrators. This staggering increase in visitation was fueled by two developments that were cited in Wright's employment documents under "justification" for his new position. The first was the completion of a year-round road into the valley in 1926. Prior to its construction, automobiles had had to negotiate the rutted and narrow old stagecoach road, which carried tourists from El Portal, the terminus of the Yosemite Valley Railroad. Many cars simply couldn't navigate it. And the second: the opening of the magnificent Ahwahnee Hotel in August 1927. Although the valley already had several lodging options, the publicity blitz around the Ahwahnee drew people from near and far. There is no doubt that Superintendent Lewis was truly excited about adding Wright to his team because of the young ranger's training and experience, but the Park Service was also desperate to hire more staff to handle the predicted winter surge of tourists due to these two improvements.

Wright's office was in the Yosemite Museum, built in 1925 and the first national park museum in the system. The museum stands to this day and still functions as offices for park staff. Wright's superior was Carl P. Russell, park naturalist for Yosemite. Russell had arrived in 1923 to work as a summer naturalist— and stayed. Not surprisingly, Russell was well acquainted with Grinnell and Dixon, and he was thankful to have Wright on his staff. With the help of Russell, Wright learned the routine of giving talks to tourists when they visited the museum, and also how and where to lead nature hikes throughout the valley. While he was acclimating to his new job, Wright still found time to observe and explore.

> The snow still lingers in patches on the north side and in considerable drifts on the south side of the valley. The elk are fighting vigorously. They are being fed hay at this time as all along since the first heavy snow covered the ground. Ranger Godfrey and I took a walk along the west boundary of the

Wright with camera, Yosemite National Park, ca. 1928. Photograph by Carl Russell. Courtesy of Pamela Meléndez Wright Lloyd.

park today. We spent the hours from nine to five today between Arch Rock and Chinquapin.[17]

In February 1928, while Wright was settling in and learning the ropes, a serious problem arose with his status as a park ranger. A regional bureaucrat reviewed Wright's paperwork and determined that at five foot four, he was too short to be a park ranger. Rangers were required to act as park police and carry a firearm, when necessary, and the height standard, though never stated, was above Wright's stature.[18] The district supervisor contacted Horace Albright, who was, on paper, working out of the Park Service's San Francisco office at the time. Albright was determined not to lose Wright. He immediately wrote a "personal and confidential" note to the acting National Park Service director, Arthur E. Demaray, who was temporarily sitting in for the ailing Mather.

> It is absolutely necessary that we keep Ranger George M. Wright. . . . This man has an income of $1200 per month and . . . he is a very generous and public spirited fellow. He has a Cadillac car which he is constantly using without cost to the Government; he is contributing books and articles of equipment to the museum; he is a fine naturalist and is doing splendid work. He has a spirit very much like that of Mr. Mather. He is the man who found the surf-bird's nest in Mt. McKinley Park—something that attracted attention throughout the United States last year. He has been in nearly all of the National Parks. Some way must be found to keep him.[19]

Albright was relentless. In a follow-up letter to the director, he specifically stated that Wright, unlike other rangers, would not have police duties, "because he is to be employed as a Ranger-Naturalist." Again, on April 17, Albright strongly asked the director to authorize Wright's new title: "We must take no chances of losing this valuable man."[20]

In late April, Director Mather, having returned to his duties, wrote to the secretary of the interior, Hubert Work, using Albright's wording verbatim from his March 1 letter. Mather implored the secretary to approve a new position, with the title of "Scientific Aid," for Wright. He was to be paid "$1,680 annually, minus $180 for quarters, heat and light."[21] The secretary approved the request, and Wright was allowed to stay.

Albright saw great potential in the young naturalist and therefore argued strongly to waive the height requirement to keep him in the service. He also anointed Wright with the ultimate compliment by comparing him to his own hero, Stephen Mather—a high honor that others would also allude to, with time.[22]

During these negotiations between Albright and the Washington, DC, office, Wright seemed to be unconcerned. There are no indications in his personal correspondence that anything was amiss. As Albright noted in his impassioned letter, Wright's monthly income from his personal trust was $1,200, almost the same amount that he was making annually as a Park Service employee. Free from financial concerns, Wright spent the next sixteen months taking full advantage of working and living in Yosemite National Park.

As time went on, the young assistant naturalist kept learning from and exploring with his boss, Carl Russell, and the two formed a strong relationship. On the occasional day off, they would often venture out for birdwatching, botanizing, and wildlife observation around the valley, as they did on February 27, 1928.

> Yesterday afternoon Carl and I scrambled 2/3 of the way up the north wall between El Capitan and the Three Brothers. . . . Two golden eagles hung about the face of the cliffs or, more correctly, sailed around them all afternoon. . . . At the same time, there was a mixed flock of ruby-crowned kinglets and bush-tits gypsying through the bushes. Our chief purpose was to visit the bear dens, these latter appeared to be entirely deserted whereas in March 1925 they showed fresh signs of occupancy.[23]

The young naturalist began many of his work days—after bringing coffee to Auntie at the Ahwahnee—with early morning, and sometimes all-day, hikes with Enid and Charles Michaels. Charles was the valley's assistant postmaster and an avid birdwatcher. Enid was the park's first ranger naturalist and considered one of the early pioneering women naturalists in the Park Service. Wright not only got to know Enid Michaels and her husband, but over the next seven years he would also befriend several other Park Service staffers who paved the way for other women to follow in their footsteps, such as Herma Albertson Baggley, who became the service's first permanent female park naturalist, based out of Yellowstone in 1931. Wright was supportive and encouraging to these trailblazing women. It is interesting to speculate if Auntie had a role in Wright's relatively liberal view of women in the Park Service. Horace Albright was also, overall, supportive of women in the Park Service, and Wright no doubt watched and listened to Albright closely.[24]

Other days he headed out with "my excellent roommate," Ranger Bill Godfrey, who also became a close friend. These naturalizing forays with senior colleagues and friends blended together with and complemented Wright's actual work duties. During 1927, for example, the park naturalist staff gave 423 lectures to almost 78,000 visitors and conducted 401 nature walks for over 6,500 people. More than 300,000 tourists flowed through the museum in 1927. These numbers increased substantially in 1928 and continued steadily into 1929. Wright and his naturalist colleagues were kept extremely busy.[25]

Wright also spent time with another type of park resident: local artists. The valley had long been a haven and inspiration for photographers and painters, and several made the valley their home off and on from the late nineteenth century through the first few decades of the twentieth. Two prominent resident painters, Norwegian-born Christian August Jorgensen and Swedish-born Gunnar Mauritz Widforss, both spent a considerable amount of time in the valley—particularly Jorgensen and his wife, Angela. Wright knew them well. He called Jorgensen "Uncle Chris," a nickname Jorgensen liked his younger friends to use. Both of these painters became famous for their work in Yosemite as well as for their renditions of other national parks and of coastal California.[26]

It is also highly likely that this is where Wright first met photographer Ansel Adams—though it could have been in San Francisco, where they were both born. They were only two years apart in age; Adams grew up in the far reaches of the Richmond District. Both spent their youth exploring the wilder corners of the city, and both were dedicated Sierra Club members.

In the small community of Yosemite Valley in the late 1920s, these two young men undoubtedly connected. Adams, however, first came to Yosemite on a family trip when he was twelve; he returned in 1920, when he was eighteen, to manage the Sierra Club's LeConte Lodge at the base of Glacier Point.[27] In 1927, Adams was spending a lot of time at a photography and landscape painting showroom known as Best's Studio, which had been operating seasonally in the valley since 1902. But it was more than photography that drew Adams to the establishment. Virginia Best, the owners' daughter, was just as important. After courting, they married in the park on January 2, 1928, and settled down to help manage the studio.[28]

As early as January of 1928, Assistant Naturalist Wright also put his high school journalist hat back on and began writing articles for *Yosemite Nature Notes*, the official publication of Yosemite National Park's education department. His natural history articles focused, not surprisingly, on birds—mountain quail, golden eagles, and songs and calls, for example—but he also highlighted the valley's deer, woodrats, and a devastating fungus that was ravaging the valley's western chokecherry. In "Fare of the Golden Eagle," Wright notes, "No eagle ever took wing over scenes of more impressive grandeur than do those which soar about the domes of Yosemite. Here, if any place, they should be epicures. But alas! By actual observation, carrion carcasses of deer seem to be the leading article of diet, on a very plebeian menu." After explaining it was truly rare that eagles kill lambs, calves, or fawns, if ever, he

Cordelia Wright, "Auntie," in her room at the Ahwahnee Hotel, Yosemite National Park, December 1927. Note Wright's hands, bottom right of image. Courtesy of Pamela Meléndez Wright Lloyd.

finished with: "The golden eagle is fast vanishing. His status would profit if it could be shown that stockmen and hunters have blackened his character unjustly or to unreasonable extent in the past."[29]

Sometime during the late summer or early fall of 1928, Ben Thompson returned to Yosemite to pursue his restaurant job again—this time at the Ahwahnee. He quickly struck up what would be an enduring friendship with Wright. At about that same time, Auntie's health began to fail. On October 11, Wright wrote to Dixon back on the Berkeley campus. "Auntie is as well as can be expected, though some little difficulties arise now and then, and she grows ever a little more weak. I hope that we will be able to keep her here through the winter, but I am always prepared for an emergency move." Two months later, on December 10, he penned another note to Dixon. "Auntie is fairly well this morning. I have just come from giving her the morning coffee. She remembers you very clearly."[30] Just nine days later, Cordelia Wright, Auntie, died in the Ahwahnee Hotel, where she had been living for over a year. She was eighty-eight years old.

From all accounts, Auntie was an extraordinary person. For her, George Wright was "My Boy." Since 1906, when Wright's mother, Mercedes Meléndez, had died suddenly, Auntie had been Wright's caring substitute parent and constant companion. Of course, Wright had an extended family in El Salvador, but he had very little contact with his brothers Johnny and Charles. And while members of the Meléndez family would occasionally come stay at the house on Laguna Street during his childhood in San Francisco, or drop by during their travels, and friendships were formed, Auntie was his family.

In Wright's field notes from January 1929 he stoically records: "From October 20 to date my outdoor activities have been nil. From Oct. 23 until Dec. 19 I was in attendance upon an ill person. Since then, except for a three day run to San Francisco, I have been in the Yosemite Museum."

Wright buried Auntie at Cypress Lawn Memorial Park, in Colma, just south of San Francisco, next to her husband—his grandfather—Captain George S. Wright.

Another octogenarian, who also considered Wright one of "my boys," was Maria Lebrado. In July 1929, Lebrado visited Yosemite Valley for the first time since she was a little girl, some eighty years before. Lebrado, also known as Totuya (Foaming Waters), was one of the last American Indians that fled the valley during the 1851 attack by the Mariposa Battalion. She was also a granddaughter of Chief Tenaya.

That July day in 1929, she arrived in Yosemite with one of her daughters, Grace, from California's Central Valley, and since Spanish was her principal language (her second husband was Mexican American), Wright served as host and interpreter. According to an article in *Yosemite Nature Notes*, Wright and Thompson (who also spoke Spanish from his upbringing in Arizona) spent a day with Lebrado, visiting the museum, walking around the valley floor, eating acorn meal she had prepared, and listening. They quickly bonded.[31]

Dixon was in the valley at the time as well and, after some negotiations, Lebrado allowed her photograph to be taken with Wright. In the images that have survived, it appears as though there was some serious storytelling taking place. In one image, she is making a point, with her arm raised and finger outstretched; head slightly tilted, Wright is listening with rapt attention. What was she saying?

Another image shows Lebrado suppressing a smile. Perhaps a small joke between the new friends? In March of 1931, Maria Lebrado fell ill and her daughters informed the superintendent of Yosemite, Colonel Charles Goff Thomson.[32] They wanted to make sure that Wright knew. Yosemite's assistant park naturalist, George Crowe, wrote to Wright in Berkeley to inform him about Lebrado and to ask, regarding her family, "If you have any suggestions I will be glad to see what I can do for them."[33] She passed away several weeks later.

Wright and Maria Lebrado, Totuya, Yosemite National Park, July 1929. Photograph by Joseph Dixon. Courtesy of Pamela Meléndez Wright Lloyd.

Although there was an "Indian Village" in the valley during Wright's time there,[34] with some sixty to seventy residents, his experience and relationship with Lebrado—an American Indian resident of Yosemite Valley from the mid-nineteenth century—served as tangible proof to Wright of an elemental fact that would come to influence his thinking about wildlife management in parks: people had been living in, and managing, so-called wilderness areas for thousands of years. The presence of people in these inhabited landscapes far predated the creation of national parks and protected areas, and this reality had to be acknowledged and accounted for as part of any management equation moving forward.

How do you restore fauna in the national parks, Wright would ask, to a "pristine state," and then manage at that level, when the question of what is pristine had yet to be determined? And, once that is determined and agreed upon, how do you manage contemporary humans—tourists—in those parks with the inevitable problems caused by people and wildlife jointly occupying national parks?

Am I Visionary, or Just Crazy?

Wright spent almost two years working in Yosemite National Park—from the fall of 1927 to the summer of 1929—learning the trade of a Park Service naturalist. During this entire time, Wright was formulating a groundbreaking idea. And it soon became all-consuming, constantly playing in the forefront of his mind as he flourished in Yosemite Valley. Finally, cautiously, he began to talk about his proposal with a few of his mentors, several close colleagues, and his new friend Ben Thompson. His idea? To organize and finance a wildlife survey for the western national parks—an undertaking that had never been pursued before.

Starting at a young age, and on his own initiative, Wright had traveled extensively throughout the western United States to visit national parks. He had explored Sequoia National Park, Kings River Canyon, and the Sierra on foot with the Sierra Club. He had dusted off his Model T and completed at least two large national park circuits as he drove around the West. And he had sailed north with Dixon, reaching Alaska's Mount McKinley National Park and conducting fieldwork for almost three months there. During his years in Yosemite, he had continued to observe firsthand how extremely out of balance the wildlife and natural systems of the western national parks were, and had been for at least a generation, if not longer.

In particular, Wright disagreed with the Park Service's tradition of feeding bears at dumps, or "bear pits" as they were called, as well as the construction of bleachers so that the public could witness massive grizzlies and their cubs in Yellowstone and black bears in other parks grovel and fight over garbage. He questioned corralling elk and bison for convenient and close observation by park visitors, and he intensely disliked the so-called park zoos (as did Grinnell), such as the ramshackle pens in Yosemite, which displayed sad and often maimed specimens of local wildlife to fulfill the same purpose: easy viewing for tourists.[1] And, like his mentor Grinnell, he railed against the indiscriminate and widespread killing of any predators found in or near park boundaries—from wolves, mountain lions, and coyotes down to porcupines and skunks.

Wright believed these practices ran completely counter to any notion of a natural and functioning landscape, especially within a national park. He considered these, and other Park Service management activities, not only harmful to the long-term health of the parks but in contradiction to how he interpreted the National Park Service Organic Act of 1916 that created the parks. The act states, in part, that the purpose of national parks "is to conserve the scenery and the natural and historic objects and the wild life therein and to provide for the enjoyment of the same in such manner and by such means as will leave them unimpaired for the enjoyment of future generations."[2] There is no question Wright was influenced in this belief by Grinnell, but he had also studied the act and would come to cite it often.

Wright was slowly, and quietly at first, mounting a challenge to what historian Richard West Sellars has termed "façade" management: the park management style that was created and vigorously promulgated by the service's first two legendary directors, Mather and Albright. Façade management, as described by Sellars, was "protecting and enhancing the scenic façade of nature for the public's enjoyment, but with scant scientific knowledge and little concern for biological consequences."[3] This was a tension born of managing for short-term aesthetic purposes and convenience over managing for long-term ecological health: tourism, trains, hotels, and roads versus what Wright would come to call science-based restoration and management of the "pristine state."[4]

In the fall of 1928, for example, Wright's Yosemite field notes contained many entries about the nonnative but endangered tule elk that had been shipped to Yosemite Valley in 1921 from California's San Joaquin Valley, then corralled and fed by the Park Service during the intervening seven years. He was also disturbed by their unnatural presence in the valley as well as the small zoo maintained there. From his viewpoint, they were one and the same. "The elk problem bothers me very much," he noted. "There are many sides to the question."[5]

Recognition that there are wild-life problems is admission that unnatural, man-made conditions exist. Therefore, there can be no logical objection to further interference by man to correct those conditions and restore the natural state. But due care must be taken that management does not create an even more artificial condition in place of the one it would correct.

                                        GEORGE WRIGHT[6]

On the same day that he recorded the "elk problem" in his field notes, Wright wrote a letter to Grinnell in Berkeley. His former professor had sent a prominent Russian zoologist and ecologist, Daniil Kashkarov, to Yosemite with a letter of introduction.[7] Wright had served as Kashkarov's guide for the day.

"My own interest in ecological studies has always been very great, if, perhaps, undernourished," admitted Wright. "However, contact with this scientist stimulated me to new enthusiasm." And then, as if sneaking in a hint about his budding wildlife survey idea, Wright complimented Grinnell on his monumental book that served as their guide that day. "As on many past occasions, it was most fortunate that we had *Animal Life in Yosemite* to fall back upon. This sort of work certainly should be carried on in all of the national parks as soon as practicable." He then let Grinnell know that he could always call on him for anything whatsoever because "I feel that it was largely through you and Joe Dixon that I find myself in this very congenial situation."[8]

Joseph Dixon and George Wright had a very collaborative and close relationship: an almost father-son, or older brother-younger brother, bond. Their Alaska trip in 1926 cemented that connection. There is no question that from the beginning, Dixon was one of Wright's thought partners and teachers as the young assistant naturalist solidified his ideas around the wildlife survey. Only later did Wright loop in his boss and friend, Carl Russell, as well as Ben Thompson, while Professors Mulford and Grinnell, and a few others, would be included in the discussions a few months later.

Dixon had four young children by 1928, and his correspondence with Wright indicates that he was constantly looking for greener pastures. Money was tight. In October of that year, Dixon informed Wright that he had taken a different approach to potential solvency. He had applied for the position of head field naturalist for the National Park Service. Wright responded that he was truly happy for Dixon, envious really, but the two had already been in talks about the wildlife survey and Wright wanted Dixon to partner with him on the project. "My wonderful experience with you in Alaska has proved to me that no one would be more satisfactory to work with," Wright lobbied from Yosemite, "However, until we can talk to one another at considerable length and really lay all of the cards on the table, I suppose it will be impossible to formulate any definite plans. But you have no idea how anxious I am for that talk to come about."[9]

Four months later, in February 1929, Wright wrote Dixon and laid out his initial plan of action for a two-year wildlife survey, while thanking him for giving him "new courage," and also fully acknowledging the daunting task before him and admitting a few personal foibles, desires, and fears. "I know myself quite well enough to be entirely confident that I would fulfill my promises," Wright continued. "When I contract to sponsor this thing for two years I'll have it bought and paid for at the start. Your salary and money for field expense can be put in an account where I can't even reach it. . . . Joe! Am I visionary or just crazy?" He signed off with "More power to our side."[10]

In those intervening four months, Wright and Dixon had slowly circulated the wildlife survey idea to a wider circle of people. Some of them thought Wright too young and inexperienced to take on such a large and important research project for the Park Service. Grinnell, although a big supporter of his former student, was apparently one of those doubters.

Early on, Wright admitted that he was intimidated by Grinnell. But this sentiment would utterly change in the years to come, as Wright and Grinnell would exchange correspondence and ideas pertaining to national park issues, as well as more social notes discussing Cooper Society events and updates from the Berkeley scene. As Wright's career in the NPS flourished, Grinnell proved to be his confidant, sounding board, and intellectual guide as his thoughts around wildlife management and wilderness in the national parks, and other park-related issues, matured.

In response to this feedback, Wright and Dixon agreed that Dixon would become the front man for the project, lending it his seniority and years of field experience. Without hesitation, Dixon took his cue from Wright and wrote to Albright, who had assumed the directorship in January 1929 after Stephen Mather suffered a stroke and resigned. Albright had already been part of earlier discussions.

"At last I think we are in a position to get real action on the proposed survey of wild life problems in National Parks," Dixon suggested to Albright. "I spent the major portion of last Sunday night going over with George Wright, the details of his offer to finance the investigation. I subsequently again went over the proposed program with Mr. Ansel Hall."

Like Wright, Hall was a Berkeley forestry graduate who had joined the Park Service early on and quickly rose to become the first chief naturalist and chief forester. The initial thinking by the Park Service was that the wildlife survey should be part of the education branch, which housed the naturalist program. Wright disagreed. He wanted it to be a discrete program: he wanted a measure of independence.

"George is very anxious that the work begin July 1, 1929," continued Dixon, "as a regular National Park project associated with the Educational Division. George is very modest and does not wish to have any undue publicity given to his part in the program. At the same time, he, like the rest of us, appreciates credit being given where credit is due."

Again, Dixon emphasized that all funds would be secured ahead of time to cover field equipment, supplies, and travel expenses for two years. Wright also wanted to buy the wildlife survey's research vehicle and not go through government procurement channels because, according to Dixon, "he wanted to have a good engine under him." Dixon let the director know that all of the members of the secretary of the interior's Educational Advisory Board, which provided advice on the Park Service's educational programs, had given their enthusiastic approval of the project.[11] In another letter on the same day, Dixon wrote to Harold Bryant, by now a senior Park Service employee in the education branch based out of Washington, DC, and also a member of the board. Dixon was delighted that the advisory board was behind the project. In particular, he mentioned the support of John C. Merriam of the Carnegie Institute (by way of Berkeley's Paleontology Department), and his practical suggestion that "some of the outstanding and most pressing problems can be defined at once and work on them started at an early date without waiting for the entire survey to be completed."[12]

Over the course of the next few weeks a fundamental shift occurred with the dynamics of the wildlife survey. Wright began communicating directly with Albright. Dixon was still intended to be the titular head of the wildlife survey, but Wright's guiding hand and confidence began to shine, and they never dimmed. Wright sent a letter to the director from Yosemite and submitted the wildlife survey plan "reduced to its simplest terms." He told Albright he looked forward to discussing it soon, during the director's upcoming trip to the valley.[13] Wright included his "Proposed Survey of Animal Life Problems in National Parks" with the letter. It spelled out, for the first time, and with quasi-legal or contractual precision, the essence of the wildlife survey:

> The object of this work shall be to make an inventory of wild animal problems in the National Parks, and (a) to seek to define the more important and more pressing problems, (b) to seek a fair appraisal of the possibilities and methods of solving such problems. To this end, specimens, fieldnotes, photographs, and other scientific data showing actual conditions affecting animal life in the National Parks shall be sought.[14]

Wright reiterated his desire to start on July 1, 1929, and agreed to deposit $10,000 in a San Francisco account that would be managed by a board of three trustees, including his former professor Walter Mulford, a Park Service representative, and a bank or other financial representative to be chosen by Wright.[15] Dixon was to receive the title of Field Naturalist, with an annual salary of $4,000 (increasing to $4,500 the second year). He then stated that during the first two years of the survey, the government must strive to procure funds to continue the survey into the third year and beyond, if necessary. He insisted that the wildlife survey headquarters would be based in Berkeley. And he established a basic annual schedule, balancing fieldwork with time in the office, allowing the team a third of each year to concentrate on their report, based on the field studies. Additionally, he wished for the assurance that the results would be published by the government within a year after the survey was completed in a form that could be useful as a reference for fellow Park Service staff in the field.

Albright replied to Wright two days later, stating in no uncertain terms that he had a "keen personal interest in you and my desire to see you continue your association with us in this tremendously interesting new field which at the present time has prospects of developing into the biggest and most important activity of the National Park Service." He thanked Wright for his "splendid offer" and looked forward to discussing the details.[16] Albright, once an architect of façade management, believed Wright's wildlife survey plan was brilliant and critical for the Park Service's future. He approved it immediately. George Wright wasn't "just crazy," as he had suggested to Dixon. He was a visionary.

In 1929, the bureaucratic wheels of the relatively new National Park Service were already turning slowly. First, there was the matter of extracting Wright from his position as assistant park naturalist at Yosemite, changing his title to park naturalist aide, then completing the "Transfer within Service (at Large)" paperwork.[17] In order to speed up the process, Wright offered to forgo his salary for two years; eventually, a legal ruling by the Department of the Interior determined Wright could continue to be employed by the service with a salary of $12 a year.

Wright was in Yosemite through April of that year until he fell ill, spending the entire month of May at Peralta Hospital in Oakland. The culprit was an acute duodenal ulcer, located in the upper reaches of his small intestine that had bothered him previously. Ironically, one of Wright's best bird call descriptions in his field notebooks was recorded from this Oakland hospital bed. A brown towhee—a decidedly plain but interesting bird—had commandeered his windowsill to start its spring histrionics. So, naturally, the naturalist recorded the towhee's behavior and calls. Grinnell wrote him in an attempt to cheer him up. "Here's trusting you'll soon be out among the hills," the professor wrote encouragingly, "away from human congestion and into the restful association with wild creatures."[18]

June found Wright back in Yosemite, still as assistant park naturalist. He was joined there by Dixon who camped out for the summer with his wife and four children. By July, however, Wright's transfer was completed, and he returned to Berkeley to continue to set up the wildlife survey's new office in the American Trust Building, located two blocks from the Berkeley campus.[19] Dixon stayed on in Yosemite until early August, then followed Wright to Berkeley. Later that month, wasting no time, the biologists drove to Yellowstone. Thompson, meanwhile, was back at Berkeley beginning his studies under Grinnell so he could join the team the following spring.

During their time in Yellowstone, both Wright and Dixon kept field notes, but Wright's, unfortunately, have been lost. The two researchers, according to Dixon's records, spent just about every day together in the field, and they concentrated on two species and their specific management issues: trumpeter swans and bears. These animals would be a focus of their fieldwork for years to come.

During the previous two years in Yosemite, Wright had often recorded information about black bears in his field notes: where they denned, arrival time after hibernation, numbers of cubs, the issue with garbage pits, and the increasing problem with bears raiding campsites and performing "holdups." Holdup bears, who were mostly female, had learned to stop in the middle of the road when a car approached, stand on their back feet, and raise their forelegs, thereby "holding up," or robbing, the tourists. (The bears had been doing this for years before Wright's arrival.) The excited tourists would inevitably stop, the mama bear would then approach the car to be fed, with her cubs in tow. It was a terrible, and sometimes fatal, behavior passed down from mother to cubs for generations.

In the very early twentieth century, many park employees advocated killing all bears in Yosemite Valley because of the damage they were doing to campsites. By the late 1920s, and operating with slightly more enlightened views, the Park Service experimented with trained dogs to chase bears away from areas frequented by people. They even designed a bear trap barrel to catch ursine offenders live and then ship them to another part of the Sierra.

In spite of these efforts, both bears and humans often behaved badly, or worse, stupidly. Tourists attempted to pose with bears, as if they were circus animals. When visitors ran out of treats, the bears became agitated. Black

Left to right: George Wright, Ben Thompson, and Joseph Dixon, Mono Lake, California, July 24, 1929. Photograph by Frances Chamberlain. Courtesy of Pamela Meléndez Wright Lloyd.

bears weigh, on average, between 150 and 250 pounds. In other words: You don't want to try to put your arm around an angry bear. Dixon reported that in 1929 alone, eighty-four people had been bitten or seriously scratched by bears in Yosemite (mostly on their hands and arms).[20] Bears that harmed people more than once, or were threatening, had to be killed, though the Park Service neither preferred that solution nor to let it be widely known.

Carl Russell, in particular, was an advocate for leaving the bears alone. He believed the problem originated with bad human behavior, not bears. Tourists and residents alike had to stop feeding bears and providing readily available garbage in their camps and houses. Needless to say, it was an uphill struggle, and the situation would not be resolved for decades to come.[21]

Yellowstone, the biologists learned, had a similar problem on its hands. There were holdup bears, as in Yosemite. But the park also had a major problem with bear raids on automobile tent encampments: the raids were constant and often lasted all night long. Even when tourists rented a hotel room or a cabin in Yellowstone and removed food from their vehicles, bears would rip open the cars' canvas tops or break doors to get in, often while the tourists were inside their cabins, just yards away. It happened nightly while Wright and Dixon were in the park, and the tourists were livid. (The biologists were camping away from the developed areas.) Over a period of several days, Dixon researched each break-in and interviewed each car owner. He inspected for food and recorded names, addresses, the make and license plate numbers of the cars. He determined that it was only one or two older black bears with bad habits, and it didn't matter if there was food in the cars or not.[22]

Yellowstone also maintained bear-feeding pits where garbage was dumped. The dump near the Canyon Hotel was frequented by black bears and grizzlies, but the more remote Lake Lodge garbage pit was the exclusive domain of the dominant bear species in the Yellowstone ecosystem: the grizzly. Female

No. 25   Subject Bear, Grizzly (four-full plate)   Reg. No. 50+
Date Sept. 11, 1929 Locality Canyon Lodge Yellowstone, N.P.   Photographer J. Dixon

Wright & Dixon

Grizzly bears at Canyon Lodge dump, Yellowstone National Park, September 11, 1929. Photograph by Joseph Dixon. Courtesy of NPS History Collection.

grizzlies can weigh up to 400 pounds, and males, up to 700. They have massive jaws, four-inch claws, and are surprisingly fast and agile.[23]

The researchers accompanied the Lake Lodge garbage truck out to the dump several times. The drivers recounted seeing thirty-two grizzlies at the dump a few weeks before Wright and Dixon arrived, and the bears had become so unruly in anticipation of their meals of garbage, the staff reported, that they had begun charging and climbing onto the truck upon its arrival. Needless to say, this not only frightened the drivers but prevented them from dumping their garbage. Rangers with shotguns soon accompanied them and fired warning shots. After this, the bears' aggressive behavior, for the most part, stopped. During one dump visit Wright and Dixon saw sixteen grizzlies at once, a sight which astonished them. It was, of course, a completely unnatural scene, but for two avid naturalists, also an incredible one. Dixon exclaimed in his notes that he had "8 grizzlies in the finder of the movie camera at once."[24]

The duo could not solve the Yellowstone (or Yosemite) bear problem after just one visit but they, and soon Thompson, would spend considerable time over the next three years attempting to do so.

During the next few weeks, when they weren't researching bears, they focused on swans. And not just any swan: the trumpeter swan. This magnificent bird, which Wright would come to call "the greatest of our American waterfowl,"[25] once ranged over most of North America.[26] By 1929, only a handful of birds survived in the greater Yellowstone area.[27] The trumpeter swan is the largest of the North American water birds, with magnificent wings that can span almost eight feet from tip to tip. The males, or cobs, can weigh close to thirty pounds, while the females, known as pens, can top twenty pounds. With graceful, sinuous necks that can reach five feet long, and brilliant white feathers with jet-black facial features, they are a spectacle to behold.

Decades of hunting had eliminated the swans from the vast majority of their historic range. The early and main culprit was the Hudson Bay Company, which employed hunters who shot thousands of birds starting in the late eighteenth century in order to export swan skins and feathers to Europe. There they were made into a variety of women's fashion products.[28] That was followed by domestic market hunting and sport hunting, which, combined, succeeded in extirpating the swans from their range. Although Wright and Dixon dedicated some days to observing other key species—elk, bison, deer, badgers, and pronghorn antelope, for example—the remainder of their time in Yellowstone was spent trying to get a basic understanding of the swans' behavior and their numbers. They also interviewed people they called "oldtimers" about the swans.

After returning to Berkeley, they continued to organize their office (with Thompson lending a helping hand) and plan for the 1930 field trip season. There was, however, one critical event that took place, which interrupted the team's planning: the stock market crash, and with it, the incremental creep of the Great Depression.[29] The stock market would continue to plummet—with the occasional, anemic spike of recovery—until the summer of 1932, when it bottomed out and depression truly gripped the land.

How opportune was it, then, that Albright had agreed to the wildlife survey earlier in the year, and that Wright had established a trust fund, in cash, to cover expenses for the next two years? The Depression, and other societal and environmental challenges that plagued the United States and the world during the early 1930s, were acknowledged by the team, but these factors would, miraculously, have only the slightest of impacts on their important work.

6

Beginnings:
The Wildlife Survey, 1930

By now, Wright, Thompson, and Dixon had deep roots in Yosemite, and in March of 1930—prior to their official departure on the survey—they visited the valley for some preliminary fieldwork. Wright's notes from the trip are both detailed and nostalgic. But this visit was different: Wright was no longer a ranger there; Thompson was far from his busboy days; and Dixon wasn't working with Grinnell. This was the Park Service's wildlife survey. This was official. After they arrived, the team checked in with Superintendent Colonel C. G. Thomson and discussed a variety of wildlife issues, then moved on to conduct a census of the valley's deer population: the stated central focus of their brief trip.

To make possible the great joy to be found in the infinite variety of the wilderness—not to thwart the desire to discover more and more of its ways—and the moral obligation to leave it unimpaired for new discoveries tomorrow, these are functions of the national parks in our general scheme of wilderness use. Here is a thing so glorious that it threatens to be impossible. How can the secret beauty of wilderness be opened to the people and remain unspoiled? This is the greatest question we have to meet if we are to save this and every other national park as truly primitive areas.

BEN THOMPSON[1]

During the early years of the Park Service, deer were a main attraction in parks, especially in Yosemite. In fact the park had a small herd of tame deer that lived around the developed parts of the valley, kept there with the express purpose of entertaining tourists. The deer had been trained by staff over time to eat out of visitors' hands, and they were considered—by visitors—as little more than domesticated pets: they were nonthreatening—cute, even. These socialized deer were wildlife that had been stripped of their wildness. Spread out across the valley, however, was also a very large herd of deer that were, for all intents and purposes, wild. And it was with this population of deer that the interests of Wright, Dixon, and Thompson lay.

The researchers knew from firsthand experience that two of the park's largest natural predators—wolves and grizzlies—had been absent from the valley for decades. Additionally, mountain lions and coyotes were constantly being hunted and trapped; their numbers were so depressed that they were rarely seen. Because of this dearth of natural predators, the biologists' basic concern was that the deer population would soon increase beyond the valley's capacity; that the deer could potentially overgraze the valley's vegetation, and, as a result, their physical condition would suffer too. "We counted 96 mule deer in the valley by covering the floor as completely as we could from the car," stated Wright. "Practically all of them were feeding in the meadows on the new grass."[2]

It was also during these first few months of 1930 that Wright purchased a car "of the latest vintage" for the survey team. As Dixon had written to Albright over a year before, when they were negotiating the approval of the survey, Wright "wanted to have a good engine under him." Translated from Dixon's tactful language, this meant that Wright had no time for a government-issued vehicle not suited for fieldwork. Wright settled on a 1930 Buick, a large and heavy-duty automobile—some sixteen feet long—from Buick's "big series" of cars.[3]

As Thompson remembered in 1987, the car was a Buick Roadster, "and three could sit comfortably in the front seat." He continued: "They cut the conventional back off, and built a truck bed on the back, like today's trucks. There was a water-tight compartment built right behind the front seat for camera equipment, books, and other things you needed to protect. Camping gear, pots, and bedding and everything else was under a tarp in the back."[4]

Customizing the Buick—which the wildlife survey team called "the truck"—took much longer than anticipated. "Mr. Dixon, Ben and I are all champing at the bit," Wright wrote to his friend and Yosemite National Park naturalist C. A. Hartwell on May 15, "We should be in the field by now were it not for delay in finishing up our field car."[5]

But, finally, the truck was ready and the team assembled on May 24: the wildlife survey was ready to begin. That same afternoon, they steered the truck toward Los Angeles and started off. With the trio comfortably settled across the front bench seat, and the back loaded down with the equipment for their first field season, it was an exhilarating moment. However, the first

A SURVEY OF ANIMAL PROBLEMS
IN THE
NATIONAL PARKS
OF THE
UNITED STATES

FIELD < 1930 > SEASON

April and early May have been spent in preparation. After numerous delays which have delayed our starting nearly three weeks we are on the way. No one can know how glad we are.

May 24. This is the first official field season of "WAS." wild animal surveys in National Parks. This party consists of Joseph Dixon, economic mammalogist at the University of California, George M. Wright, scientific aide, U.S.N.P.S., and Benjamin H. Thompson, field assistant. We start in a car of latest vintage (registering 160 miles only) which the members of the party have had built from an idea of their own. The summer will be spent in the National Parks and in travelling the roads which connect them with San Francisco. It is hoped to glean such facts as we may, concerning the wild animal life in the parks and then to interpret them for the use of the National Park Service. This project was

Wright's field note recording the beginning of the Wildlife Survey, May 24, 1930. Courtesy of Pamela Meléndez Wright Lloyd.

day of travel was not one of wildlife and wild scenery. Instead, it was spent "laboriously" driving south, and in place of camping out embraced by the spectacular landscape of a national park or monument, the trio unceremoniously threw down their bedrolls in a "stubble field just south of Kings City."[6] But they didn't mind: at long last, they were on the road.

Wildlife survey truck, with Wright behind the wheel, Steamboat Rock, Fredonia, Arizona, May 1930. Photograph by Joseph Dixon. Courtesy of Pamela Meléndez Wright Lloyd.

In Los Angeles, they were delayed again, spending two days to have the Buick's rear springs strengthened. Their cargo alone weighed 1,160 pounds, and the vehicle plus the team tipped the scales at three tons. With the truck fortified, the team finally left that "go-getter" city, as Wright called it, and turned southeast. After brief stops at Zion National Park in Utah and Pipe Spring National Monument in Arizona, they arrived at Arizona's Grand Canyon National Park on the afternoon of May 30, 1930.

At the Grand Canyon, the survey's first official stop, the biologists laid down the groundwork for what would become an invaluable routine upon entering each park. They began by meeting with the superintendent, Miner R. Tillotson, at Grand Canyon Village headquarters. As in Yosemite, the team's initial focus was on deer. Tillotson informed them that state game officials wanted to raise the local hunting limit for mule deer in the fall to an impressive ten thousand animals, due to what the officials claimed was the "overstretched" winter feeding range.

The Kaibab Plateau forests sit at seven to eight thousand feet of elevation, and the Grand Canyon carves the plateau in two: the northern and southern Kaibab.[7] In 1930, it was estimated that some thirty thousand deer thrived across the northern Kaibab Plateau on National Park and Forest Service property. Come fall and cooler temperatures, these deer migrated downslope from the high forests of the Kaibab Federal Game Refuge, outside the park, and onto additional Forest Service lands and other public properties, where they were pursued by hunters.

Wright had visited the park before, and he knew that, in recent history, overgrazing had been a major problem in the region, both inside and outside the park. However, he doubted that the previous winter's range was as severely overgrazed as claimed, because the deer he and the team inspected looked "better than any mule deer I have ever seen coming off winter range." In fact, park staff said that the previous late summer and fall were comparatively moist and winter conditions were good for deer. Tillotson and his rangers shared another theory about why the new proposed bag limit was set so high: The preceding season some 3,800 deer were shot outside park boundaries, netting $22,000 in state and local hunting fees. In short, they believed the decision to increase the bag limit was based strictly on economic considerations, and that it had nothing to do with grazing conditions that year, let alone any science-based range analysis.[8]

Regardless of the factors, from the financial to the biological, the Kaibab deer herd had been at the center of the regional and national debate for several decades. In 1903, President Theodore Roosevelt, a renowned hunter, visited the Grand Canyon, the Kaibab Plateau, and its deer herd. By 1906, he had established the 727,000-acre Kaibab Federal Game Refuge. This was followed by his declaration of the 1,279-square-mile Grand Canyon National Monument in 1908, bringing much-needed protection to the canyon and adjacent lands as well as an additional safeguard for the deer population. By 1919, the monument lands had become Grand Canyon National Park.[9]

The Kaibab deer herd was famous for its size, and it became still more so, but for the wrong reasons, after the winter of 1924–25. Throughout the previous years, the size of the herd had been surging, and, as a result, the Forest Service called for an organized culling of roughly half of the herd. Park Service Director Mather, however, disagreed. He simply didn't believe that the large deer herds were detrimental, and, more importantly, the spectacle was appreciated by visitors to the Grand Canyon region.[10] As a result, thousands of deer died over the course of that winter due to starvation. It is a case study in wildlands management that scientists and conservationists have analyzed, and disagreed about, for decades.[11]

Another problem Tillotson brought up to the biologists was that cattle had been grazing in the park. The survey team saw this for themselves, too. "Old-timers are still permitted to graze cattle in the park," Wright lamented. "Grazing in the past has reduced the range to a deplorable condition. Bunch grasses are in poor shape and the scrub oak browsed so that only tops out of reach remained intact while the smaller bushes were almost 100% dead brittle stubs."[12]

"It is a strange feeling," Wright went on to note, sarcastically, and with a historical reference to explorer John Wesley Powell, "to have a white faced steer standing and gazing at the 'Sublime Spectacle' in an atmosphere of congeniality with the park visitor."[13]

"I believe that the Kaibab will yield more over a long period of time in <u>deer</u> hunting than it ever would from the few cattle that could range there," Wright continued. "As it is now the <u>deer</u> will go down. Then there will be a cry to stock more <u>cattle</u> on the extra range and there will be a temporary increase of revenue from these grazing fees."[14]

This was a tug of war the team would become all too familiar with: caring for wildlife and its habitat versus maximizing grazing for livestock. Across the West, cattle and sheep ranchers wanted to keep park boundaries as limited as possible and to increase removal of deer, elk, and bison to "free up" range for their animals. The wildlife team's field research, on the other hand, sought to achieve the exact opposite result.[15]

The presence of cattle, and the status of the Kaibab deer, was, however, just a sampling of the drama that came with managing Grand Canyon National Park. For many years, entrenched interests throughout the Grand

Canyon landscape had relentlessly butted heads with the Park Service, and the opposition was formidable. Topics of contention also included the potential for timber harvesting across the plateaus as well as the possible expansion of the park's boundaries. This was, in no uncertain terms, contested terrain: a crossroads of conflicting interests. Forest Service lands surrounded the park to the north and south; existing private inholdings and mining claims within the park proved to be troublesome; and the Office of Indian Affairs and local tribes—the Navajo, Hopi, Havasupai, and Hualapai—were also, understandably, sensitive about any threats to their lands. The Arizona Cattle Growers Association, local timber interests, politicians (both state and federal), and sporting groups also had extremely strong positions about their interests tied to the park.[16] And it is important to note that whenever a national monument transitioned to a national park—as the Grand Canyon (one of the earliest to go through the process), Acadia, Bryce Canyon, Carlsbad Caverns, Lassen Volcanic, and Zion had done—the lands transferred from the Forest Service to the Park Service. This was a constant source of irritation to the Forest Service and created a long-simmering culture of competition between the two agencies.

The team learned of these tensions firsthand, yet they were undeterred. Their focus was on gleaning "such facts as we may concerning the wild animal life in the parks and then to interpret them for the use of the National Park Service." This collection of federal, state, county, tribal, and private interests—in different combinations—would be encountered by the trio wherever they went. However, under Wright's guidance and example, his team would become skilled in the art of listening, negotiation, and persuasion. This evaluation and practice would, too, become part of the routine of each visit to come.

Around the same time that the wildlife team was in the Grand Canyon region, there was a conversation taking place about the park—specifically, about increasing its size. It was a topic that Director Mather, in particular, had pushed for from early on in his tenure. The concept was to absorb the inholdings, slowly remove domestic animals from within the park's boundaries, and move the borders out to help protect wildlife—among other objectives. These issues were all very controversial, but at the time, enlarging the park was the Park Service's top priority for Grand Canyon. And the goal was to bring a more scientific perspective to the question of park boundaries. As historian Michael F. Anderson has noted, the boundaries of national parks and monuments in the early twentieth century were not determined by wildlife biologists but instead by a consortium of "congressmen, land managers, and an assortment of private sector allies."[17] Wright aimed to change that, and he and his team would soon lobby to be at the table when park boundary decisions were negotiated in the future.

In early 1930, Director Albright had written Dixon at the Berkeley office asking for the team's advice regarding potential Grand Canyon expansion. Albright had had a meeting with a Park Service adviser, John C. Merriam; Robert Y. Stuart, chief of the Forest Service; and Paul G. Redington, chief of the United States Biological Survey. (Prior to being appointed chief of the Biological Survey, Redington had been a career Forest Service man.) They had discussed the possibility of enlarging Grand Canyon National Park and agreed to have a feasibility report produced. Vernon Bailey, a forty-plus-year employee of the Biological Survey, prepared the document with the help of the Park Service. It was sent to Stuart and Redington for "comment and criticism."

Before discussing the matter further, however, Albright wanted advice from the wildlife team about potential "policies of game preservation" in the document.[18] Dixon conferred with Wright, and Dixon responded with a clear and concise letter that stated the wildlife team's early and solid stance on these matters. "The problem," wrote Dixon, "boils down essentially to one basic principle, which is: Should the boundaries of a national park be extended so as to include the complete, year-round habitat of the important animal life involved? It is futile to protect them at one season within the park and to let them starve outside the park at another season."

"A basic function of the national parks," Dixon argued, is to "preserve, in as much as nearly possible the condition in which white men first found them, the distinctive biological as well as scenic features of these parks for the inspiration, education and enjoyment of this and future generations."[19] Therefore, he concluded, extending park boundaries to include year-round habitat was consistent with the major purpose of creating a national park. In fact, he continued, by not including this habitat, the Park Service, or any other agency, was not fulfilling its responsibilities.[20]

At present, not one park is large enough to provide year-round sanctuary for adequate populations of all resident species. Not one is so fortunate—and probably none can ever be unless it is an island—as to have boundaries that are a guarantee against the invasion of external influences.

FAUNA NO. 1[21]

Vernon Bailey's report stated, in detail, what the Park Service wanted: 620 square miles added to the park to help preserve sufficient habitat for the

park's wildlife and plants. Stuart and Redington sent Albright their comments. They opposed it.[22]

Once again, Albright had run up against the differing opinions and objectives of the "sister" government agencies that managed the nation's natural resources. The Forest Service had little interest in seeing national parks expand,
particularly when it resulted in relinquishing their forested and economically
valuable lands. The Biological Survey agreed. Both organizations—and the
lumber, livestock, hunting, and mining interests—saw no need for parks
to become comprehensive game preserves, either at the Grand Canyon or
anywhere in the West.[23] And, until Wright began to influence Park Service
thinking, no one inside that organization had suggested expansion of parks
based strictly on wildlife considerations either. Albright and the wildlife team
waited for another day to make their argument a reality.

The Biological Survey that joined forces with the Forest Service against the
expansion plan was created in 1885 as the Division of Ornithology and Mammalogy in the Department of Agriculture. Its name was changed shortly after
1900. Its first chief, C. Hart Merriam, became one of America's greatest scientists and field naturalists. A physician by training, his discoveries, theories, and
publications in the biological sciences are simply too numerous to list. "The
Division of Ornithology and Mammalogy," wrote Merriam in the Biological
Survey's first publication in 1889, *North American Fauna*, "is engaged in mapping the geographical distribution of birds and mammals, in addition to the
study of their economic relations. The purpose of this work is to ascertain the
boundaries of the natural faunal areas of North America." Merriam recognized
that the bureau had "two distinct classes of readers—farmers and naturalists."
The bureau was both economically based—to assist the growing number of
ranchers and farmers streaming into the American West by identifying potential pests—and science-based (for the naturalists). Because he served two
audiences, Merriam began writing scientific articles in *North American Fauna*
and also a series of bulletins and reports for farmers and ranchers.[24]

To assist him with his fieldwork, he recruited an impressive group of field
naturalists who would work for the Biological Survey for decades: Vernon
Bailey, E. W. Nelson, and E. A. Goldman, among many others. Instead of
highly educated academic types, Merriam looked for "farm boys" who knew
the land and its plants and animals. He wanted young men who had an interest in natural history and could take care of themselves for extended periods
far afield. This trio of early hires is legendary among today's field biologists.
Their stellar research across the western United States, Alaska, and Mexico—
often under unimaginably harsh conditions—and their numerous articles
and publications impress and astound to this day.

On June 2, Wright, Dixon, and Thompson promised their colleagues at the Grand Canyon that they'd return in the fall. They then repacked the truck and drove north. The next day, they briefly visited Bryce Canyon National Park in southern Utah before continuing on. A few days later, they camped at the Bear River Marshes, approximately five miles west of Brigham City, Utah, on a bay of the Great Salt Lake where the edges of the Pacific and Central flyways converged. The marshes had been preserved as a migratory bird refuge just the year before by the Biological Survey, to provide sanctuary for the thousands of birds that surged through to refuel before continuing to their northern nesting grounds. Many species also lingered there to nest throughout the marshes. The wildlife team was eager to see the spectacle.

The team was in ornithological heaven. It was the height of the nesting season and the team spent hours measuring the size of fledglings. They then used that data to approximate breeding dates for the different species. Dixon captured as many photographs as he could of the birds as well as of their young, nests, eggs, and habitats. All three waded out through the dense tules to a large rookery shared by cattle egrets and innumerable white-faced ibises.[25] And the sheer number of curlews, avocets, stilts, willets, and phalaropes was startling to them. "We have heard about places like this," Wright wrote. "It is a paradise for marsh loving birds."[26]

The team rolled into Yellowstone National Park on June 8 and made camp along the Lamar River, about three miles east of Tower Junction and a quarter mile from Trumpeter Lake. They would work out of this site for the next twenty-three days. On occasion, the team took advantage of an empty cabin offered by a park they were visiting, especially during stormy weather, but those accommodations were few and far between. Besides, they preferred to sleep out in the elements, next to the truck, and away from developed areas of the parks; closer to the wildlife. They soon drove into Mammoth Hot Springs, home to park headquarters, to check in with Superintendent Roger W. Toll. Over the coming weeks, they returned to headquarters a few times for supplies, a hot meal, and to tend to correspondence. Over the coming years, Wright and Toll became trusted colleagues and dear friends.

Several times we have heard coyotes howling in the distance. Last evening we heard them just before dark and previously it was about nine in the morning. At 11:45 last night one howled may times from the immediate vicinity of camp. A meadow lark sang twice. Strange duet, I thought, then turned over.

GEORGE WRIGHT, YELLOWSTONE NATIONAL PARK[27]

Whereas Dixon's field notes from his and Wright's previous year's visit to Yellowstone contained a few scant pages dedicated to trumpeter swans, this season the team focused on the swans almost exclusively. In fact, the vast majority of Wright's thirty-five pages of Yellowstone field notes concern swans. In Dixon's forty-three pages of field notes, fully three-quarters of them record his detailed trumpeter observations. (Other species covered in both men's notes were badgers, elk, moose, mule deer, pronghorn antelope, marmots, porcupines, white-tailed jackrabbits, and an extensive list of birds.)[28]

The concentration on trumpeter swans was logical and timely. The wildlife team, and biologists across North America, knew next to nothing about these swans. Very few of the birds were left in the United States, or anywhere for that matter, and therefore they were considered endangered. That much was understood, but there was a dearth of reliable data on how many swans existed or where those birds lived. Nesting pairs had been documented in Yellowstone and possibly in southern Montana and eastern Idaho. Yet their basic life history—from breeding and nesting to eating and migration patterns— was all but a mystery. They had been mentioned in the field notes of explorers and some naturalists for decades, but only in passing.

Milton P. Skinner, for example, the first naturalist for Yellowstone National Park, wrote a brief observational note about the birds, as did his successor Edmund J. Sawyer. The renowned ornithologist Arthur Cleveland Bent, in his classic 1925 book *Life Histories of North American Water Fowl*, detailed some of the historical information and more contemporary personal observations about trumpeters, but the author made it clear that nobody had truly studied them in depth.[29]

What the team accomplished in Yellowstone proved to be the foundation for obtaining those fundamental facts about the species: the information needed for writing articles and the science required to form the building blocks—the incremental beginnings—to forge a plan to rescue the swans.[30]

Dixon and Wright had found a pair of swans on Trumpeter Lake in 1929. When they revisited that site the day after arriving in 1930, a pair was again tending an active nest just offshore.[31] It was decided that Dixon would dedicate himself to Trumpeter Lake so he could observe the nest and the six eggs it cradled. He spent the next three days camped out at an observation post behind a large granite boulder, some 150 yards away from the nest and a quarter mile from the team's Lamar campsite. It was an open grass-and-sage-covered landscape, so distant observation was possible. Binoculars in hand, he watched, all the while his notebook and cameras at the ready. At one point, he dropped to the ground and slowly crawled on his stomach toward the swans, carrying his camera, to test how close he could get before being detected. Not far: the male saw him almost immediately and called out loudly.

During this period of observation, Dixon's notes paint a fascinating, and at times moving, portrait of an endangered species on a small and shallow lake in the heart of the country's oldest national park.[32] He would routinely wake at 5 a.m. so he wouldn't miss a thing. And once he began the day at 3:40 a.m., after he heard the male calling, and he went to investigate.

The nest itself—a large mound of dead tules—was roughly 6½ × 7 feet at the base and 3 feet tall—with the nest cavity perched on top. Dixon discovered that the mound was, in fact, an active muskrat den; the swans simply took over the top floor (this, they would discover, was very common). The female incubated the eggs exclusively while the male stationed himself at the base of the mound. One day Dixon watched as the female "reached her bill backward between her wing and body and probed around a bit apparently turning one of the eggs."[33] However, when she raised her head, a large piece of egg shell was in her beak. She had just helped her sixth baby swan, or cygnet, hatch. The new cygnets squirmed under their mother, while their parents renovated the nest cavity into a wider depression so that the entire family could fit at night.

In his notes, Dixon describes how the female carefully slid off the large nest into the lake with a "toboggan like motion";[34] how the adults gracefully drank water; how they preened their sweep of snow-white feathers between jet-black bills; and how they probed their long serpentine necks into the water to extract tender tule shoots to eat. He recounts the cygnets' first swim; how the female gently dried them off with her bill once they clambered back up into the nest; and the baby swans' attempt to climb onto their mother's back.

But before the cygnets had hatched, while the pen was still incubating the eggs, she would carefully cover the eggs with plant debris before leaving to eat, in an effort to deter predators, specifically, as Dixon wrote, that "destroyer of bird eggs": the raven.[35] And the ravens came, frequently. But both swans were on constant alert and would fly back to the nest to chase the marauders away.

The ravens infuriated Dixon. He watched as they strategically raided all of the other nests in the thick stand of tules that ringed the lake. He tracked them on foot—as only he could do—south to their nest, a mile and a half away, high up on Specimen Ridge at over nine thousand feet. Through his binoculars, he observed the parents as they brought back the still-living nestlings of other birds—coots, grebes, blackbirds—and dropped them whole into the gaping maws of their young.

Incensed, Dixon went back to the Lamar campsite, retrieved his collecting shotgun from the truck, and brought it to Trumpeter Lake. The next time he saw the ravens approaching the swan nest, he opened fire.

The biologist's rage was not an isolated event: Dixon and his team were committed to a real solution. "A general campaign of control of ravens or other enemies of the swans throughout the park would not only be desirable, but it is absolutely necessary, if the swans are to survive," he wrote. Eventually, the wildlife team also added otters and coyotes to that list of the swans' foes.[36]

Dixon was very serious about how he recorded observations. Straightforward. As he was taught. For the most part, he left editorial opinions and conjecture for the numerous articles he wrote. But even the seasoned naturalist waxed poetic in his field notes during his days with the swans. Here he describes the lake's resident male as it chased away another male: "As they wheeled in turning their tremendous spread of white wings and bodies against the blue waters of the lake in which were reflected the passing wind-driven fleecy white clouds of the sky it made a picture never to be forgotten."[37]

While Dixon was stationed behind his boulder at Trumpeter Lake, Wright and Thompson explored other bodies of water looking for swans. They concentrated on a trio of pine-rimmed lakes south of their campsite: Fern, Tern, and White. These were about an hour's drive away, then a short hike in. The lakes were separated by a mile and a half mile, respectively. In this wooded terrain, the duo spotted swans over several days, but they couldn't, at first, determine if they were watching one pair that moved between the lakes, two pairs, or more. After they quickly hiked between the lakes several times, they discovered that, in fact, there was a pair at each lake.

The swans at Tern Lake were the only nesting pair, so Wright and Thompson concentrated on them. Wright, like Dixon, was often on-site just after 5 a.m. watching the nest. He likely camped out there at least a few nights as well. One day, when the parent birds were on another part of the lake, he and Thompson observed a raven swoop down, poke around the nest and then "Rap four or five vehement strokes, it's whole body jerking with each movement."[38] The predator had succeeded in opening an egg, and it flew off with its prey. The parents returned and protested, but soon nonchalantly swam to the other end of the lake.

It was perplexing behavior, Wright thought, for the swans to simply swim away after an egg had been destroyed, but in it he saw his opportunity. The two biologists took off their clothes, slipped into the water, and carefully waded out to the nest; Wright notes the water was up to his neck (remember, he was five feet four inches tall.) They quickly examined the nest. The

Wright with rubber boat for studying trumpeter swans, Yellowstone National Park, summer 1931. Courtesy of Pamela Meléndez Wright Lloyd.

five remaining eggs were safe, warm, and in advanced stages of development. They took measurements, covered the eggs, and eased back to the shoreline, completely unnoticed by the adult birds.

While Wright's field notes are concise and observational, like Dixon's, he—much more frequently than his mentor—worked in meditations on the marvels and beauty of the park: the scenery, the sun and clouds, or the animals that he was privileged to observe. He also wove in everything he could about wildlife, vegetation, people, and management issues in the parks he and his colleagues visited.

Birds, and bird calls, were of particular interest to the young biologist. Along the Lamar River, he noted the abundance of the meadowlark. "Their clarion song rings out with particular emphasis in the quiet time after sundown."[39] While watching a sandhill crane slowly circling above his head, gaining altitude, before lining out to its final destination, he believed that the bird's call sounded like "the noise of a mallet on a hallow wooden box."[40]

"This association of the <u>sandhill crane</u>, <u>Canada geese</u> and <u>Trumpeter swan</u>," he continued, "is very thrilling when one considers the desperate status of two of them, and the acute case of the third."[41] And when a lone wood ibis was spotted in late June—a rarity for Yellowstone—he wrote, "The naturalists on the Lamar were treated to a rare ornithological delight today."[42] (Dixon, meanwhile, captured the bird, typical of southern, warmer climes, in a series of black-and-white photographs.)

At each stage of the survey, Wright also peppered his field notes with questions. He highlighted, in particular, interviews with "old-timers" who had lived in or near a given park as well as rangers and other park staff with long, local tenures. What wildlife was there ten, twenty, or thirty years ago? What about predators? When did you last see a wolf, grizzly bear, or mountain lion? What was the condition of the range for native game? When did cattle and sheep move into the country? And, in Yellowstone, where have you seen trumpeters?

At times, Wright comes across as mildly distracted in his field notes, as if split between conducting the basic science of the survey, which he did, and the big picture management issues that were increasingly becoming clear to him: What's to be done about the killing of predators? How to improve the range for wildlife in parks and eliminate cattle and sheep? What is the best strategy for strategically increasing—based on wildlife needs—the size of the parks? Why is this species endangered, and how can we save it?

But he was part of a team, a team that he had created. He wasn't alone while grappling with the multiplying issues rolling out before him, from park to park. That was the key reason he supported, encouraged, and depended on Dixon and Thompson with such fidelity. He needed them. He relied on them for their exceptional fieldwork, assistance, ideas, and friendship.

Wright publicly acknowledged Carl Russell, his friend and former boss in Yosemite, as one of the architects of the wildlife survey idea. And in the summer of 1930, Russell transferred to Yellowstone as a field naturalist. He and his wife, Betty, would spend time in the field with Wright over the next few seasons.

As part of his duties in Yellowstone, Russell authored a document entitled "A Concise History of Scientists and Scientific Investigations in Yellowstone National Park." In the section describing the work of the wildlife team, Russell recorded their respective duties: "Dixon, Birds; Mammals. Thompson, Birds. Wright, Birds; Mammals; Management."[43] As evidenced here, Dixon and Thompson were focused on the fundamental—and critical—fieldwork. But Wright was already also juggling fieldwork with the Park Service bureaucracy in his effort to change management practices while highlighting and improving wildlife conditions in the parks.

On June 26, six days after his twenty-sixth birthday, Wright was at park headquarters in Mammoth Hot Springs to collect his mail and write some letters. He commonly had mail forwarded to parks if his schedule permitted. And it was on that day that Wright sent a note to Superintendent Thomson in Yosemite National Park. "The further we go and the more we see of the parks," wrote Wright, "the greater grows the longing for that first love, Yosemite. If there can be a best, among such a priceless collection, I think that Yosemite must be acclaimed the jewel." But Wright wasn't just writing the superintendent to express his love of Yosemite. He also wanted an update on a project that moved deer from Yosemite Valley, to ease the population pressures there, over to the Hetch Hetchy area, north of Yosemite. And he requested reporting on the "knotty bear problem."[44]

He further took the opportunity to share some thoughts with his colleague, many years his senior. "To say that the three of us are as happily busy as we can be with a sense of being unable to cover the field, is to admit that we feel that organized research in wild life management is an essential factor in intelligent park administration." Wright continued to state that he understood that visitors had to be educated when they came to the parks, though he wished the "so-called educational department," under which the survey operated, could function under another title. And that wildlife—what he refers to as the parks' "stock in trade"—should be the center and guiding focus of all park management: "I feel that at the present time only a very few officers, of whom you are one, realize that these other functions can only be operative if the parks' stock in trade is first preserved in the best condition possible."[45]

"Representatives of scientific institutions are gathering data continually in the national parks, and their findings are of inestimable value to us. But," he continued, envisioning the need for what today are called resource managers in the parks, "we need men within our own organization to actually work out animal problems for immediate, practical application. . . . In several of the parks at least, each superintendent will require the full-time services of one trained worker in this department."[46]

On the last day of June, the team stopped at Lake Lodge, on the shores of Yellowstone Lake. That night they took in the "bear show" at the Old Faithful

bear-feeding ground, which was actually just a dump. A black bear entertained the tourists at first, then three grizzlies appeared and the black bear
scurried away. Eventually, there was some "scrapping" among the grizzlies,
and then a scrum of last year's grizzly cubs tumbled in, wrestled on the platform, and ran around as the adults ambled off.

The ranger giving the bear talk—while mounted on a horse trained not to
be spooked by the bears—was Phillip Martindale. Martindale was locally famous for his presentations at the bear "lunch counter." He was an old-school
ranger who had been around for decades. But this was exactly the type of
supremely unnatural entertainment the team disliked: a wildlife spectacle
they would work hard to eliminate from Yellowstone, Glacier, Yosemite, and
Sequoia National Parks for the sake of the bears, and humans. "Martindale
gave a fairly good bear talk," Wright commented in his notes later that night.
"It was coloured up to interest his audience the more, and contained some
rather questionable statements, though in the main, his facts were accurate
enough."[47]

The next day, Wright and his colleagues left Yellowstone for the season.
But he'd be back. Eventually, Wright would concentrate on this park more
than any other. Between 1929 and 1933, he spent two hundred and twenty-
seven field days there—almost seven and a half months. Yosemite was his first
love, but Yellowstone would become his intellectual challenge and passion.

The team headed east to Casper, then south through Chugwater and Chey-
enne, Wyoming, before reaching Colorado's Rocky Mountain National Park.
At headquarters in Estes Park, they checked in with Superintendent Edmund B.
Rogers. He told them a "timber wolf" had been reported by a man named
Hutchins, a naturalist employed by Grand Lake Lodge, but that he doubted
"the scientific value of *anything* Hutchins would report." A park staff member,
however, whose opinion was "absolutely sound," had seen one near Long's
Peak within the last year. Meanwhile, the black bear population, once severely
reduced by hunting, was resurging and bears had begun raiding resorts and
camps. (The last known grizzly in the park had been killed in 1910.) Not surprisingly, the black bears were a growing management issue. The superintendent wanted to start a bear show, as in other parks, claiming he was going
to "educate them from the start." Wright no doubt thought this naive and
wrongheaded, but he made no comment.

Rogers also informed the biologists that it had been confirmed that
buffalo had once roamed through the region, and that staff had reportedly
found their skulls, even fairly high up in the mountains. Too, wolverines and

martens, once common top predators, were now very rare. And even though antelope had been missing from the ecosystem for decades, Wright believed that antelope belonged "in all the parks."

The destruction of our once abundant wild-life resources, through waste and neglect, constitutes one of the sorriest chapters in our national history.

THE WILD-LIFE RESTORATION COMMITTEE[48]

In fact, everywhere they went, the team recorded observations and noted discussions about whether or not the landscape provided good antelope habitat. But while Yellowstone had a sizable population of the animals at the time, elsewhere they were few and far between.

Pronghorn antelope once roamed vast areas of North America, from Mexico to southern Canada. They inhabited the same landscape as tens of millions of bison, and many scientists believed pronghorn numbers once exceeded those of their ecological consorts. One of those believers was E. W. Nelson, who had been appointed chief of the Biological Survey in 1916, replacing C. Hart Merriam. In his classic *Status of the Pronghorned Antelope, 1922–1924*, Nelson argued that "the most beautiful and graceful of America's big-game animals" needed immediate help, and that government agencies and conservation organizations should work together to establish pronghorn refuges.[49] After extensive fieldwork, he believed that approximately thirty thousand pronghorn survived from Mexico to Canada, living in small, disjunct herds (the population maps he created in the publication are impressive). In this way, pronghorn and their cause became the symbol of the American conservation movement at the time.[50] And Wright and his team would become part of the effort.

The conversation with Superintendent Rogers then turned, as it often did, to predators. The Rocky Mountain coyote and mule deer populations were healthy in the park, and the superintendent had no active control program for coyotes. Historically, the park had carried out intense predator control efforts, starting in 1922 under Superintendent Roger Toll, before he moved to Yellowstone. In this effort, Toll had had the help of Stanley P. Young of the Biological Survey, who had suggested a lethal mix of hunters, dogs, and poison bait to kill as many mountain lions, bobcats, wolf, fox, lynx, and (especially) coyotes as possible during a five-to-six-year period.[51]

Rocky Mountain's elk population had been all but hunted out by late nineteenth-century pioneers and early settlers, ending only when the park was created in 1915. In fact, the remaining three-hundred-plus elk were descendants not from the park's native population but rather from about a dozen elk that had been imported from Yellowstone in 1912.[52] And while the numbers of this new population had greatly benefited from the predator control efforts of the 1920s, seasonally the elk trickled out beyond park borders and, like their predators, caused issues with local landowners and farmers. "Last year the elk season was opened up in five counties bringing hunting south & west of the park," reported Wright. "The result was the slaughter of elk bulls, cows, calves, horses, cows, pigs etc. etc. Such a hue and cry was raised that it is not likely the season will be opened again."[53]

In mid-July, Wright peeled away from his colleagues and traveled back to California. Dixon and Thompson, however, stayed on in Rocky Mountain until late July to continue studying the cross-section of issues detailed by the superintendent. In particular, Dixon and Thompson focused on elk as well as Rocky Mountain bighorn sheep. Populations of both species appeared robust, though the discussion over the park's boundaries, and the seasonal move-ment of the elk, would remain a subject of their study over the next few years. To find the sheep, meanwhile, Dixon and Thompson climbed Specimen Mountain several times, to over 12,400 feet, in order to observe the animals and take photographs. One morning in the rarefied air, Thompson counted a sizable gathering of fifty-three sheep in one extended group.[54]

This separation of the team during the field season—a kind of divide-and-research approach—became a common occurrence over the next few years. Increasingly, Wright dispatched Thompson, particularly to the Southwest where he was raised, for specific research and to attend key meetings, while Dixon often returned to Sequoia or Yosemite National Parks to continue his research alone and also be closer to his family. Wright, meanwhile, focused on Yellowstone, but he would unite with his colleagues at other parks on his research circuit.

This particular side trip for Wright, however, during the heart of the research season, had a specific purpose: He was traveling to Santa Barbara to propose to Bernice "Bee" Ray. Bee Ray and George Wright met at Berkeley when they were both students. She was two years younger than Wright—she graduated in 1929 with a degree in political science. Wright and Ray were, indeed, en-gaged in Santa Barbara in July of 1930, possibly when the Ray family was vacationing there from their home in Los Angeles. A spring wedding was an-nounced for the following year.

Around this time, Wright was not in the field for almost two months. It is not clear what he was doing, though it is probably not hard to surmise.

Bee Ray and George Wright, Yosemite National Park, ca. 1930. Courtesy of Pamela Meléndez Wright Lloyd.

His correspondence—that of it which remains—is minimal but, just before his departure for the coast from Rocky Mountain, it does include a note to the MVZ from Estes Park. The correspondence pertained to two grizzly bear skins and skeletons he had obtained in Yellowstone and had shipped to the museum. His note was not to Grinnell but instead to another of Grinnell's PhD students, E. Raymond Hall. Hall would go on to become a renowned mammologist and advocate for stopping predator control programs.

"Though our stay in each park is necessarily limited because of the necessity of making a general survey of our problems," Wright wrote, "it seems only right that we should be of service to the museum whenever possible."[55] He then promised a moose specimen before signing off. Grinnell wrote back. "Dixon and Thompson were certainly heroic," observed Grinnell, "to rough out those 'ripening' skeletons. To go through with that sort of job depends upon an ironclad digestive system!" The director then expressed his extreme appreciation for the grizzly specimens and his enthusiasm for their work with the swans. "Congratulations on landing the batch of facts concerning the life history of the Trumpeter Swan. Be sure and get Dixon all primed to give Cooper Club a 'preview' of the appertaining pictures—to accompany the story itself."[56]

In mid-August, while Dixon was traveling south from Yosemite, down the Sierra to Sequoia National Park for more fieldwork, and Wright and Thompson were in Berkeley, Director Albright finally sent out an official memo to all Park Service superintendents and managers of park operations (hotels, lodges, stores) about the wildlife survey and the team's work. "One of the most important of the newer activities of the National Park Service," stated the director, "is our wild life research branch." He thanked Wright for his "generosity and spirit" for creating and funding the survey but promised additional funding soon. He asked all personnel to "extend all practicable courtesies and assistance" to the team, including mechanical help, provisions, and facilities. "Finally, let me say that there is no work going on in the National Park Service today that interests me more than the undertaking of Mr. Wright and his associates. Therefore, any assistance and courtesies extended to them personally, as well as officially, will be appreciated by me."[57]

In late September, the team traveled directly north to Mount Rainier National Park in Washington State, then slowly south, hoping to avoid early winter storms that might overtake them. Wright knew Mount Rainier well from his many trips throughout the West. Prior to their visit, he wrote his friend and head naturalist of the park, Frank Brockman, to let him and the superintendent know when they might arrive. "I have not been there since the time we climbed the peaks several years ago," Wright remembered to Brockman.[58]

Mount Rainier is one of the older parks in the national park system. It was established by an act of Congress in 1899, after Yellowstone, created in 1872, and California's trio of Yosemite, Sequoia, and General Grant National Parks in 1890. Rainier was declared almost exclusively for its scenic beauty: the snow-covered, volcanic mountain that gives the park its name soars over 14,411 feet above the pleated skirt of heavily forested parkland below. Gouged by dozens of glaciers, the iconic mountain dominates the skyline for miles.

The park was purposely created "to protect and preserve unimpaired the majestic icon of Mount Rainier, a glaciated volcano, along with its natural and cultural resources, values, and dynamic processes."[59] In particular, the Park Service wanted to ensure that the enabling legislation stood in well-defined contrast to the use of natural resources emphasized by the newly formed federal Division of Forestry. An early and clear distinction between the two services was established.[60]

In addition to the magnificent volcano, the park also sheltered a diverse range of wildlife. So upon their arrival, Wright's team, as was their custom, checked in with Superintendent Owen A. Tomlinson, Chief Ranger A. H. Barnett, and Brockman, and were told a similar tale to those of the other parks they had visited. The men informed the team that wolverines were scarce, but martens seemed to be holding their own. Beavers were abundant, after being completely trapped out during the previous few decades. The chief ranger stated that the last wolf in the park was killed in 1911 and that none now lived there. Cougars were "pretty well cleaned out" too, though a few might remain.[61]

Black bears were also making a comeback and quickly becoming a management headache, as in Rocky Mountain National Park. They harassed campers, shredded tents, and broke into cars. Around Paradise Park, on the park's southern edge, the local ranger believed most of the damage was done by three or four old "rough neck" bears who had no fear of humans.[62] Staff had tried relocating some of them, but they had returned within a week or two, because, as Thompson pointed out, the park was too small.[63]

Similarly, black-tailed deer were increasing, but the lack of winter feeding grounds within the park forced them downslope, outside the park and onto Forest Service lands, where they were shot with abandon. Thompson reported that deer were killed year-round outside the park, which was illegal but unchecked due to a lack of enforcement.[64]

The elk story paralleled the deer report. Elk were abundant in the park, but come winter, they spilled over onto lower-elevation Forest Service lands where they were relentlessly pursued by hunters. Wright recorded that the Forest Service representative they interviewed said the killing of elk was necessary in order "to clean them out as they were taking the range from cattle and sheep." Additionally, a Park Service ranger told them he shot as many "large hawks" as possible because they killed grouse, a favorite game bird.[65]

As with Rocky Mountain National Park's herd, Mount Rainier's elk had been hunted so severely during the previous fifty years that Yellowstone came to the rescue once again. Starting in 1912, Park Service staff had been herding elk into cargo train cars and shipping them to Rainier.[66] However, in this region of the country, from the western edge of the Cascade Mountains to the coast, the native elk were Roosevelt elk, not the subspecies thriving in Yellowstone, Rocky Mountain elk. So if any Roosevelt elk had survived the late nineteenth- and early twentieth-century onslaught around Rainier, they likely had already crossbred with the introduced Yellowstone elk.

This concerned Wright, who believed the practice of sending elk, bison, deer, and other animals from one park to another across the West, and beyond, was not ecologically sound—distinct populations of species should not be mixed and matched with no consideration for regional differentiation. His mentor, Grinnell, agreed, and they would both work to change this practice in subsequent years.

Rainier is known for its native mountain goats, and in 1930 the herd was robust. Park staff estimated two hundred and seventy-five individuals thrived on the slopes of the mountain. However, they voiced concern for the herd, as the goats frequently moved out of the park toward the high peaks on the eastern edge of the Cascades. And during this trek, they, as with so many other species, were ruthlessly hunted. Because of this, the superintendent wished that the park's boundary on the east reached "to the top of the Cascades Divide" as originally planned. Livestock owners and other interests, however, had long stood in the way of that expansion.

"This outside area is beautiful, scenically," noted Thompson about this eastern edge after a day in the field, "and naturally belongs with the region west of the divide for summer deer & elk range."[67] He also believed lands to the south—in the Ohanapecosh and Clear Creek region—needed to be added to the park for the same reason.

On the last day of September of 1930, while Dixon ascended Burroughs Mountain to a large marmot colony for a day of observation, Wright and Thompson drove south to the country around the Cowlitz and Ohanapecosh Rivers for a long hike. After their conversations with park staff, interviews with locals, and a general orientation, getting into the backcountry was important for the researchers.

It happened to be the day before the deer hunting season started, and the woods outside the park were teeming with men and rifles. One hundred and fourteen hunters were counted at one location alone. "Game simply could not stand a chance against such persistent hunting," noted Wright. They also came across a settlement along the Cowlitz River, likely occupied by people recently displaced by the Dust Bowl and deepening Depression. Wright was not sympathetic or impressed with what he saw. They were "West Virginia mountaineers popularly called 'razorbacks.' They are poor, ignorant, and not exactly lawbiding. They believe in their primordial right to take game as they see fit. Consequently, there is a great deal of winter killing of deer and practically no effective prosecution."[68]

The duo continued into the park on foot through dense forests, crossing waterways and clambering over ridges. To their utter delight and obvious excitement, they found wolf tracks on the west side of the Cowlitz Divide. "They were made in the trail and were fresh," recorded Wright, "there having been a shower about an hour before." Thompson measured the tracks carefully, to share with the real expert, Dixon. The track was well defined and, as the two noted, "it could not have been a cougar's track, and it was much too large for coyote. There are no dogs in this region."[69] By the time they had returned to their vehicle it was 6 p.m., and dark. They had hiked twenty-seven miles. Over the next several days, they would explore different sections of the park—the four cardinal directions—focusing on the borders where park lands turned to national forests across a seamless blanket of green.

Before leaving Rainier, Thompson wrote a section in his notes with the heading "General Impressions of the Park." "Rainier is almost an isolated island from the game & forest point of view, and with the converging of the 3 new highways at Chinook Pass, the park area will need every protection available."[70]

At the recommendation of Superintendent Tomlinson, the team drove west to Seattle and then dipped down and around Puget Sound, to Mount Olympus National Monument. Their goal was to interview three "old-timers" who knew the region well: Asahel Curtis of Seattle, Chris Morganroth in the northern peninsula city of Port Angeles, and E. B. Webster near Crescent Lake, also in the north. All three men had lived in and explored the peninsula for decades.

All three of these old-timers, the team discovered, believed wolves existed on the peninsula. And although all were self-proclaimed Roosevelt elk experts, their estimates of the monument's population varied from one thousand to eight thousand. They all concurred, however, that the borders of the monument needed to be adjusted to create better winter feeding grounds for the elk. It might be a matter of simply buying out three to four homesteaders along the Hoh River, they suggested, on the west side of the monument.

Wright and Dixon were particularly interested in what Curtis said about predators. He believed there was an "improved attitude" toward predators in eastern Washington, where he had recently visited. He said that all of the coyotes had been poisoned there and a severe rodent plague ensued shortly thereafter. Now, he stated, "the residents wished that they might have the coyotes back."[71]

Earlier in the year, Wright had communicated with both Crater Lake National Park's superintendent, Elbert C. Solinsky, and Chief Ranger William Godfrey. He had worked with both of them in Yosemite, and both had recently transferred to Crater Lake in Oregon. Solinsky, another Berkeley graduate, had been assistant superintendent at Yosemite under Thomson, while Bill Godfrey was Wright's "excellent roommate" when they were both new to the service.

Godfrey and his wife Elizabeth, or "Bab," were very close to Wright. Their correspondence is both familial and a little silly. In a three-page letter—including a handful of amusing stick figure drawings—acknowledging Wright's planned trip to Crater Lake, Godfrey replied they were really looking forward to his visit. "Since this will be your sixth visit to Crater Lake," Godfrey entreated, "Bab joins me in asking you plan your trip so that you can spend more time here than you had originally planned to spend."[72] The team arrived at Crater Lake's park headquarters on October 11 and stayed for about a week.

Crater Lake National Park was another early addition to the system. Established in 1902, again by Theodore Roosevelt, it was similar to Mount Rainier in that its stunning geologic features were the main attraction of the park—centered on the water-filled ancient caldera, Crater Lake. Historically the area was also very important to Indigenous Peoples, including the Klamaths, who lived east of the lake, and the Molalas, Takelmas, and Umpquas to the west. Even the Modocs of northeastern California, to the south, knew the lake. They all visited the area during the summer months, and they all handed down stories through countless generations of how the ancient volcano erupted, some seven thousand years ago.[73]

And, of course, there was the wildlife.

Although a few elk could be found along the edges of the park, it was really the local deer herd that was of concern to the biologists—and a main topic of their discussions with Solinsky and Godfrey. As in so many other parks, come fall and cooler temperatures, the herd moved downslope, out of the park, and straight into the path of waiting hunters and poachers on the Forest Service lands that all but surrounded the park.

Again, it was a matter of improper winter forage due to the park's limited size and artificial boundaries. Godfrey thought an extension of the park's western boundary downslope toward the Rogue River watershed would help the herd tremendously.[74] Dixon, after some investigation, suggested they should work to have a six-mile buffer zone, or "game refuge," declared on Forest Service lands and other properties encircling the park. It was a management technique being used successfully in several other western parks—most notably, the 727,000-acre Kaibab Federal Game Refuge north of Grand Canyon National Park.[75]

The team learned that the park was cleared of staff during the winter months due to the severe weather around the lake; the caldera's rim reaches eight thousand feet. Most staff moved to Medford, but Godfrey and his wife stayed on, traveling downslope to housing in Munson Valley. They talked about seeing poached deer on the margins of the park during the winter as well as illegal trap lines inside the park.

In addition to what they absorbed from park staff, Thompson conducted several old-timer interviews. He sat down with Judge William M. Colvig, a local resident since the 1850s, John Mayben, and Fort Hubbard. Thompson gleaned that grizzlies were once abundant in the mountains, but the last one—known as "clubfoot," according to the judge—was killed in the late 1870s. By the turn of the century, elk had also been removed from the region through intense hunting. Wolverines were rare, if there at all. And wolves and cougars had been systematically killed by the Biological Survey and state hunters.

Crater Lake didn't have a bear show, but the bears here too were quickly adapting and becoming problematic, thanks to some helping hands. "All of the bears are great pets," noted Dixon. "They hang around the mess cook house where they are fed by the workmen after each meal." When park staff closed down the buildings by the lake for the winter, service employees had to cover all windows and doors securely with galvanized wire fencing that was "pig-tight and bull strong" to keep the ursine intruders out.[76]

One day, the team hiked with Godfrey up to Union Peak, just outside the park to the southwest, to inspect the mountain pine beetle's extensive damage to the lodgepole pine forest that stretched out below them in all directions. He showed them how the beetles had ravaged the trees and killed off thousands of lodgepoles.

Pine beetle infestations were an extremely serious problem both on Forest Service lands and in national parks, particularly during extended droughts. But the die-offs were of concern for different reasons to the respective agencies: harvest yield versus aesthetics and habitat. Although most western parks suffered from beetle infestations in the 1920s and the 1930s—albeit sometimes because of a different species of beetle and a different host tree—Crater Lake National Park, and the surrounding Crater Lake National Forest, were the epicenter for beetle eradication efforts, especially from the Park Service's perspective.

Eradication programs started in the early 1920s, and between 1929 and 1931, an estimated 43,000-plus trees were "treated."[77] Treatment consisted of cutting down the trees, lopping off their tops, debarking them, exposing them to the sun, or piling them and lighting them on fire. It was a process they called "fell, peel, and burn." It was clear-cutting and destruction on a massive scale, all for the sake of killing the beetles and their larvae. The infestations and the "cure" were both devastating for the forest industry and visually and ecologically disturbing to the park.

The team's primary concern was the huge impact this process had on all forms of wildlife. Habitats were eliminated or radically altered, and with them, food sources and shelter disappeared. Although the bark beetle problem was deemed "under control" in the Crater Lake area in 1934, the park and all western states would continue to suffer tremendously from episodic outbreaks that would decimate hundreds of thousands of acres—up to the present day.

It was an issue that Wright, a trained forester, and Adolph Murie, a future team member, would soon revisit.

"We arrived (Dixon, Thompson, Wright) in the late afternoon. Not a cloud broke the heaven's blue." So penned Wright on October 29 after reaching Grand Canyon Village for the second time in five months.[78] The team spent almost two weeks on the edge of and in the canyon: hiking, observing, talking with park staff, and conducting another round of interviews with a cross-section of longtime residents.

Some days they covered between ten and twenty miles on foot, in and out of the canyon, along the rims, across the southern plateau, and zigzagging the Kaibab to the north. On their first foray, they dropped down to Indian Garden from the south rim, about two-thirds of the way to the Colorado River, via Bright Angel Trail. They were on their way to conduct fieldwork in general, but their real mission was to find the pronghorn herd at Indian Garden.

In 1924, a dozen pronghorns had been transplanted to the wide and sparsely vegetated valley sheltering a riparian, oasis-like strip of towering cottonwood trees. The pronghorn had been donated from animals obtained in Nevada.[79] The herd had diminished, according to the superintendent's 1930 annual report, but was "holding its own." Wright, Dixon, and Thompson found them far too tame, and a bit disappointing, as the animals passively ate

Pronghorn, American
No. 12 ⁓ Subject Antelope, Pronghorn — Male on guard   1905
Date Oct. 31, 1930 Locality Indian Garden, Grand Canyon National Park   Photographer J. Dixon

George M. Wright

Pronghorn antelope, Indian Garden, Grand Canyon National Park, October 31, 1930. Photograph by Joseph Dixon. Courtesy of NPS History Collection.

out of feeding troughs, built by the park to keep them in the valley so that the tourists could get close.

During the next few days in the canyon—exploring the Tonto Plateau and meandering along the Hermit Trail—they kept up the search for additional pronghorn, but to no avail. "As a general impression," recorded Thompson, "there was very little evidence of mammalian or reptilian life down in the canyon. Water & food seem to be a limiting factor, but not such as to account for the scarcity now prevalent."[80]

The team also explored an area outside the park to the southwest, back beyond the opening to Havasupai Canyon. It was an open, high and dry landscape, dominated by piñon pine, juniper, sagebrush, and other chaparral plants. Thompson believed it to be perfect for pronghorn—particularly the more open, prairie-like sections—as well as for deer. "It could serve as a game preserve for the park as well as supply for hunting outside its boundary," he wrote.[81]

The quest for pronghorn continued as they drove the seventy-five miles across a desert track to the W-Triangle Ranch—again, south and west from the park. A herd of one thousand pronghorn was reported living across the grasslands of the vast property, and one ranch hand had seen over a hundred animals a few years prior. But all that the team found were two thousand head of cattle and fourteen hundred sheep.[82]

Deer on the Kaibab continued to be the serious management problem that the team had encountered on their very first visit to the park. Overgrazing by deer was evident everywhere, and in spite of heavy losses during the previous hunting season, the Forest Service estimated the deer population hovered around thirty thousand.[83] And perhaps a tenth of that was within park boundaries along the north rim.

Superintendent Tillotson believed that, instead of hunting, trapping the deer and restocking them to different parts of the country, where populations had diminished, was the answer. The Park Service, in conjunction with the Forest Service, Biological Survey, and State Game Department of Arizona, was studying the situation.

In the meantime, park employees, with the help of the other agencies, had been moving fawns from the north to the south rim for several years to build up a population around Grand Canyon Village and park headquarters. They too wanted a semidomesticated herd as an attraction for tourists, like the one in Yosemite. The baby deer were driven around the canyon by truck or flown over the canyon by one of the park's early concessionaires, Scenic Airlines.

This practice of moving deer, or any other species, from the Kaibab to the south rim was, as already noted, opposed strongly by Wright. He believed that it would "invite disaster" and that "it would be destroying all of the significance of the canyon as a natural barrier between related forms of animal life." He went so far as to suggest that the few bridges at the bottom of the canyon crossing the Colorado River be guarded somehow so that animals could not unnaturally cross what was a significant ecological barrier.[84]

An additional problem in the park was the inability of the canyon's bighorn sheep to rebound after the park was created and they were ostensibly protected. Superintendent Tillotson believed the park's countless wild burros—voracious living reminders of the region's mining past—were eating vegetation that would otherwise be available for the sheep. "We saw no sign of the once abundant <u>wild burros</u> that 'took the range' within the cañon," recorded Wright, "Evidently, the kill of 1100 in the park's extermination program has been very effective in reducing their numbers."[85] The burro eradication program, started in 1924, would continue for years. But the wildlife team only saw bighorn tracks and scat.

On another trip near Havasupai Canyon, the team stopped at the remote Pasture Wash Ranger Station. By the front door, leaning against the wall, stood two "drying boards" with coyote pelts nailed to them for curing. On their first trip to the park, Wright had interviewed a seasoned ranger who reported that trapping in the park the previous winter had been very good. The ranger killed numerous coyotes and "wild cats" (bobcats), but he also, "by mistake," took some badgers, foxes, and other mammals. Wright thought the practice very questionable.[86]

Many early rangers were local outdoorsmen, lightly educated, and what Horace Albright called "old-timers." "Particularly the veterans in the ranger service," Albright wrote, "are born men of the mountains, gifted with a working knowledge of woodcraft, of trail-blazing, of the ways of wild life, and with sufficient instinctive resourcefulness in the mountains and the forest to be able to take care of themselves and others under any circumstances."[87]

Rangers commonly augmented their meager incomes by trapping animals and selling their pelts for a government-paid bounty, with the approval of the Park Service. Prior to the creation of the service, rangers, or "scouts," were hired locally by the political appointees managing parks, and eventually, by the superintendents, with very few professional standards in place. (Those would come later, under Stephen Mather.) Of the first five rangers hired in Yellowstone in 1915, for example, two were brought on specifically to kill predators.[88]

One day, Wright asked to look at the office files at headquarters in Grand Canyon Village. He wrote a note listing how many park animals had been killed by staff since 1922: 293 coyotes, 75 wildcats, 19 foxes, 2 mountain lions, and 1 wolf.[89] Like Grinnell, Wright would become a dedicated and leading opponent of predator control and of unregulated hunting in and around parks. However, he didn't oppose hunting in general. As a field biologist he had collected dozens, possibly hundreds, of specimens. (Many of these are still held by the MVZ in Berkeley.) More than once, Wright notes how, during research in a given park, the local ranger he was traveling with would stop the car he was riding in, or jump down off his horse, rifle in hand, to shoot at a coyote. Shoot first, then observe. There was no hint of reprimands from Wright. He simply watched and took notes. Yet when Wright came across coyotes on his own, he would not shoot but rather stalk them for as long as possible, detailing their behavior.

Wright's reaction was consistent when he was told by park employees how they trapped coyotes and when Yellowstone's "Buffalo Keeper" informed Wright that he had been dynamiting badgers inside their dens to clear the range and prevent riders from going down when their horses got a leg stuck in a den hole.[90] His response was a variation of: "I think this practice very questionable." For the most part, in these scenarios, he was dealing with Albright's old-timers and he wasn't there to lecture or reprimand. He was there to observe, to conduct research, gather facts. He would then take this information, share it, and digest it with his team, and then he would make recommendations back to the director, as agreed.

The predator statistics Wright gleaned from the files at Grand Canyon head-quarters paled in comparison to what had taken place since the early twen-tieth century throughout the West in national parks, across Forest Service holdings, as well as on other public lands.

As European Americans pushed west in the latter half of the nineteenth century, wolves in particular were pursued tirelessly by frontiersmen. But af-ter 1900, when the Biological Survey began focusing on predators, mostly in the West, the killing campaign increased exponentially. As early as 1907, the Biological Survey staff assisted the Forest Service in killing 1,723 wolves in thirty-nine National Forests and 23,208 coyotes in seventy-seven National Forests.[91] By 1915, the Biological Survey was experimenting with a suite of killing methods for various predators—shooting, trapping, poisoning—and when they obtained funding for predator control work in 1916, they let loose hundreds of hunters across the West.

The thriving livestock industry was elated, and it served as a constant booster and supporter of the Biological Survey's efforts. The stockmen also had the ear of western politicians. This was true of the early managers and superintendents of western national parks as well, who welcomed Biological Survey hunters with open arms. In 1916 alone, they "destroyed" 424 wolves, 11,890 coyotes, 1,564 bobcats, 9 mountain lions, and 2,086 "miscellaneous wild animals." They also carried out strychnine poison programs "with ex-ceptional vigor" against prairie dog towns. Prairie dogs, it was believed, de-stroyed range that could be used for livestock.[92]

The following year, under the leadership of the new chief, E. W. Nelson (the author of the pronghorn study), the eradication effort became an all-out war. By 1923, Nelson gleefully proclaimed that, thanks to their work, wolves "are being so reduced in numbers that over most if not all of the West their end is in sight."[93] Between 1916 and 1928, the grim death totals accumulated by the Biological Survey are staggering: 8,370 wolves, 324,915 coyotes, 1,877 mountain lions, 36,597 bobcats and lynxes, 1,277 bears, countless numbers of prairie dogs and ground squirrels, and innumerable nontargeted species. And yet these "official" numbers for animals killed reflect only a fraction of the total: these were only the corpses "that could be counted." For coyotes alone, for example, the bureau stated that the actual total was two or three times their official number—approaching one million dead—because many of the animals that were poisoned wandered off before dying, thus disappear-ing into the landscape before becoming a statistic.[94]

In addition to the relentless hunting, trapping, and the placement of millions of strychnine baits on tens of millions of acres of public lands, the Biological Survey also discovered the efficiency of "denning." Hunters would find the dens of wolves and coyotes after pupping and kill all of the young inside. The Biological Survey also placed full-time hunters along the Mexican border, where known wildlife corridors existed, with orders to shoot any predator that passed by, but especially the "red wolf"—today's Mexican gray wolf.

Before the 1930 wildlife survey season began, Dixon wrote to Director Albright, informing him of a visit to the wildlife team's office in Berkeley by Paul Redington, chief of the Biological Survey (he had taken the reins from Nelson in 1927). The chief was accompanied by his colleague, Stanley Young, who managed the Biological Survey's predator control program. Redington and Young no doubt had heard about the new wildlife survey, and they wanted to know the team's plans for predator control within national parks. Dixon reported that Wright and Redington agreed that no poison should be used in parks. The wildlife team informed the Biological Survey men that the Park Service and its rangers were fully capable of any control issues that might arise in the parks. Dixon let Albright know that was the wildlife team's preferred policy: to keep predator control, if necessary, within the Park Service.[95]

"We have no intention whatever of giving up any of our authority over predatory animals in the national parks," replied an agitated Albright, "and we expect to be guided in our control of these animals by the recommendations of Mr. Wright and yourself."[96]

The tensions coursing beneath these words highlight a shift in what had once been a cozy relationship between the Biological Survey and the Park Service. The essence of this growing divide was the mounting discontent in the academic community, conservation organizations, and the general public over the Biological Survey's relentless pursuit of predators: their unfettered killing of mammals and in particular their exorbitant use of poison. And yet this discontent wasn't exactly new.

I believe it is wrong, economically, scientifically, esthetically and on humanitarian ground, to use poison of any kind, against birds or any species whatsoever, anywhere.
JOSEPH GRINNELL[97]

As early as 1916, Joseph Grinnell and Tracy Storer had written an impressive article in *Science* entitled "Animal Life as an Asset of National Parks." Among its many prescient ideas about parks and their values, the article also zeroed in on the predator issue. "As a rule," the authors wrote, "predaceous animals should be left unmolested and allowed to retain their primitive relation to the rest of the fauna, even though this may entail a considerable annual levy on the animals forming their prey."[98]

The resistance and professional tension that would come to define this debate began in earnest in the mid-1920s. In 1927 E. W. Nelson resigned as chief of the Biological Survey, after a forty-plus-year career there, and Redington took over. Instead of Nelson's upbeat commentary on the numbers of predators "destroyed," with detailed stories from the field—typically placed near the front of each annual report—the killing totals in Redington's reports between 1927 and 1930 were moved to the back of the document, behind more mundane topics, in a futile attempt to appease the outcry from scientists and the public.

A single organization at the time reflected this rift between the Biological Survey's field biologists and their academic and institutional friends and colleagues: the American Society of Mammalogists. Founded in 1919, the association soon became ground zero for the controversy surrounding the Biological Survey's vigorous control programs. In spite of differing opinions, and, no doubt, a handful of personality clashes, the organization survived and continues to this day. C. Hart Merriam, who had retired as chief of the Biological Survey in 1910, was the organization's first president. Grinnell, Dixon, and other professionals from "their side" were fully integrated into the association as well. Grinnell, in fact, was on the committee that created the association, and Dixon soon chaired the Committee on Economic Mammalogy. Wright was elected to that committee in 1930. Both Grinnell and Dixon also wrote numerous articles for the association's journal.

After a 1924 symposium organized by the association to debate the growing concern about the killing of predators, their publication, the *Journal of Mammalogy*, published several of the papers that were presented at the meeting. Lee R. Dice, from the University of Michigan, wrote, "Every kind of mammal, as well as every other type of organic being is of great scientific significance, and the world can ill afford to permit the extermination of any species or subspecies."[99]

Dixon, after he studied the stomach contents of over a thousand predators (he had four hundred more preserved in formalin) found that "certain so-called predatory mammals such as the wildcat and the skunk are, in the aggregate, beneficial and not harmful to human welfare." In essence, he found, they ate a lot of rodents. In contrast, E. A. Goldman, by now a Biological Survey legend, concluded his article by stating: "Large predatory mammals, destructive to livestock and to game, no longer have a place in our advancing civilization."[100]

In the spring of 1930, one hundred and fifty-two of America's top natural scientists, academics, museum directors, and conservationists—including a dozen members of Berkeley's MVZ—signed a petition, "A Protest," against the wholesale killing by the Biological Survey. They pointed out that the killing was being carried out by "irresponsible hunters" being paid by the federal government, "in a manner strongly opposed by almost all of the American experts on the subject, and without consultation with such experts."

They sent this petition, with a cover letter, to "every US senator, every US congressman, the editors of all nature, outdoor, sporting and agricultural periodicals, the officers of all of the more important farm granges, the editors of a selected list of some five hundred daily newspapers, the chief of the Biological Survey, and the secretary of agriculture."[101] Changes needed to be made to the Biological Survey's predator program, and this vocal collection of professionals wouldn't stop until they achieved success, no matter how partial it might be.

Why did Wright and his team continuously ask about grizzlies, wolves, mountain lions, coyotes, bobcats, and wolverines at every single park they went to? Why did they repeat those questions to the old-timers they interviewed? Because, in the preceding decades, these top predators—indicators of a healthy ecosystem—had been killed or removed from every single western park and surrounding lands. This also explains their excitement at finding signs of hope, like wolf tracks at Mount Rainier, where wolves, they were told, no longer existed. The national parks were, in other words, incomplete. And Wright knew it.

The team left the Grand Canyon region and, after a stop in Monument Valley, headed to Mesa Verde National Park, arriving on November 8 to interview Acting Superintendent Marshall Finman. Although they explored Mesa Verde and environs for several days—including the park's fascinating archaeological resources—nothing unusual was reported other than an infestation of bark-eating porcupines. Twenty had been shot in the past year.

So they kept on the move, crisscrossing the region before dropping back down to the Kaibab Plateau to inspect the deer herd once again and, finally, head home. "These four days were spent as happily as any I have ever known," recorded Wright. "The desert scenery, for color, and fantastic formations surely must be as fine as any in the world."[102]

While leaving the plateau and driving up to Jacob's Lake at almost eight thousand feet, the three men got stuck in a sudden and heavy snowstorm. They made do until they could dig their way out the next day. At the same time, unbeknownst to the wildlife team, almost a thousand miles to the northwest, at

Crater Lake, their friend Bill Godfrey had ventured out on foot into a similar snowstorm, attempting to reach some men at a work camp within the park. But the snow kept coming—some forty-two inches were reported—and Godfrey, unprepared, got stuck. He was found the next day, frozen to death.

"We are just back from a rather strenuous trip to Mesa Verde and Grand Canyon national parks," Dixon wrote somberly, after their return to Berkeley. "On our way back we were blocked by the snow and were unable to make a hill near Jacobs Lake on the Kaibab Plateau. We had no inkling at the time that this same storm was bringing tragedy to Bill Godfrey, at Crater Lake, whose funeral we have just attended."[103]

Wright wrote Superintendent Solinsky at Crater Lake. He expressed his sorrow about Godfrey's death and sincerely thanked the superintendent for taking Godfrey in, giving him confidence and responsibilities, and making his life at Crater Lake pleasant and professionally satisfying. "We came to know each other pretty well rooming together at the Rangers Club," Wright wrote, "and we often talked of our hopes and ambitions."[104]

The Intangible Beauty of Nature, 1931–33

In 1931, Wright, Dixon, and Thompson revisited most of the eleven national parks and monuments surveyed the previous year, either as a team or separately. They also pursued preliminary fieldwork in several additional parks: Lassen Volcanic (California), Grand Teton (Wyoming), Glacier (Montana), and Carlsbad Caverns (New Mexico). And they traveled to Pinnacles and Death Valley National Monuments (both in California). It was a very full field season. Their fieldwork through the end of 1933 followed a similar pattern.

They also began work on their first publication, one that would change how the Park Service managed wildlife for decades to come: *Fauna of the National Parks of the United States: A Preliminary Survey of Faunal Relations in National Parks*, Fauna Series No. 1. Historian Richard West Sellars has described *Fauna No. 1*, as it came to be known, as a landmark document that "proposed a truly radical departure from earlier practices."[1]

A Wedding in Bed

Straddling the new year, Wright and Thompson were sent to the Everglades region of Florida by Harold C. Bryant and Albright because it was being considered by Congress for a new national park.[2] They spent approximately a month and a half on an ambitious driving trip that started in late November, 1930—logging, eventually, some ten thousand miles.

Uncharacteristically, there are very few field notes by Wright covering their investigation of the Everglades, but Thompson did record their basic itinerary and the spectacular bird life they saw. In a reflection from a day motoring along the Tamiami Trail in mid-January, Thompson wrote: "The great

flocks of birds were a tremendous sight. At a signal, so it seemed, they would
all rise into the air then gradually settle back out of sight."

After the Everglades, the new year started out on a precarious note for
Wright: he contracted a severe case of malaria, which was perhaps one of his
reasons for not recording notes. In the sunshine state and across the southeastern United States, this debilitating ailment tormented generations of residents and travelers well into the 1930s, killing thousands annually.[3] It caught
up with Wright in Arizona as he and Thompson motored back to the West
Coast. It might be that they stopped in Phoenix because Thompson's family
lived just northwest of town, in Glendale, or it could be that Wright simply
could go no farther without medical attention. Whatever the reason, Thompson admitted his colleague to a hospital.

Wright was a very logical, thoughtful, and organized young man. He believed in making numbered lists of what might be called "life objectives"—
reminders and projects to pursue—and he kept them in a notebook. He once
penned a simple note with the lofty heading "To live best I want: . . ." It started
reasonably with health, followed by financial independence, employment,
culture, social life, and leisure. Several of these were detailed with subpoints.
However, perhaps the most important of these listed goals was family.

Wright dearly wanted a family because his had, over the years, slowly
faded. His parents and his beloved Auntie were gone. His younger brother
Carlos—who was raised by relatives in El Salvador—had been shot and killed
by a Meléndez cousin during an argument in that country the previous year.
His relationship with his older brother, Juan, who was eight years his senior
and had a young family in El Salvador, was also limited. George (or Jorge,
as they knew him in El Salvador) and Juan communicated occasionally, but
mostly through brief letters that were more formal than familial. Wright had
many cousins, and at least one, Mercedes Quiñónez, exchanged long letters
with him, but again, this was no close bond.

He did, however, have his fiancée, Bee Ray.

Within days of his hospitalization, and after talking with Bee by telephone,
Wright lassoed a few dear friends and cajoled them to come to the hospital
in Phoenix. Bee arrived with her sister, Jane, and their parents. Bee's favorite
cousins, the Foots, also made the trip. Wright's good friend and colleague
Ben Thompson was, of course, there too, and Francis L. Chamberlain, from
Berkeley and Yosemite days, traveled to the desert as quickly as he could from
San Francisco. Finally, and perhaps most importantly, Thompson's father, the
Reverend H. A. Thompson, who knew Wright well, came down from Glendale. Once gathered in the hospital on February 9—with the patient still in
bed—George and Bee were married by Reverend Thompson, months earlier

Slide C-16-3 Wapiti, American —
No. 6 Subject Elk: Calf by small lake. Comparison of size with Mrs. Wright. 2324
Date May 30, 1931 Locality Junction Butte, Yellowstone National Park Photographer G. M. Wright

Bee Wright
(Beatrice)

George M. Wright

Bee Wright with elk calf, Yellowstone National Park, May 30, 1931. Photograph by George Wright. Courtesy of NPS History Collection.

than their planned wedding—and most certainly not in Southern California style. George Meléndez Wright and Bee Ray Wright were officially family. Their new life together had begun.

Why Wright wanted so desperately to be married earlier than planned, and in a decidedly unique fashion, is not known, but it could be that he believed his illness might get the better of him. His logical mind may have determined that if the worst-case scenario were to unfold, and he didn't recover, at least the woman he loved would inherit what was his and hopefully go on to have a full life.[4]

What is known: Wright improved, and he and Bee soon moved into the Biltmore Hotel in Phoenix for their honeymoon. The wedding party also stayed at the hotel for a few days and a muted celebration ensued. The newlyweds then traveled to the ecological antipode of the humid, mosquito-filled Everglades: La Quinta Inn, in the arid desert near Palm Springs, California. After some more recuperation, and more celebration, the couple headed back to Berkeley and the house on Thousand Oaks. Once home, Wright finally wrote to Park Service Acting Director Arthur E. Demaray to explain his lapse in communication. "Let me beg the excuse of a long trip home, and an unexpected sickness resulting in a wedding in bed in Phoenix."[5]

With his marriage to Bee, Wright had not just gained a life partner, he also added another unofficial member to his fieldwork team. "Bee had no background in biology," Thompson would recall years later, "but she strongly supported George in his work. After their marriage she went with him on nearly all of his trips into the parks, collecting information on wildlife conditions, and often camping in remote regions, as in the upper reaches of the north fork of the Flathead River in Glacier National Park, and in the Bechler River country of Yellowstone. She had a fine social sense and their home was a center of many festive parties."[6]

> The antelope fawn uttered a cry as it went along. At the first outcry the female antelope . . . came running over like a flash of greased lightening to where my wife was standing with the cameras. I did not see this, but my wife did, and fled for dear life with the cameras.
>
> GEORGE WRIGHT, YELLOWSTONE NATIONAL PARK[7]

La Familia Meléndez

George Wright only traveled to El Salvador once with his father and brothers in order to meet his Salvadoran relatives, most importantly his maternal grandmother: Mercedes Ramírez Meléndez, or "Mamita," the family matriarch. She lived a long and productive life after her husband left her a widow at thirty-seven, with ten children. She quickly took charge of the family businesses and, by all accounts, was very successful.

In 1930, Wright planned a trip to El Salvador to visit with Mamita, his brother John and his wife Teresa and their three young children as well as the rest of the Meléndez family. For untold reasons, however, the visit never happened. His cousin, Mercedes Quiñónez, wrote him expressing "great pity" that he changed his plans, but he should reschedule soon, she pleaded, in order to learn about his heritage. "You could get a fair idea of the family and of its history and tradition," she lobbied, "you could get acquainted with those who being gone forever are cherished by us all and live in our memories."[8]

But Wright never rescheduled. In 1931, he wrote a letter to his brother John about transferring some bank shares to him that belonged to their deceased younger brother, ending with: "I have not heard from you in a long while and I look forward to the time when you shall have the opportunity to write." A year later, Mercedes and her parents fled to Paris due to the changing political winds in El Salvador. She wrote Wright several times, repeating a sentiment she had expressed to him before: "I am so happy that you, at least, were kept away from our dangerous, but how beautiful, country. My best love to Bee."[9]

The Case of the Trumpeter Swan

The Wrights started out their marriage, and collaboration, by traveling to Pinnacles, Death Valley, Carlsbad Caverns, and Colorado's Mesa Verde. Thompson accompanied them on these trips, while Dixon stayed back to conduct research in Sequoia and Yosemite National Parks.

By May, the Wrights were in Yellowstone to focus on swans. So intense was Wright's interest in and concern for trumpeter swans that he spent countless hours tracking down potential nesting areas inside and outside of Yellowstone. He often chased down enticing stories he heard of the birds nesting on this or that lake. More often than not, when he followed the leads, they ended at a lake once home to trumpeters but now abandoned. On other days, back in the park, he would stay in one location observing general swan behavior "during a typical day in the incubation period."

Wright and his team were mystified by the startlingly low survival rate of the cygnets. They knew ravens opportunistically ate swan eggs, and they suspected otters and coyotes were culprits too, but they had very little proof in spite of weeks of observation, including the analysis of scat from the suspects: they found feathers and bones of other birds, but not of swans.

The day was cloudy but mild in temperature. The sun shone through a little around midday. Bee accompanied me. We took three censuses, Bee recording as we went.
GEORGE WRIGHT, YELLOWSTONE NATIONAL PARK[10]

One night, Dixon, who joined the team in June, slept on the shores of Trumpeter Lake once again, not far from a nest with four cygnets. When he awoke at 5 a.m., there were only three. He was perplexed. He hadn't heard any commotion or seen anything during the night, and he found no tracks along the shore near the nest. (Reading through his field notes, it seems as though he often "slept" with one eye open and one ear listening.) He finally surmised the perpetrator must have been a great horned owl he heard calling in the middle of the night.

By August of that year, the Wrights had moved on to Glacier National Park to conduct general fieldwork and to search for swans in particular. They found no trumpeters, not even at Swan Lake, south of the park. After camping out for a couple of days and undertaking several prodigious hikes, they stayed in the small town of Belton, Montana, just outside the park.

From the shores of the Middle Fork of the Flathead River, Wright organized his first serious report for the director detailing the plight of the swan and suggesting a possible course of action. That four-page memo was likely the first such document concerning the trumpeter swan written by any American biologist. "In the field of conservation of bird life in the United States," Wright began, "the case of the trumpeter swan is one of the first magnitude."[11]

Wright then detailed the interest in swans that he had discovered everywhere he traveled, from government officials to local residents. As far as he was able to confirm, by midsummer 1931, the US trumpeter swan population consisted of twenty adults and fifteen cygnets, all located in the greater Yellowstone region. In his memo, Wright explained some of the potential reasons for the species' decline, and he laid out tentative "protective measures," including publicity campaigns and even the possibility of captive breeding as a last resort:

> Unless the Park Service is quick to accept the challenge to do everything within its power, we will surely suffer the opprobrium of our own and future generations for our laissez-faire attitude. . . . My personal feeling is that a bright star would be added to the National Park Service's crown if it stepped out with a courageous and long-sighted program, a real attempt to save for posterity the greatest of our American waterfowl, the trumpeter swan.[12]

Wright's sentiments were echoed by Dixon in an article he published based on their fieldwork together. "It is our belief that the trumpeter swan is a species that has reached a critical stage of existence," Dixon wrote. "We believe that if a 'do nothing' attitude prevails, this magnificent bird will soon be numbered with the passenger pigeon and other extinct species."[13]

After Wright received a tacit green light on the swan project, he fashioned a more detailed proposal for his superior, Harold Bryant. He expanded on the various points in his August report, but he also focused on the need for two Park Service researchers to be dedicated to the Yellowstone swans between April and migration in the late fall. He wanted to have these individuals keep watch, night and day, for at least two weeks at a single nest, after the cygnets hatched, in order to identify predators.

Overall, Wright presented a holistic approach to the problem: research, collaboration, community involvement, communications and outreach, and contingency plans.[14] He did not receive those two dedicated researchers he requested. Instead, he spent four and a half months over the next two years—

Neg.No. 5474

No.10   Subject Swan, Trumpeter   (Eggs did not hatch)

Date June 18-20,   Locality Red Rock Lake, Montana
1932   Photographer Dr. Oastler

George M. Wright

Trumpeter swan by nest, Red Rock Lake, Montana, June 1932. Photograph by Frank Oastler. Courtesy of NPS History Collection.

with the help of his team, and often with Bee—conducting the basic fieldwork he had suggested to his superiors. Most of this research, not surprisingly, was based out of Yellowstone, where he was also able to enlist some key colleagues from the park. Superintendent Roger Toll was already 100 percent behind Wright and his efforts, as was Joseph Joffe, the assistant superintendent. And for real, on-the-ground help while Wright was away, his friend and Chief Ranger George Baggley stepped up, sending him regular swan observation reports.[15] Wright also asked that Baggley remind the Yellowstone rangers of the importance of "recording everything possible relative to the winter status of this species. Little by little we are piecing together a picture which is going to be the most valuable thing of all in securing the perpetuation of the trumpeters."[16]

At 8:10 pm I was startled by a loud wailing which could only have been coyote. While looking for the source of this sound I spied a black form moving through the sagebrush across the Creek. It was a large grizzly bear, the first I have ever seen away from the immediate vicinity of a feeding platform. The grizzly did not see me, though moving leisurely it covered ground at a rapid rate. The large size, the grizzly cast to the dark coat, the hump & dish face made identification exceedingly simple and certain. It looked so ready for mischief that I found myself quite cowardly willing to hurry on.

GEORGE WRIGHT, YELLOWSTONE NATIONAL PARK[17]

The next season, 1932, Wright saw photographs of swans at two lakes in Montana, due west of Yellowstone: Upper and Lower Red Rock Lakes. After his first visit to the area, he proclaimed "Lower Red Rock Lake is the best lake I have ever seen for trumpeters."[18] On a subsequent trip, Wright and Thompson, positioned on a ridge high above the lake, counted twenty-one swans and three active nests. Those photographs, and that first visit to Red Rocks, changed the trajectory of Wright's swan work. Immediately afterward he expanded the geographic scope of his research, and he spent the next several years "piecing together a picture" by working on both the conservation of swans in Yellowstone and the preservation of their habitat at Red Rock Lakes.[19]

Charmaine and Pamela

In the spring and early summer of 1932, the Wrights stayed in Yellowstone National Park for two and a half months, with the occasional foray over to Montana and Red Rocks. The first week of July they drove west, then south, en route to Berkeley and home. Bee was eight months pregnant. On August 14 Charmaine Wright was born.

That November, just three months later, the Wrights tucked Charmaine into a sturdy basket with a gauze window above her head. They snugly packed her behind the driver's seat of the wildlife survey's truck and drove back to Yellowstone for another five weeks of work based out of a cabin.[20] It was an undertaking that could not have been easy for the new parents: "Last night the minimum thermometer recorded -21.5°F," Wright noted several days after their arrival. "A real cold snap for the time of year."[21]

A year later, he typed a note to Joseph Grinnell from the small town of Kalispell, Montana, southwest of Glacier. Thompson had been traveling with him. Dixon was back at Sequoia. Bee was in Berkeley with Charmaine, and she was very pregnant with baby number two. "I would have little hope for acceptance of this apology for delay in correspondence excepting that as a fieldworker you are experienced in the difficulties involved and hence will be sympathetic," Wright wrote to Grinnell. "Progress . . . has been satisfactory, but we have long, long progress to make where wild life values are

concerned. . . . My spirit is in Berkeley now, for reasons you can easily surmise. For the same cause, you may be sure that nothing can keep me from
returning by October first."[22]

He did make it home on time, and Pamela Wright was born a few weeks
later. The new father wrote to Superintendent William E. Branch and his wife,
at Platt National Park in Oklahoma, where Wright had been in July to study
the introduced herds of elk and bison. "Our second little baby was a girl, born
on October 17, so now we, like you, have two small daughters to love and
care for."[23]

The Suicidal Effects of Overgrazing

Thompson had stayed behind in the Southwest at the beginning of the 1931
season for a variety of fieldwork; then he joined the others in Yellowstone.
He focused on livestock, overgrazing, and their impacts on native wildlife in
and around parks and monuments. This issue wasn't a simple annoyance to
the biologists—the fact that nonnative herbivores grazed inside parks—but
rather a serious and entrenched management issue.

Ben is back like a fresh gust of wind and with lots of news for us. It was so sad a thing to
me to have to go away from the park during the height of the season and while all our
projects were the most interesting. But next to being there myself it is nearly the same
having Ben there. We think and work so nearly along the same lines that it is like one
person divided.

GEORGE WRIGHT[24]

At Utah's Zion National Park, for example, several thousand sheep grazed
inside the park on inholdings, but they also roamed throughout the entire
park. "I think this region is one of the most outstanding examples of the sui-
cidal effects of overgrazing," noted Thompson, "especially by sheep."[25] Dixon
found four to five thousand sheep thriving within nearby Bryce Canyon National Park in 1931. He was told that all decisions regarding grazing were managed by the Forest Service and its local grazing board, not by the Park Service.[26] Two years later the situation had not improved. "The attitude of the
sheepmen," he reported in 1933, "is that the grazing both outside and inside the
park belongs to them and that it isn't any of the park's business what they do."[27]

Because the wildlife team was so concerned about overgrazing and its severe (and often deadly) impact on native wildlife, they built a series of "fenced
range study quadrates," or plots, across the Kaibab Plateau. This allowed the

researchers to compare the growth of important plants inside the enclosures to the vegetation outside the fencing on an annual or biennial basis. The team eventually established similar sets of enclosures across the Grand Canyon's south rim and in Mesa Verde, Zion, Yosemite, Sequoia, Rocky Mountain, and Yellowstone National Parks.[28]

Overgrazing also plagued the northern, mountainous parks. Yellowstone, however, presented an exceptionally challenging and unique management issue, due to a native species: elk. Prior to the US Cavalry arriving in Yellowstone in 1886 to take over management, Yellowstone's large mammals had been shot to near annihilation, either by individuals for subsistence or by the rapacious market hunters who infested the park during the 1870s.[29] The military eventually put a stop to the excessive hunting and, over time, ungulate and bear populations increased. Of particular interest to park management— and in later decades, to nearby hunting groups—was the status of what was referred to as the northern elk herd. Spread out across the Lamar and Yellowstone River basins, and up the northwest-trending Yellowstone River valley— into Montana, and outside the park—the herd benefited from its protected status and thrived. Some hundred linear miles to the south, adjacent to Grand Teton National Park and Jackson Hole, another large herd existed, secure within the National Elk Refuge, created in 1912.[30]

By the early 1930s, Wright and his colleagues had determined that the northern herd had grown too large. "The area is frightfully overgrazed in my opinion," recorded Wright. "Junipers were cleaned right up to the reach of the deer. Elk had eaten the aspen twigs as high as they could reach. Even the sage had taken a severe beating."[31] Although the wildlife team deduced this for themselves after several years of fieldwork, they also leaned heavily on local expertise to bolster their opinions and eventually their management recommendations. In 1927 Yellowstone's first naturalist, Milton P. Skinner, wrote a lengthy article that highlighted, in part, the history of elk and their ecological status within the park. And William M. Rush, a Forest Service biologist, published the results of his three-year northern elk herd study in 1933.[32] Meanwhile, Olaus Murie, with the Biological Survey at the time, weighed in with dire warnings about Yellowstone's elk in early 1931.[33]

All of these biologists concurred that the elk imbalance was the result of a convergence of factors. Elk predators, for example, had all but been exterminated from the park and surrounding forests. Biologist Adolph Murie (Olaus's brother) noted that between 1900 and 1935, 121 mountain lions, 132 wolves, and 4,352 coyotes were killed in Yellowstone—and those were just the official numbers.[34] Additionally, grizzly bears had changed their natural

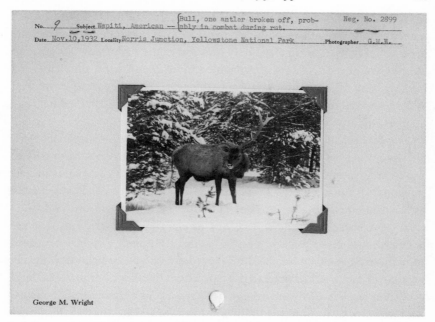

Bull elk, or wapiti, with damaged antler, Yellowstone National Park, November 10, 1932. Photograph by George Wright. Courtesy of NPS History Collection.

feeding patterns. Instead of taking down the occasional elk, they were entertainment at the "bear shows" and addicted to piles of garbage. A further, albeit uncontrollable, element impacting elk habitat was the extended drought in the lower forty-eight states from the late 1920s to at least 1935; less rain simply meant less forage for the growing herd and other species.[35]

As Wright pointed out during the early 1930s, the spring and fall range in the northern reaches of the park were overoccupied almost year-round by an estimated 10,000 elk, 1,000 bison, 800 mule deer, 600 pronghorn, and 125 bighorn sheep for large portions of the year. Rush estimated the elk population as even higher, between 12,000 and 14,000 animals.[36] Rush and Skinner also complained about the herds of horses—between 200 and 300 head—kept on the park's northern range by a commercial tour operator.

To the north of the park, on the elks' traditional winter range, sheep, cattle, and horses spent seven to nine months of the year eating all of the vegetation to the ground. Additionally, lines of hunters at the park's northern border not only killed the elk in a disorganized and uncontrolled fashion every fall and winter during migration—taking an inordinate number of cows and calves—but they also succeeded in driving most of the elk back into the park and away from their traditional winter range. This created unnatural congregations of animals in the wrong part of their range at the wrong time of year. This "firing line" of hunters was particularly irksome to the biologists. "Disgraceful hunting conditions," as Rush commented in his report. And after visiting a hunting camp himself, just over the park's northern border one November, Wright referred to it, in a lengthy and damning entry, as "a jumbled ugly human community."[37]

It was a critical situation created, ironically, by decades of successful wildlife restoration management within the park that converged with restrictive and unnatural park borders. And outside those borders was a powerful livestock industry that kept too many animals on too little land—all augmented by basic human avarice, manifested during every hunting season.

In 1932, seven thousand acres of traditional elk range were added to the northern border of the park, west of Gardiner. Though Wright lobbied for and approved of this purchase, he believed it wouldn't be helpful to the elk for a long time, as it had been so degraded from decades of livestock use and needed to recover. Rush and Wright both argued for a more regulated hunting season, what Rush termed a "limited license system" that would specify the number of hunters allowed, where and when they could hunt, and what age and sex of elk they could take.[38] By 1932, the Park Service had negotiated a three-day pause—a cease-fire—between periods of shooting that allowed the elk to move north to their winter range unmolested.[39] Combined, these changes would allow hunters to bag their elk, while not completely blocking the herd from moving north.

Despite these steps forward, both Wright and Rush were determined to continue working with the Montana Fish and Game Commission to further improve the situation. A 1932 handwritten note by Wright, simply titled "Northern Elk Herd," summarizes the basic steps he sought to implement on behalf of the Park Service in order to help the species. In addition to revamping the hunting conditions and increasing the number to be killed, he suggested more land purchases, the removal of fences, and the reseeding of some lands.[40]

Even taking these plans into consideration, and the small positive steps they had already achieved, Wright and Thompson both believed there was one key management step that still had to be taken by the park. "If there are 10,000 elk in this northern herd," wrote Thompson, "it is my opinion that they should be reduced to 5,000. Unless the elk are immediately reduced the range will continue to deteriorate. George suggests that the elk be reduced 1,000 per year, by hunting, until the carrying capacity of the range is reached, and range recovery is apparent."[41]

The concept of shooting, or culling, the elk to reduce numbers wasn't an original idea in wildlife management, but it was a novel idea in relation to the northern elk herd of Yellowstone. Wright and his colleagues didn't have to look far, however, to see how it might be managed. After all, the park's bison—the other species of particular interest to park management, and to many Americans—had been intensely cared for since they came back from near extinction in the late nineteenth century.

In 1900, perhaps forty bison survived in the park.[42] A recovery program began in 1902 and, thirty years later, the herd numbered over 1,100. The bison—America's most iconic animal—had been treated like domesticated cattle in order to achieve those numbers. The strategies to success—all run out of the Buffalo Ranch in the park's Lamar Valley—included yearly fall roundups, corralling, winter feeding, and veterinary checkups.[43] Some bison were shipped to other parks and zoos. And the Park Service also reduced the herd through the strategic shooting of bison, principally to remove older steers and adjust the sex ratio of the herd. The meat from the culled buffalo was given or sold inexpensively to the local Indian Agency for distribution to nearby reservations.[44] With the bison herd stable in the early 1930s, Wright also lobbied to reduce this intense management to slowly return the Yellowstone bison to "the wild state insofar as the inherent limitations of the park will permit."[45]

With the lessons learned from the bison's success story, the wildlife team had the beginnings of a plan for elk management. It was now just a matter of convincing Park Service senior staff that reducing the herd size by aggressive and carefully planned shooting was the right management choice to make. It wouldn't be easy.

We cantered across the flats where the hay is harvested, our eyes on the buildings of the ranch beyond the tall cottonwoods, our minds on a dinner long delayed. We were in twilight but the sun reached out to the Absarokas above Soda Butte Creek on one side and above the Lamar on the other, lighting their snows vividly. Sunset rose glowed in the clouds that hung stilly above their summits. We have had a great day.

GEORGE WRIGHT, YELLOWSTONE NATIONAL PARK[46]

Like a House with Two Sides Left Open

In November of 1933, Olaus Murie wrote Wright to congratulate him on the birth of his second daughter, Pamela, but he soon pivoted to the issues before them. "It seems to me that in game management we are inheriting a lot of trouble from the fact that boundaries of National Parks and perhaps other reserves were not made with a view to providing decent winter range for our animals. Today we sometimes meet opposition when trying to rectify these mistakes. Apparently game needs are not yet understood by many people."[47]

Boundary issues were documented and discussed by Wright and his team in every park and monument they visited, as was the matter of insufficient winter range for migrating ungulates—a related result of linear borders that looked good on paper but which disregarded on-the-ground wildlife requirements to create what he called a "biographically self-sufficient unit." After several visits to Mesa Verde National Park, for example, Wright lamented the inappropriate perimeters of the park. "On the south and west sides of the park there are no present natural boundaries. It is like a house with two sides left open."[48]

In 1931, Wright produced a report analyzing Carlsbad Caverns National Park, in southeastern New Mexico, and the ecologically connected Guadalupe Mountains just over the border in Texas. Carlsbad Caverns was created to preserve its vast limestone caves and not necessarily its wildlife.[49] However, Wright detailed the wildlife issues in and around the park and in the mountains to the south. He then focused on the need to adjust boundaries in general. "Every member of the staff, as well as myself," wrote Albright after receiving the document, "regard this report as one of the most important that have come into the Washington office during the year."[50] Director Albright and the national office began to listen to Wright on boundary issues.

Carlsbad Caverns: Trip down bat cave with G. M. W. It seemed inconceivable that so much life could live in such darkness.

BEN THOMPSON[51]

Wright and Roger Toll had known each other for several years due to Wright's extensive fieldwork in Yellowstone. Additionally, during at least one trip to the Park Service's San Francisco office, Toll had stayed with the Wrights in Berkeley. And so, on the strength of Wright's Carlsbad report and with Albright's encouragement, Toll and Wright began collaborating on park boundary issues. Toll was Mather's, then Albright's, go-to man for special assignments. These consisted principally of reconnaissance trips to evaluate potential new parks and to research the possible expansion of borders for existing parks. Toll, a former mountain climber born and raised in Denver, Colorado, was a tall and imposing figure (particularly when standing next to the diminutive Wright).[52]

"The Washington office has expressed approval of the principle that a preliminary investigation of the wild life of any areas where new park or extension projects are contemplated should be made," Wright informed Toll in January 1932. "We here believe this to be very important, for a consideration of the wild life requirements of the proposed park or extension will often result in the establishment of the correct boundaries in the beginning."[53]

Toll responded enthusiastically to Wright's note and the "excellent program" he laid out. The Yellowstone superintendent then listed which parks and monuments he suggested Wright evaluate and report on first.[54] Wright replied immediately, commenting on each park and what needed to be done. He insisted, for example, that the secluded Darwin Falls be included in a Death Valley extension. "We really feel this is important," he wrote.[55] One of the only year-round, spring-fed watering holes in the Death Valley area, Darwin Falls not only supports lush vegetation in the middle of the desert but also provides a key habitat and water source for everything from amphibians to birds to bighorn sheep—and countless generations of humans.

Regarding the Everglades, Wright declared that, "If there ever was a situation which presented a brief for the importance of wild life conditions, it is here. What an unparalleled opportunity in the Everglades to do something big."[56] He lobbied to join Toll in the redwoods of Northern California, voiced concern about the Roosevelt elk at Mount Olympus National Monument, and argued that the trumpeter swans would benefit from an enlargement of Grand Teton National Park.

In total, there were thirteen locations that Wright and Toll agreed to focus on. However, Wright also informed Toll he wouldn't be taking any trips specifically for this new assignment. "We will keep the list of the projects now before you at hand," Wright promised, "in order that they may be included in our itineraries where possible."[57] Yet there was one place where Wright did want to "do something big": the Everglades.

Approximately a year after this exchange with Toll, Wright's frustration with developments in the Everglades became apparent. Even though Albright had sent Wright and Thompson to southern Florida in the winter of 1930–31 on a reconnaissance trip, and Wright stayed up to date on most aspects of the park's status—both in Florida and Washington, DC—boundary decisions were being made without his team's input. Instead, the federal General Land Office had apparently been to the region and was beginning to design potential borders working with a large consortium of public and private parties.[58]

"Inasmuch as the wild life of the Everglades is a paramount reason for making a national park of this area," Wright wrote Albright, emphasizing the fact that this was to be the first park designated primarily for its wildlife and not for outstanding geologic features, "we urge that the Service's own wild life experts be given an opportunity to go over the ground before any final delimitation of boundaries is made. This is necessary because only within our own organization has the concept of what is required to make of a national park a biographically self-sufficient unit been established. Perhaps this suggestion may seem to you to be too premature. It is, however, all too evident from past experience that park boundaries have usually been laid out first and the actual wild life requirements considered later when it is almost, if not entirely, too late to do anything about it."[59]

Harold Bryant responded to Wright's letter on behalf of the director, acknowledging the need for the input of wildlife experts and the importance of having "experts investigate proposed boundary lines." Bryant then added, "There is growing sentiment favorable to an Everglades National Park, and it is bound to become an actuality sometime."[60] Almost two years later—long before Everglades became a park—Wright, Bryant, Toll, and the Park Service's deputy chief engineer, Oliver G. Taylor, traveled to southern Florida on a five-day reconnaissance to study the border issue.[61]

By his action, man can restore a needed range to a park provided he is willing to do it, but there is absolutely no way he can keep every unfavorable influence out of that park—not so long as boundaries are artificial, and some of them must always be that.

FAUNA NO. 1[62]

We Shall Never Make Any Moves without Mr. Wright and His Associates

When Director Redington of the Biological Survey and his colleague Stanley Young stopped into the Berkeley wildlife office in the fall of 1929 to inquire about the biologists' plans for controlling predators in national parks, the team knew the issue had quickly moved to the front burner. They also knew—after Dixon informed the director about the visit—that Albright wanted to be "guided in our control of these animals by the recommendations of Mr. Wright and yourself."

During the following year, the first official year of their survey and after numerous in-person conversations with superintendents and rangers in all of the western parks, a predator policy began to develop. In reality, these were more than simple conversations: the team, and specifically Wright, were subtly and simultaneously educating and lobbying their Park Service colleagues.

In March of 1931, Wright wrote to Bryant about the predator control policy the Park Service was going to issue. It was a document the biologists had a major role in writing, but Bryant was in charge of finalizing it, and it would then be released under the director's name. "May I say that I think this statement of the National Park Service's policy relative to predatory mammals to be fine in every way? This, of course," joked Wright, "is to say that it coincides exactly with my own ideas on the subject."[63]

The following May, the National Park Service's "Policy on Predatory Mammals" was published in the *Journal of Mammalogy*.[64] Although the new policy left the door open for some control when predators, specifically coyotes, were "making serious inroads upon herds of game or other mammals needing special protection," the statement constituted a dramatic change from the days of beaming Park Service employees posing with dead mountain lions and of the Biological Survey's free rein to track down predators in the parks and sprinkle poisoned meat and grain across the landscape. It was a break from the past that could not have happened without the persistence and persuasion of Wright as well as his team, conservationists, and academics.

"The National Park Service believes that predatory animals have a real place in nature," the policy affirmed, "and that all animal life should be kept inviolate within the parks." Predatory animals were now to be "considered an integral part of the wild life protected within national parks." In conclusion, the policy's last paragraph declared: "It can be seen, therefore, that within the national park system definite attention is given to that group of animals which elsewhere are not tolerated."[65]

To say the least, it was a rough transition for many superintendents and their rangers. They understood it and, for the most part, they agreed with it. The numerous conversations Wright, Dixon, and Thompson had with their colleagues assuaged their fears. And yet, sparing predators ran counter to years of practice within the parks—not to mention a loss of income for some rangers who had been allowed to sell the animals' pelts.

Copying the wildlife office, Superintendent Tillotson of Grand Canyon National Park wrote the director after the policy was announced and expressed the need to adapt. "I have discussed this at some length with Mr. Wright and Mr. Dixon on the occasion of their visits to the park," the superintendent stated. "As a result I have definitely come to the conclusion that we have for the present gone far enough, or perhaps too far, in the extermination of such predators." He continued on to suggest that the rangers he typically deployed to kill predators in the winter could instead switch their attention to coordinating with the Forest Service to eliminate wild horses on the north rim of the park.[66]

Wright, not missing a beat, replied to Tillotson, approving of his "very sound" decision not to resume predator control. He encouraged the superintendent to "keep a detailed account" of the wild horse removal, "not only for scientific reasons but for the future historical value of such a record." And, he suggested, some of the rangers who previously worked in predator control could instead study them and their relationship to other fauna in the park. Wright was deliberately trying to recruit help within the park for his team's research from a colleague he knew well.

To make it easier for Tillotson, Wright included a memo with "some thoughts along this line." It was a memo he had written the director previously, suggesting that rangers, if properly trained, could perform some basic wildlife research in the parks: an effort he would not give up on.

In addition to the predators that had been persecuted for generations, the biologists also became involved, to a lesser degree, with issues ranging from mosquito abatement to how best to remove skunks from under park buildings to gassing gophers in Yosemite Valley. Perhaps one of the most intriguing issues they had to deal with, however, involved trout. More precisely, who was eating the trout that many Park Service employees and fishermen believed belonged to them—trout that thrived for years, for the most part, thanks to Park Service fish-stocking programs. Wright, an avid fly fisherman, pursued this issue with great interest.

Some parks, such as Glacier, were seriously considering shooting fish-eating birds such as mergansers, kingfishers, cormorants, seagulls, and osprey to protect fish for visiting anglers (most likely they had already started doing this on the sly). In a letter to the superintendent of Glacier, E. T. Scoyen, Wright warned about the precedent that could be set by removing the birds—as well as several fish-loving mammals. One suggestion he offered was instead to plant trout fingerlings that were a minimum size of six inches so it would be harder for birds to catch them.[67]

Wright strongly disagreed with the need to remove these "trout predators" unless a situation arose "when control was imperative." He simply wasn't convinced that it was a real management problem. "I might add," Wright continued, referring to his recent trip to Glacier, "the fishing in Red Eagle Lake is good. I took out a limit of fine native trout in the afternoon, and this at the end of the season when the lake had been very heavily fished, according to the district ranger."[68]

One trout-eating bird that did not escape the wrath of humans was Yellowstone's white pelican. These large birds—"grotesque on land and superb in flight," as Wright mused—had been nesting on the Molly Islands, in the southeast arm of Yellowstone Lake, for decades. Ben Thompson had focused on the white pelican for his master's thesis while he was studying under Grinnell. During his travels with Wright and Dixon, he was given the opportunity to conduct fieldwork for his thesis with the team. Now the biologists found that, without an official management plan yet in hand, Park Service employees had begun controlling the pelican population as early as the 1920s in order to "protect" the lake's trout.

In a rather chilling entry in his field notebook, Wright recorded what he discovered about this supposed wildlife management effort from a park document. "The confidential report indicates that control work began in 1923 and has resulted in reduction of the colony from about 600 to 250." He then recorded, year by year, how many eggs or young pelicans were destroyed by the Park Service.[69] In the margin of the notebook, he wrote "do not type." (All field notes were typed up in Berkeley by the wildlife office secretary during the winter).

Wright wanted this information to stay in his notebook and not be widely circulated, because it was not wildlife management. It was, he believed, instead simply a cruel culling of a species that was thought to be impacting the trout population based on absolutely no research. He proceeded to work with Superintendent Toll on the issue—along with many others—and Park Service employees soon stopped the practice.[70] Thompson's master's thesis, *History and Present Status of the Breeding Colonies of the White Pelican (Pelecanus erythrorhynchos) in the United States*, was approved by Grinnell in 1932, and shortly thereafter it was printed by the Park Service.[71]

I wanted you to know how important, for science, I think Ben Thompson's work with the pelicans is. What he is finding out with regard to the behavior of colonies is, I think, new. You are fortunate, I am convinced, in having absorbed into your Service such men as George Wright and Ben Thompson. I have the utmost confidence in the sound judgement of these men, as well as in the wide scope of their scientific knowledge.

JOSEPH GRINNELL TO HORACE ALBRIGHT[72]

"The matter of predatory animal control has become more and more a subject of controversy." So began a memo written by Acting Director Arno B. Cammerer on September 10, 1931, to all superintendents of national parks and custodians of national monuments. The shift in policy led to a rough transition indeed. It would take several years for old habits to fade—but it was a solid beginning. Cammerer refers to the Park Service official policy printed the previous May in the *Journal of Mammalogy* and which was attached to the memo. "We hope you will read it carefully, and be prepared to defend its pronouncements."[73]

Wright and Thompson with survey truck, Hayden Valley, Yellowstone National Park, May 20, 1932. Photograph by Frances Chamberlain. Courtesy of Pamela Meléndez Wright Lloyd.

Wright and Bryant were on the same page pertaining to the policy and the need to continue educating superintendents, rangers, and the public. Over the next few years, Bryant wrote letters to Wright and his colleagues, and he strategically copied various superintendents, supporting the new policy in no uncertain terms. "In my opinion," he wrote in September 1931, copying Glacier's Superintendent Scoyen, "destruction of wild animal life of any kind seriously interferes with the main duty of the National Park Service, which is, to keep the parks in an unmodified condition. At present there seems to be an unfortunate tendency on the part of some members of the Park Service to advocate predatory animal control and for several others to defend their value."[74]

The following year, Wright sent a note to Director Albright, expressing frustration at the recalcitrance of some field staff regarding predators. "Throughout the park system as a whole I believe that there are many who have not yet come to truly understand our ideal, to recognize that what is known as a predator on a game ranch does not have the same status in a national park."[75] Albright, Cammerer, and Bryant agreed with him and vowed to keep to the policy. And they did make progress. Superintendents adjusted and, in turn, worked to drive home the information to their chief rangers.

One such superintendent was Wright's former boss from Yosemite, C. G. Thomson. He explained to his head ranger that coyotes were to be left alone unless problems arose, and that hawks were no longer to be shot on sight. "Mr. Wright's accounts to me that hawks are being studied more carefully and that most species are now coming into regard as of not only interest, but also of practical influence. Hereafter, please bear in mind that in Yosemite we shall never make any moves whatsoever without the prior study on the ground of Mr. Wright and his associates."[76]

Don't Feed the Bears: It's Dangerous

When the biologists left Yellowstone in the summer of 1930 and stopped at the bear "lunch counter" presided over by Ranger Martindale, they promised to spend more time researching and attempting to solve the bear issues so prevalent in the western parks. They already believed it wasn't really a bear problem: it was a human problem. "The bear problem is due very nearly 100 percent to the abnormally intimate contacts which human beings have sought to establish with the bears," Wright wrote, "and not to the innate ferocity in bear nature."[77]

For example, when the handheld treats ran out along Yellowstone's "bear jams"—long lines of backed-up cars behind the holdup bears—accounts increased of people who were bitten or smacked by powerful paws. In 1931 alone, some seventy-six people reported bear injuries in Yellowstone; 163 visitors informed the park about damages to their equipment or cars; and eighty-two requested compensation from the federal government for their losses.[78] It was not, then, surprising that by the early 1930s tourists were becoming furious and park administrators frustrated.

And yet the bear shows continued. The spectacles were too popular and too ingrained in the culture of several parks. Nowhere was this combination of issues and behaviors more manifest than in Yellowstone. (Yosemite and Sequoia came in close seconds, however, and hand-feeding was common in other western mountain parks as well.) A complicating factor in Yellowstone was that Director Albright absolutely loved the bear shows and was very vocal about that fact.

While superintendent of Yellowstone, from 1919 to 1929, Albright had highlighted the bear shows. There were three feeding sites in the park. Of these, the Otter Creek location was the biggest stage, and Albright made sure there was log seating for up to 250 tourists to enjoy the nightly feeding, accompanied by a ranger talk. But Roger Toll, who succeeded Albright as superintendent, wrote in his 1929 annual report that "the bear population of Yellowstone seems to have reached a point where they were somewhat of a nuisance." By 1931, he admitted the problem was "acute."[79] And although Wright and Superintendent Toll were close colleagues, they gently disagreed about what to do with the bears. It was a disagreement they would work out over the next couple of years.

In the summer of 1931, Dixon inspected several cars by Yellowstone's Lake Lodge whose interiors were slashed and destroyed by scavenging bears. The irate tourists said that nobody had warned them about the bears, and that of all the western parks they had visited, Yellowstone had the worst bear problem by far. After his inquiries, Dixon made a very simple but logical suggestion. Every tourist that arrived to the park by vehicle should be handed a slip of paper by the entrance ranger that told visitors: don't leave food in your car, stay 15 feet away from bears, and "Don't feed the bears, it's dangerous."[80]

There is no evidence that his suggestion was immediately adopted. However, the official park booklets handed out to visitors soon warned against feeding bears, and that feeding was dangerous and against park policy. For the most part, however, tourists ignored the warning.[81] Additionally, Albright did not approve of negative messaging about the bears. To his mind, the bears were the celebrities that drew the tourists into the park. If there were a few incidents here and there, so be it.

"Don't feed the bears, it's dangerous"—a simple yet obvious idea—soon became a point of dry humor among the biologists and rangers in Yellowstone and in other parks with bear issues. Wright began to sign off his letters to colleagues in these bear parks with that refrain. Yellowstone's Assistant Superintendent Joffe responded jokingly to one such letter from Wright with, "We have heeded your warning about not feeding the bears. We prefer to let them enjoy themselves at the expense of our garbage cans."

The unique charm of the animals in a national park lies in their wildness, not their tameness, in their primitive struggle to survive rather than their fat certainty of an easy living.

FAUNA NO. 1[82]

Bear humor aside, the big difference in Yellowstone, compared to the other two parks with bear shows, was the addition of the resident grizzly bear. It was one thing to have black bears marauding campsites and holding up cars—and they were responsible for the vast majority, if not all, of that behavior—but grizzlies mixing with humans, due to their enormous size and strength, was a recipe for disaster. When Wright found out that two grizzly cubs had become tame in the area around Old Faithful and had been fed by hand, he was extremely alarmed. "This will not do and must be stopped before it is well started or the bear problem will be worse than ever."[83]

One July evening, Thompson was at Yellowstone's canyon bear-feeding station to accompany Frank R. Oastler, a member of the Educational Advisory Board that supported the Park Service. It was common for board members to spend the summers visiting the parks, and they often sought out the team of biologists in the field to accompany them in their fieldwork. Oastler, of New York, was an avid photographer and naturalist, and he knew the western parks well.

As Thompson and Oastler stood off to the side, away from the tourists, a mother grizzly, with three cubs in tow, suddenly turned to them, locked in, roared, and charged them at full speed. They frantically ran to the closest pine trees and climbed as fast as they could. Thompson got clear, but Oastler didn't, and the massive bear, standing up at the base of the tree, swept one of her huge paws upward, perhaps some nine feet high, and snagged Oastler's foot. He struggled to hold on as the bear tried to pull him out of the tree; finally he was able to yank his foot free and kept climbing. "The attack was unprovoked," recorded Thompson, back at camp, "except that we were standing in an unusual place." Thompson also noted, rather nonchalantly, that Oastler's mangled foot survived, minus one toe that had to be amputated at the park's hospital.[84]

Thompson returned to the feeding platform the next night with a ranger. After the crowd dispersed, they shot, and instantly killed with a single rifle bullet, the mother grizzly that had attacked Oastler.[85] With new dedication, Thompson spent many days after this experience researching the bear problem in Yellowstone with the team and several rangers. He wanted to know who generated large amounts of garbage and what they did with it. How much garbage went to each feeding site? How could it be managed better or even reduced? Could they move the feeding sites?

Thompson deliberated with Chief Ranger George Baggley and two assistant chief rangers about erecting a fence around the tourist seating areas at the feeding sites. For the campgrounds, Thompson wanted to explore constructing iron and concrete food boxes, perhaps introducing the first-ever bear-proof food containers. They also attempted to discourage the camp-raider and holdup bears from returning by spraying them with various chemicals inserted into a "Pyrene Gun" (a handheld extinguisher manually pumped to achieve pressurization). All experiments failed: "All of the control measures are to be kept from the public as much as possible," wrote Thompson, referring specifically to situations which resulted in shooting bears. "The problem is to be treated as a local problem. No lengthy report is to be sent to the director."[86]

The wildlife team agreed the bear issues were growing more complex every year, particularly in Yellowstone. They acknowledged that bears that were acclimatized to humans and had become aggressive had to be moved or eliminated, but they insisted more research was necessary in order to inform a long-term management plan for each park where bears and humans collided. As author Alice Wondrak Biel has pointed out, the different viewpoints on the bear issue—Mather and Albright's "aesthetic conservation" approach versus the biologists' forward-thinking and science-based method—"indicated a growing power struggle between two forms of national park preservation."[87] Although the bear shows would eventually be eliminated by the early 1940s, the intractable issue of bear and human interactions would take decades to solve, and then with only partial success.[88]

The Bible for All Park Biologists

Since the beginning of the biologists' fieldwork in the fall of 1929—and most likely before, while he was in Yosemite—Wright had wanted to create a manual for Park Service staff regarding park wildlife and its management. *Fauna of the National Parks of the United States: A Preliminary Survey of Faunal Relations in National Parks*, or *Fauna No. 1*, as it became known, was that manual. The 157-page, fully indexed, 6″ × 9″ booklet was illustrated with numerous black-and-white photographs and adorned with a simple yet elegant etching of a deer on its soft cover. And it fulfilled a key condition of Wright's from back when Albright had approved the wildlife survey: that the team could publish its research findings as an official Park Service publication in a form that would be "most useful as a reference book on existing conditions and problems of the animal life in the National Parks."[89]

When the 1931 field season wrapped up in November, Wright returned to Berkeley and the wildlife office to attempt to finish writing *Fauna No. 1* with Dixon and Thompson and to prepare for the next field season. He walked just over two miles from his house on Thousand Oaks to campus every morning, birdwatching and recording notes on species and numbers seen. Although all three biologists were credited as authors of *Fauna No. 1*, Thompson would later acknowledge that the conception, organization, and most of the writing was Wright's.[90]

In 1931, the wildlife team had moved onto the Berkeley campus, to Hilgard Hall, home to the Department of Forestry, and where the Park Service education program had maintained a field office since 1925.[91] Wright's office was, at most, a five-minute walk to the Museum of Vertebrate Zoology and Grinnell's office. Although they did meet to talk, as well as to attend Cooper Society meetings together, they also continued the formality of writing letters to one another. "As I will be leaving for Yellowstone within a month," Wright informed Grinnell in early 1932, "I have been very busy trying to complete the report of the preliminary wild life survey. However, I am very anxious to have a talk with you before starting out. Your suggestions are so valuable as really to be an inspiration for the work on hand, and I would not miss them."[92]

Wright and his team finished *Fauna No. 1* on time. The publication date on the report was May 1932, but it did not leave the government printing offices until January of the next year. It opened with the team's "Approach to Wildlife Administration": a dry-sounding title underneath which was an introduction that contained concepts that historian Sellars has described as "the threshold to a new era in Park Service history."[93]

A major issue the team wrestled with was the need for a specific point in time from which to pursue their objective in the national parks, "to restore and perpetuate the fauna in its pristine state by combating the harmful effects of human influence." The discussions around what was "pristine," what was "primitive America," and when that elusive time existed, were fraught with a variety of historical, biological, and cultural challenges in the early 1930s, as they are today.[94] The team chose the time period when European American culture largely replaced that of American Indians and actually altered the physical environment. The biologists fully acknowledged the symbiotic relationship that Indigenous People had had with the flora, fauna, and landscape of North America for millennia, but they couldn't conceive of what that precisely looked like, nor fully understand the varied connections the country's diverse Indigenous Peoples had developed with wildlife.

"We can know little of the other pictures that preceded this period," they wrote, "and [of the] violent changes [that] occurred immediately afterward." Wright admitted that wildlife had always been in a "state of flux" since the "continents first rose from the sea," and that changes to the "faunal structure" of North America was likely incremental before Europeans. Therefore, he reasoned, no one time or wildlife condition could be called "the original one." It was easier, they believed, to instead try to pinpoint what had happened when European Americans arrived in the West and changed the cultural and biological landscape of North America forever.[95]

Something Wright and his colleagues addressed in passing was the fact that the first national parks were created through a brutal process of dispossession of American Indians. These wild and uninhabited regions—the primeval conditions Wright pegged and used as his reference point—were in fact artificially created, with human suffering scattered across the landscape as a by-product. Wright had learned this firsthand during his time in Yosemite with Maria Lebrado, Totuya. To the north, across Canada, First Nations people endured a similar fate in order for that country to build its world-class park system.[96]

In the 1930s prejudice against American Indians was widespread, but powerful reforms would soon take hold within the Office of Indian Affairs and in certain sectors of society. Wright's thinking relative to American Indians and the parks appeared to reflect this emerging and more liberal viewpoint. Nowhere was Wright's attitude toward American Indians more on display than in his fieldwork and ideas concerning Glacier National Park's eastern border, the adjacent Blackfeet Indian Reservation, and his desire to reintroduce bison to the area to benefit the park, the bison, and the Blackfeet.

During a five-week trip with Bee to Glacier in the summer of 1931, Wright verified that bison had once been abundant there. He spent a day horseback riding with Dixon, then hiking up to Red Eagle Lake, on the park's eastern flank. There Dixon examined a bison skull and bones, unearthed by a trail crew. Wright later interviewed a veteran ranger who told him similar bones had been found just north, near Sun Camp on St. Mary's Lake, and at Many Glacier close to Swiftcurrent Lake.[97] And from his historical review and additional interviews, Wright knew that bison had been an integral part of Blackfeet culture. The Blackfeet Reservation's extensive western boundary abutted the park—their former lands. The sites where the bones had been found were no more than five miles away from the reservation's border.

Wright soon advocated for the reintroduction of bison to the region not only to help the park but also the Blackfeet. It was a unique and creative concept for the young biologist. His reasoning was that bison, shipped in from Yellowstone and comanaged by the Park Service and the tribe, would use the higher elevations of the park for their summer range and the lower reservation lands during the winter, as they had for millennia. "The bison," he wrote, "was the principal factor in the economy of the Blackfeet Indians and without it the pageant of life on the east side is sadly incomplete. Looking into the future, the interests of park and reservation, far from being at variance, are seen to be surprisingly akin."[98]

Although often discussed and supported by NPS headquarters, the concept didn't take hold. Wright fully understood why: "The Indian council," he wrote, "suspicious that the real purpose is to deprive them of more of their lands in order to extend Glacier Park, has been unwilling to accept the plan as yet."[99] He didn't blame the Blackfeet. Wright understood then what the authors of a Glacier resource management document wrote years later: wildlife policy could not drive social policy. Discouraged, he and the service abandoned the plan.[100]

In *Fauna No. 1*, Wright, Dixon, and Thompson advocated not just for conservation of wildlife but also for "constructive wild-life management" restoration that would "challenge the conscientious and patient determination of biological engineers: a science which itself is in its infancy." After running through the origins of the wildlife survey, *Fauna No. 1* highlighted the fact that the team already had accumulated 2,523 photographic negatives, "accompanied by prints all filed and indexed in readily available form." Additionally, field notes on 279 species were recorded. Their objectives were to create a "well-defined" wildlife policy for the service, to help superintendents solve urgent wildlife issues, and to create a report that presented the status of animals, park by park, analyze problems, and then outline a plan for the "orderly development of wild-life management."[101]

While focusing on the urgent needs of the parks, Wright also pulled back to the larger, systemic solutions that were necessary in his mind. "It would be analogous to placing a catch-basin under a gradually growing leak in a trough and then trying to keep the trough replenished by pouring the water back in. The task mounts constantly and failure is the inevitable outcome. The only hope rests in restoration of the original vessel to wholeness."[102]

It was in *Fauna No. 1*'s final two pages, "Suggested National Park Policy for the Vertebrates," that the "radical departure" for biologists and managers across the Park Service was detailed. The text recommended, in part, that proper and healthy habitats be maintained for all species, and that "natural faunal barriers" be used to determine park boundaries—particularly for new parks. Prior to any management plans, proper scientific research should be required to inform those decisions. And interfering with species should only be allowed if it was believed a species might go extinct or that populations were otherwise out of balance. *Fauna No. 1* also noted that artificial feeding should only be carried out as a last resort. Predators were to be considered "special charges" of the national parks and protected. Fish-eating animals—otters, mergansers, kingfishers—were not to be persecuted. And, likely with Albright's feelings in mind, they included a subtle yet pointed jab at the bear shows, stating that "presentation of the animal life of the parks to the public shall be a wholly natural one."

It is proposed: That a complete faunal investigation, including the four steps of determining the primitive faunal picture, tracing the history of human influences, making a thorough zoological survey and formulating a wild-life administrative plan shall be made in each park at the earliest possible date.

FAUNA NO. 1[103]

After the release of *Fauna No. 1* in 1933, Wright wrote to Harold Bryant at NPS headquarters in Washington, DC. "It makes me very happy to have your favorable comments on the Report," he said, "and to know that both yourself and Mr. Albright are satisfied with the reception which it is receiving."[104] *Fauna No. 1* and its suggested policies were approved as official Park Service doctrine later that year.[105]

After *Fauna No. 1* was published and distributed, a memo was sent from the Washington office to all field offices with reviews from twenty-seven prominent biologists and academics. It was an interesting internal public relations move on the part of headquarters to lend gravitas and legitimacy to the report.

"I think it is a fine piece of work," stated Grinnell, "which the years to come will show to be sound in both fact and principle." Olaus Murie wrote, "I have read the entire bulletin and feel impelled to write to you expressing my enthusiasm for its contents." Walter Mulford took a decidedly personal approach with his endorsement: "I am so pleased . . . that I cannot refrain from sending each of you good friends a note of sincere congratulations. You know how deep and loyal is my interest in you three and in the pioneering which you are carrying on so effectively. It is all a source of such great satisfaction to me and my mind often turns in your direction with real happiness."[106]

Field biologists, as they gradually began to populate the Park Service, also agreed with the reviews. Lowell Sumner had a career as a prominent, tough, vocal, and long-tenured biologist with the Park Service. He had met Wright in the late 1920s on the Berkeley campus, where he was studying mammalogy, ornithology, and ecology under Grinnell. When Sumner was twenty-seven, in March of 1935, he joined Wright's team in the Berkeley Office. In 1983, reflecting back on years of biological research and management in the parks, he stated that *Fauna No. 1* was the "working bible'" for all park biologists as soon as it was printed.[107]

But our national heritage is richer than just scenic features; the realization is coming that perhaps our greatest national heritage is nature itself, with all its complexity and its abundance of life, which, when combined with great scenic beauty as it is in the national parks, becomes of unlimited value. This is what we would attain in the national parks.

FAUNA NO. 1[108]

Until the Light Really Should Come

In the spring of 1931, a series of letters was exchanged between Park Service headquarters and the wildlife team at their Berkeley office. The subject, initially, was a further clarification of the mission of the wildlife survey—even though it had been approved in late 1929.

The team was already deep into its second full year of work, but the biologists were compliant, answering questions when they could, despite the fact that the documentation had already been submitted and accepted. This unexpected bureaucratic stepping-stone was the result of a request by Washington, spurred on by an active discussion—initiated by Wright—regarding the potential to create a "Wild Life Research Division."

On August 26, from Belton, Montana, just outside Glacier National Park, Wright sent a letter to the director.[109] "We have gained the perspective that was sought," he began, in reference to their survey work. He went on to explain that they were formulating a plan not only to manage the wildlife problems but also to organize a Wildlife Division. Wright attached a memo that detailed the potential division: *Thoughts on a Permanent Organization Plan for the Wild Life Division.* "It is crudely organized," he modestly offered, "and contains nothing more than the gist of the idea."[110]

It might have been brief and "crudely organized," according to Wright, but read today the memo is precise and clear. Wright suggested the division should help manage wildlife in all of the national parks, not just in the West. He wanted to place a properly trained wildlife specialist in each park. Then, for each of the Park Service's districts at the time—Eastern, Southwest, Rocky Mountains, Pacific Coast—a qualified district wildlife officer, in turn, would supervise the various wildlife specialists. The division's main office didn't have to be in Washington, DC, he explained, with a "highly paid executive" in charge. Instead, one of the district officers could manage the entire division. Wright was no doubt angling for the Berkeley office to serve as headquarters. He proposed that this cross-section of personnel could be separate from, but closely collaborate with, the education department. By doing so, the division could assist those colleagues with data, photographs, and the preparation of skins for the popular park museums they managed.[111]

Additionally, Wright postulated that the Wildlife Division staff could assist with the evaluation and identification of boundaries for new parks to "facilitate adequate consideration of wild life requirements." He also wanted to see that these specialists in the field were up to date on the status of flora and fauna outside of their parks by developing relationships with, among others, the fish and game commissions, the Forest Service, and sportsmen's organizations, as the "welfare of animals within the park is vitally influenced by the external factors."[112]

Approximately a week later, Wright, still in Belton, sent another note to his boss, Bryant, expressing frustration that they had missed each other in Glacier by only a day or two. Wright then explained why his proposal for the Wildlife Division was delayed several months: "I did not want to advance anything until the light really should come, until the pieces of the puzzle should fit together into a definite proposition which I could really believe in, myself, before suggesting it to someone else."[113]

Wright also felt strongly that in order to be successful, wildlife administration should be handled by men who lived in the park and worked closely with their colleagues. The job was, he believed, too difficult for service biologists that only passed through several times a year. And he added, "wild life men must be long on personality qualifications as well as having the proper scientific training."[114]

Albright and Bryant had also written the team with some of their ideas regarding how to "present game as a spectacle in large numbers" for the enjoyment of tourists. "Our aim in this work is to keep wild life conditions in the parks primitive," the team responded in a strong but diplomatic statement, "We are trying to present more than the animal as a mere spectacle. You can't present the intangible beauty of all the delicate interactions of nature to people unless they are sensitive and energetic enough to go and observe it in all its mysterious ways. . . . We haven't truly seen an animal until we have seen all the delicately balanced and interactive forces of nature which go to make up that animal. Our policy is to recommend no measures which are purely to embellish nature, but, rather, to recommend measures which will compensate for an unnatural and upset condition."[115]

By January of 1932, Washington and Berkeley were on the same page, and the biologists had the final say. Albright approved their suggested lines of inquiry, their position on presenting game, and field plans for the 1932 season. "We are pleased with Wright's program and itinerary for the Wild Life

Survey," Albright confirmed, "It has seemed to us that you have attacked the big problem of wild life in the national parks in a very satisfactory manner."[116]

The parallel discussion about the creation of a Wildlife Division continued for over a year. Bryant—who by now was assistant director and still managed the education department—informed Wright that he doubted they could create as many wildlife positions in the parks as the biologist had suggested. Bryant pointed to the likely opposition from the Biological Survey, saying that they would undoubtedly protest that "we are encroaching upon its work by getting 'biological experts' in the national parks." Additionally, and perhaps more importantly, he wrote that it wasn't feasible "because of necessary economic measures in these days of depression."[117] Albright also informed the wildlife team that the creation of the division must be considered as something that couldn't be immediately accomplished. It did take time, but by early 1933, the Wildlife Division had become a reality, and with Wright as its chief.

On March 1, 1933, three days before he left the White House and the presidency, Herbert Hoover approved Wright's promotion justification document with an official "Approved by the President" stamp. "This position will be filled by assignment of a former employee of the National Park Service, who has been acting in an advisory capacity at a salary of $12 a year since 1929." Wright had paid for the first two years of the wildlife survey. But by mid-1931, the service had begun covering approximately half of the biologists' costs. When the Wildlife Division was officially created in 1933, the service assumed all expenses for the team. Wright began to receive a salary of $3,200 annually.[118]

During 1931, President Hoover, with one eye on the upcoming election, had tried desperately to revive the American economy and stanch the rise in unemployment and widespread poverty, but to little avail. As historian David Burner notes, the true depth of the situation was confounding to many in Washington, and "the contours of a solution still remained unclear." Combined with the president's unproductive relationship with Congress, no major initiatives took shape until the end of the year when the Reconstruction Finance Corporation was conceived and then approved the following January. And yet the economy unrelentingly spiraled downward as the Depression clamped down even harder on North America and the world.[119]

In 1932, the situation devolved still further: the Dust Bowl had reared its ugly head in the heart of the country. For decades, dedicated "sod-busting" farmers had converted the fertile, tallgrass prairies of the central United States into sprawling, productive farms. But the extended drought of the late 1920s created a disaster, with the topsoil of those once-verdant farmlands turning to dry powder and blowing like bilious clouds over the landscape. Spread across the south-central plains—Oklahoma, Texas, New Mexico, Colorado, and Kansas—the unnaturally brown and sooty clouds intermittently spanned over an estimated one hundred million acres, uprooting not only the region's soil but hundreds of thousands of people in the process.[120]

One Hundred Days

Franklin D. Roosevelt, FDR, inherited this political and ecological disaster on inauguration day—March 4, 1933—and immediately started what famously became known as the First Hundred Days.[121] Unemployment was nearing 25 percent and almost thirteen million Americans were out of work. According to historian John Meacham, the pace of activity was "dizzying" as FDR and his staff, working closely with Congress, created a flurry of legislation, passed numerous new laws, and developed five major initiatives.[122] The initiatives were created in order to help breathe life back into the country by aiding the poor, assisting and boosting farm production, encouraging industrial recovery, and building dams to provide water and electricity.

Most historians agree, however, Roosevelt's "pet project" was another initiative: the Civilian Conservation Corps (CCC). It was, in fact, the first initiative to be passed by Congress, on March 31. The corps' formal name was Emergency Conservation Work, or ECW, but the program was much more commonly referred to as the CCC after FDR used that term during his second Fireside Chat on May 2. Wright and his colleagues used both acronyms.[123]

Roosevelt's new secretary of the interior, the outspoken Harold L. Ickes, recognized in Horace Albright a seasoned and savvy Washington insider (as had Mather—an old friend of Ickes—and all the previous secretaries Albright had worked under). The secretary assigned Albright to serve as a representative of the Interior Department to the Public Works Administration Council, and because of this, Albright played a prominent role in creating the CCC.[124] The entire program was overseen by Robert Fechner, an American union leader.

FDR, who was a major booster of the national parks, encouraged Ickes and Albright to establish as many CCC camps in the parks as possible. By that summer, the Park Service had built seventy such camps in national parks.[125] And because the service was adept at overseeing a variety of national parks across the country, it was put in charge of creating and comanaging, with state partners, another 150 camps in the country's fledgling state park systems. Overall, by July 1, 1933, more than 250,000 young men were employed in fully operational camps across the country.[126] Similar aggressive efforts were pursued in the national forests and other Department of Agriculture bureaus. It was a move that helped, if only slightly, to take a bite out of the 25 percent unemployment that was gripping the country.

The CCC camps, based on military-style organization, engaged these unemployed young men in a variety of conservation projects that included tree planting, firefighting, and soil erosion efforts.[127] However, as Sellars points out, although the program had "conservation" in its title, it was really more of a "utilitarian conservation" effort that the men practiced. In the parks, that translated into the construction of road, trails, and buildings. For that reason, the newly formed Wildlife Division was presented with both a new problem—and, eventually, an incredible opportunity.

After the release of *Fauna No. 1* and the successful creation of the Wildlife Division, Wright wrote to the Baggleys, his dear friends in Yellowstone, thanking them for their congratulatory letter. The new salary was a "life-saver," he replied, and their praise of *Fauna No. 1* was very important to him, especially as it came "from people who are really so thoroughly familiar with the problems involved." He ended the note by reminding George Baggley that they needed to keep on top of the bear management work, lest they lose momentum. "And," he added, "now the CCC camps will make the situation worse."[128]

Dixon, who was in Sequoia National Park midsummer, had helped to manage the CCC camp that seemingly sprung up overnight. "With 800 men available and more in the offing," he wrote in his field notes, "it is decidedly important that this work be carried on in such a manner as will do the least damage to wild life."[129] Thompson, meanwhile, was in the Grand Canyon that June and traveled to Point Sublime in order to inspect some new "camp equipment" installed by the CCC, including tables, benches, a "comfort station," signs, and an incinerator. "They are unsightly and unnecessary," he wrote in his field notes, "and greatly detract from the point."[130]

That was the division's new problem: thousands of young men let loose in the national parks. CCC camps revolved around six-month enrollment periods. Just when the recruits had learned the rules of working in a park, another fresh crew would show up, and the education process would start over.

Superintendents were ultimately responsible for the camps within their parks, but they had the assistance of the division's wildlife experts, hired crew supervisors, and Park Service foresters, architects, and engineers. They all followed the "development requirements" of each park, as recorded in six-year plans. However, there were constant issues with proper supervision and planning.[131] The corps were being managed, and kept busy, but their youthful enthusiasm led to a series of issues that needed immediate correction: they brought dogs and cats into camps; they harassed wildlife and fed the bears; and there were the random acts of habitat destruction. With the help of the Wildlife Division, park superintendents and rangers moved quickly to put a stop to these unfortunate consequences of the otherwise positive CCC camps, but they lingered for years, reemerging each time new recruits arrived.

Within this dilemma was also the division's new opportunity: Wright pushed to have "wildlife technicians" placed in each park, paid for by tapping into the emergency funds. It was the realization, albeit partial, of how he had envisioned staffing the Wildlife Division. The idea would gain momentum and importance in subsequent years. As Sellars explains, "Fauna No. 1 provided policies and the CCC provided funds for the Park Service to develop its own more scientifically informed natural resource management."[132]

It Was a Raw Day

In late September of 1933, Wright was in one of his favorite parks: Yellowstone. With a new title and new responsibilities, the biologist saddled up early on the morning of the twenty-third with a cross-section of Yellowstone men he had been working with for years: Superintendent Roger Toll, Chief Ranger George Baggley, and Ben Thompson. It was a bitterly cold morning as they rode from Tower Station across the Lamar River and Little Buffalo Creek, climbing northward until they reached the north boundary of the park. "It was a raw day," he wrote. "There was ice on the higher ponds & brooks."[133]

They had ventured out to inspect the winter range of the northern elk herd; they were also on the lookout for pronghorn. As they rode, they encountered small herds of both species on a range that was desiccated and scarred with large areas completely devoid of vegetation. "We were appalled at the poverty of the range," recorded Wright. "Two small bands of elk were seen. Later there will be thousands here."[134]

Seven years before, on the shores of the Savage River in Mount McKinley National Park, Wright had put pen to paper and recorded his observations on page 1 in his first field notebook. On that cold day in Yellowstone National Park, in another field notebook, he wrote on page 542. It would be his final field note entry. The young but very experienced biologist was now the chief of the Wildlife Division of the National Park Service and his work would increasingly take him away from the field, down the hallways of the Interior Department in Washington, DC, and into an office. He would still travel but far less frequently.

Wright had traversed thousands of miles in between those pages. It was a young life well spent, exploring the West and Alaska, and retracing those

Bechler River, Yellowstone.
June 8, 1931.

Wright

The rangers are after a poacher who is in this district trapping live marten for disposal to fur farmers.

There was also mention of another poacher living to the south who goes for beaver.

Madison River, Yellowstone
June 9, 1931.

Several pairs of Canada geese have been noted nesting on little grassy islands in the river. We saw one bird still incubating. The location of the nest was like this

Canada goose nest
bird facing upstream
as at prow of boat

Yellowstone Lake.
June 9, 1931.
Russell and I, saw two large flocks of Barrow's golden-eyes on the lake. One contained 43 birds of male sex and 2 females. The other was estimated at 55, two of these were female.
On the Yellowstone River we saw a muskrat on the bank eating some green grass.

Sample field note by Wright. With the permission of the Museum of Vertebrate Zoology, University of California, Berkeley.

very same routes for six years as an employee of the Park Service. He had seen hundreds of species, climbed fourteen-thousand-foot peaks, trekked across Death Valley, and logged hundreds of miles by foot and horseback in the western national parks—and one mosquito-infested park in Florida. But it was time to move on.

New Deal, Old Problems

The wildlife survey didn't conclude with a big celebration or fanfare in late 1933. There was no widespread recognition from the Park Service's top brass of a job well done, no written accolades from the many colleagues and collaborators Wright, Thompson, and Dixon had worked with for over three years while crisscrossing the United States.

In fact the survey didn't so much end as it pivoted. Its duties expanded; its objectives matured. The pieces of Wright's puzzle finally fit together—his Wildlife Division was up and running. This translated into less on-the-ground research for the team in 1934 and 1935 but more managerial obligations. But it was all undertaken with the same intense central focus of the previous three years: the pursuit of science-based management of wildlife and the preservation of wilderness in the national parks.

This new beginning for Wright and his team transpired without Albright at the helm of the Park Service, as he left in 1933 to become an executive in the US Potash Company in New York. Albright didn't rise to the level of a key mentor for Wright, but the two spent a significant amount of time together, especially during the last six years of Albright's directorship. And of course it was Albright who had approved the concept of the wildlife survey.

From 1927 forward, in Yosemite, Berkeley, and San Francisco, Albright and Wright had talked at length about the role of wildlife management in the parks and the need for science-based research. They didn't always agree—especially regarding predator control and the need to "present" wildlife to tourists—but they negotiated and then they moved forward with the best ideals of the national park system at heart.

After Albright's retirement, Wright began to work with the new director: Arno B. Cammerer. Cammerer in fact had been running most of the daily

operations after Albright had been commandeered during the first days of
the Roosevelt's presidency to help with the creation of the CCC. Wright had
known Cammerer almost as long as he had been acquainted with Albright.

Cammerer was personally recruited by Stephen Mather in 1919 to join the
Park Service, and after 1929 he served as Albright's associate director. This bespectacled Park Service veteran, like his predecessor, knew the halls of the Interior Department well. However, he never clicked with the opinionated and
acerbic Secretary Ickes, a self-described "curmudgeon" and "sour-puss"—an
unfortunate situation that continued throughout Cammerer's tenure.[1]

Despite this uneasy and awkward relationship, the Park Service was, thanks
to the New Deal, given vastly more responsibility and financial support from
the middle of 1933 onward. In addition to funds made available through the
CCC, the service also received resources from the Public Works Administration and, in 1935, the Works Progress Administration. In 1933 and 1934,
well over $20 million was allocated for road and trail construction, with
the vast majority of those funds marked for roads.[2] Additionally, the service was asked to assume the management of numerous Civil War battlefields, approximately forty national monuments—transferred from the Forest
Service—and the national capital parks and buildings.[3] After this handover
was official, the service's name was changed to "Office of National Parks,
Buildings and Reservations." This cumbersome title appeared on the letterhead for approximately a year before the service reverted to its original
name in 1934. Not surprisingly, this transfer of monuments did not sit well
with the Forest Service, especially since it helped improve the standing of the
Park Service.

The Better Will Be the Opportunity

President Roosevelt was an outdoor enthusiast. Although not an avid hunter
like his distant cousin and fellow president, Theodore Roosevelt, FDR enjoyed birdwatching and was particularly interested in forestry. He also loved
being on the water, boating and fishing. These passions stemmed undoubtedly from growing up on his family's Hyde Park estate, just north of Pough-
keepsie, New York. At its largest, the Roosevelt holdings stretched for almost
two miles along the wooded shores of the Hudson River and encompassed
1,522 acres.[4]

Throughout 1934, the president acted on these lifelong interests by craft-
ing a flurry of projects focused on America's wildlife and forests, with ample
input from his staff and several old friends. "Roosevelt shrewdly put wildlife restoration under the banner of retiring submarginal land and relieving

drought," historian Douglas Brinkley explains, "thus procuring for wildlife a modest portion of the federal moneys that were being spent to alleviate human distress."[5] These restoration efforts also helped jobless Americans. Unemployment had improved slightly from a staggering high of approximately 25 percent in 1933 to roughly 20 percent by 1935, and the economy enjoyed "a steady, if undramatic, recovery, particularly after 1934."[6]

The Fish and Wildlife Coordination Act was also passed during this period, authorizing the secretaries of agriculture and commerce to collaborate with other federal agencies and states to increase the populations primarily of game species, fur-bearing animals, and fish. On the forestry front, meanwhile, the president consulted with his friend Gifford Pinchot for advice and assistance. Pinchot was governor of Pennsylvania at the time, but he had long been at the center of American forestry. Together with Acting Forestry Chief Ferdinand A. Silcox, FDR engaged thousands of young CCC recruits in national forests and state parks across the country, specifically to remove diseased or dead trees and to undertake tree-planting projects.[7]

Perhaps FDR's most visible effort as part of his "New Deal for Wildlife" was the creation of the Committee on Wild-Life Restoration. The committee, organized in early January 1934, was charged with writing a report that was to encompass "a national wild-life restoration program of the broadest scope."[8] The committee consisted of just three individuals, who represented an interesting mix of both experiences and political orientation.

Thomas Beck, editor-in-chief of the New York–based *Collier's Magazine*, was the chair. He was an "aristocratic" friend of the president, a New Deal booster, and a conservationist.[9] Beck wrote FDR in 1933 to express his alarm at the rapidly declining populations of waterfowl in North America. This was especially acute throughout the greater Mississippi River watershed, which encompasses the adjoining Great Plains to the west. Across this vast region of middle America, it is estimated that between 50 and 85 percent of waterfowl habitat—millions of acres of wetlands, streams, prairie potholes, and grasslands—had been drained, diverted, or reclaimed for farming and other uses after the arrival of European American settlers, primarily since the 1880s.[10]

The second committee member, Jay Norwood "Ding" Darling, was a well-known and widely syndicated political cartoonist at the *Des Moines Register*. Darling was also an outdoorsman and a passionate duck hunter as well as a recognized conservationist. He often used his cartoons to editorialize about conservation issues of the day, and he was a vocal critic of the insufficient number of federal wildlife refuges as well as their management by the Biological

Survey. He was also a Republican, a Hoover supporter, and an unabashed anti–New Dealer. Roosevelt was fully aware of the cartoonist's opinions and reputation—in fact, FDR was lampooned several times by Darling—but the president viewed the appointment as an opportunity to have Darling—with the exposure of his front-page cartoons and his large following—participate in the solution instead of simply complain about the problem.

Aldo Leopold rounded out the committee's roster. In 1931, the former Southwest Forest Service ranger had authored his "Report on a Game Survey of the North Central States."[11] And in 1933 Leopold's book *Game Management* was published—which would, with time, be considered a classic. He would go on to pen the equally timeless *Sand County Almanac* in 1949. An avid life-long hunter—with a particular interest in waterfowl and upland game birds—Leopold, like Darling, was also a Republican—though he was far more interested in game than politics.

With Beck and Darling—two high-profile and media-savvy professionals—it is no surprise that the committee's work garnered attention. After their first meeting in Washington, DC (Leopold was back in Wisconsin), the *New York Times* ran a piece with the headline, "Duck for Every Puddle." The article detailed that "Mr. Beck and Mr. Darling agreed that they were interested primarily in restoration of the wild duck, geese, snipe, swan and upland fowl that the old-timers remember."[12]

Although the committee name suggested a far-reaching examination of wildlife across the United States, the report truly did focus on the serious loss of habitat and the consequential population decline of America's waterfowl and upland game bird species. Nonetheless, the report was daring and sweeping in its conclusions and recommendations. It boldly suggested a budget of $50 million in order to purchase and restore some seventeen million acres of habitat. The committee also wanted to see extensive removal of grazing rights on public lands, particularly in national parks and national forests.[13]

Though there were some vigorous disagreements among the committee members, they all agreed that the Biological Survey was doing a terrible job in managing federal wildlife refuges. The Biological Survey, they wrote blisteringly, was "a misnamed, quasi-scientific bureau quite unequal to the present task." Additionally, they had no confidence in Paul Redington, the longtime chief of the survey and the same person who had butted heads with Wright and his team over predator control in national parks. Darling later reiterated that Redington was a " 'totally inarticulate' spokesman for the cause of wildlife restoration."[14]

FDR and his secretary of agriculture, Henry Wallace, drastically reduced the committee's proposed budget for wildlife restoration to $8.5 million. Action

on the recommendations was slow, but the committee and its vision nonetheless excited the conservation community, and changes, slowly, started mani-
festing themselves throughout the refuge system.[15]

Darling, for his part, went so far as to complain to FDR about the cutbacks
and delays. The president responded by offering him the position of chief of
the Biological Survey. Darling accepted and he moved from Des Moines to
Washington shortly after the publication of the report. He focused on improving the nation's wildlife refuges for the next eighteen months.[16]

Between January and March 1934—when the committee was formed, and
its report written, then published—Wright was wrestling with several inter-
related Wildlife Division issues simultaneously. The first was generated by
Frank Oastler, a member of the Park Service's Educational Advisory Board,
and the man who almost lost his foot to a grizzly bear at a Yellowstone bear-
feeding station. Oastler had lodged a complaint that the Wildlife Division
was not moving fast enough in placing wildlife staff in each of the parks. It
is highly likely that Oastler had read the Wild-Life Restoration Committee's
report and noted the media generated around its formation and suggestions.
He no doubt felt as though the Park Service was lagging behind the new national effort.

The second issue was that a few superintendents and old-school rangers
were, apparently, still not adhering to the service's official wildlife policies, as
set down in *Fauna No. 1* the previous year.

Wright tackled both problems in a four-page letter to the director and
assistant director. "I have some very definite ideas relative to the place of the
national parks in the wild life restoration plan," stated Wright, addressing
Oastler's concern, "and also as to how we should proceed on wild life matters
generally from this point." He informed them that a detailed report would be
in the mail the following day.[17]

Wright then diplomatically pointed out that, prior to 1930 and the creation
of the wildlife survey, there was no concept of wildlife management in the parks
(with a few exceptions), and that in three years they had both created and elevated the discipline to the forefront of the National Park Service. Resources, he
explained, in the heart of the Depression, had been very scarce, so the Wildlife
Division could not staff up as desired. Furthermore, the majority of park rangers lacked the "requisite knowledge" and time to carry out research—and the
wildlife survey team could only do so much training while in the field.[18]

Wright explained that he didn't want to "advocate the development of
elaborate plans" that looked impressive on paper, and that would generate
news, only to have those grand ideas wither away on the crowded desks of

superintendents "with no feasibility of practical accomplishments." He was, however, positive that the designation of "wild life rangers" was forthcoming, made possible with CCC funds. "It is with this in mind that I have consciously endeavored to build up the ideal plan among ourselves and then deliberately set about accomplishing it by moving a step at a time and educating the park administrators as we go." Eventually, this was enough to assuage Oastler's concerns.[19]

To counter the second issue regarding noncompliance of wildlife policies within the Park Service, Wright recommended a precise communications plan—or a "campaign"—to reeducate superintendents and head rangers and to reinforce how they should be managing wildlife. Between March and May, he wanted to send out four memos, staggered by a few weeks each, which he offered to write.[20]

The first two were to be issued under the director's name, the last two under Wright's. In sequence, they comprised, first, a reference to the new, nationwide wildlife restoration movement and reinforcement of the Park Service's official wildlife policy; second, a detailed note on how the wildlife ranger program was going to work; third, a customized memo for each park regarding its specific wildlife management needs; and, finally, a request for a report from each park regarding progress made on wildlife management planning. Wright suggested this planned release of shorter memos in lieu of one large dispatch in order to keep the superintendents' attention.[21]

Cammerer and Bryant approved the plan, and two weeks later, the director sent out the first three-page memo. When Wright drafted the document, he wanted to include some very specific commentary about the Wild-Life Restoration Committee and the fanfare around its report. "President Roosevelt took the preliminary step toward a nation-wide wild-life restoration program when he appointed the Committee on Wild-Life Restoration," he wrote. "It is to the credit of the Park Service," he continued pointedly, "that it recognized the fundamental principles as applicable to the national parks and recorded them on paper long in advance of the work of the special committee. We wish to continue our fine leadership in this field and would protect our proven ability to administer park wild-life with the minimum of regulation from the outside."[22] What was "recorded" on paper, a year prior to the committee's report, was *Fauna No. 1*.

He then turned to the service's official wildlife policy and reminded them that it should be followed in each park. What followed was a twenty-point review of the policy, the very same twenty points at the conclusion of *Fauna No. 1*—including, once again, a clear reminder about predators. "The rare

predators shall be considered special charges of the national parks in propor-
tion that they are persecuted everywhere else."[23]

Another issue, captured in a round of correspondence, focused on what
Wright termed "a major policy which guides the Service: that national parks,
'shall be preserved in the natural state.'" This problem began in December
1933, when it became known that Colonel Thomson, superintendent of Yosemite National Park—and Wright's former boss—had approved a plan of
"vista clearing" around the giant sequoias in the park's famous Mariposa
Grove. His staff had cut down other tree species as well as brush in order to
make it easier for tourists to see the mighty giants. Wright didn't approve of
the action, and he wrote to the director and copied Superintendents Thomson and John R. White at Sequoia National Park to the south.

"Though scientific ecology has not progressed to the point where all environmental factors bearing upon the welfare of the Sequoias within a grove
of trees can be given exact proportional values," Wright proffered, "I believe
that any competent ecologist would consider the removal of an associated
species such as white fir, or the establishment of clearings, as something to be
viewed with alarm." Nothing should be done, he stated, "without years of preliminary experimentation."[24] Thomson did not appreciate the pushback from
the young chief, and he let it be known. He questioned, as well, the Wildlife
Division's insistence on managing to the "primitive" or "natural state."

Again, Wright sent off a letter to the same trio, but this time he looped in
Ben Thompson and Duncan McDuffie. McDuffie was a California business-
man, a noted conservationist, a recent past president of the Sierra Club, and
well known to the superintendents. Wright didn't hold back. This was, after
all, the central tenant of *Fauna No. 1*, and the focus of all of his and his team's
work to date.

> Since Superintendent Thomson and other sober thinkers among us who share
> this view, believe that this policy is a shibboleth, a principle of administra-
> tion whose impossibility of application makes it potentially ruinous to the
> Service, I believe that the future welfare of the Park Service demands that such
> policy be put on trial. Let the arguments on both sides be fully heard and fairly
> judged. When a judgement has been handed down, let all abide by it for in
> failure to do so we definitely sow the seeds of ruin.[25]

Wright then recalled the early days of the wildlife survey and stated: "We
foresaw that it would prove a stupendous job to maintain and restore primitive conditions but that this ideal, though it might never be realized to perfec-
tion, was the only goal worth striving for."[26]

He continued with a quote from *Fauna No. 1*: "Protection, far from being the magic touch which healed all wounds, was unconsciously just the first step on a long road winding through years of endeavor toward a goal too far to reach, yet always shining ahead as a magnificent ideal. This objective is to restore and perpetuate the fauna in its pristine state by combating the harmful effects of human influence."[27]

After this pointed response, however, he became the diplomat, once again: "I am glad that this whole episode has served to bring forth the vital question as to whether we shall or shall not conduct all park activities with the object of restoring and preserving natural conditions."[28]

White, who was also an old acquaintance of Wright's, wrote the biologist separately after this exchange, letting him know he agreed with him and saying that "there is a great temptation to doll up the forest and, of course, any such dolling up involves ecological changes which must affect the flora and fauna."[29] Roger Toll was also looped into this circle of correspondence. He posited that whatever was done regarding sequoias, the trees should come first and people second. Wright, again, responded to all parties and stated, "I do believe with you that for the most part we have been talking at cross purposes, seeing in blurred vision three stars which in focus are but one."

Soon after this intense exchange of ideas and conflicting philosophies about the "major policy" that guided the Park Service, Director Cammerer informed Wright that he was needed in Washington, DC. In a clear sign of endorsement of his young chief—on all fronts—Cammerer wanted Wright to manage the Wildlife Division out of headquarters for a period of time, while also assisting with the exigencies of the New Deal. In early April, Wright sent a letter to a friend in Yosemite. "Bee and I with the two babies are leaving for Washington, D.C., next week. We shall be there for some time and then will work in the Rocky Mountain section before returning to the coast, so I may not see you until next summer."[30]

Every Year Ought to Be National Parks Year

In July of 1934, FDR began a monthlong boat trip aboard the USS *Houston*. His ship set sail from Annapolis, Maryland, and ventured south to the Caribbean, with stops in Puerto Rico and the Virgin Islands. Then, via the Panama Canal, it entered the Pacific Ocean, steered northwest to Hawaii, and eventually anchored in Portland.[31] On August 5, FDR and his entourage motored east from Portland to the snow-covered peaks of Glacier National Park—his first visit—where he gave an animated radio address from the park's Two Medicine Chalet. He shared highlights of his extended trip with the nation and spoke of these fellow Americans, in the distant lands he had visited, that were suffering because of the Depression. He then expressed his "thrill and delight" at touring through Glacier.

"The Secretary of the Interior in 1933 announced that this year of 1934 was to be emphasized as 'National Parks Year,'" the president continued in his distinctive voice. "I am glad to say that there has been a magnificent response and that the number visiting our national parks has shown a splendid increase. But I decided today that every year ought to be National Parks Year. . . . They are not for the rich alone," he reminded Americans. "There is nothing so American as our national parks."[32]

Wright, now living with his family in Washington, DC, was tapped by the administration to deliver a national radio address as part of National Parks Year. He gave a talk entitled "Big Game of Our National Parks." In it, he tailored his words carefully for a wide range of Americans. Wright also tried to give a clear idea of the status of the country's "big game" and how it was still possible to view these animals in the wild. "A hundred years ago," he began, "wild game still abounded from the Atlantic to the Pacific in numbers that totaled millions. In a century's time this vast game field vanished like a continent sinking into the ocean. Where once it was continuous, now only small islands of game remain." He then highlighted all of the big-game animals in the parks that people could experience, including "strange parti-colored antelope of the deserts and the sagebrush mountain slopes"; mountain goats, when seen from a distance on a far slope, that "look like so many white sheets spread out to dry on the fresh green grass"; the "tall dark stranger with the broad palmed antlers" that is the American moose; and the grizzly bear, "an animal of another temperament. Lord of all the lands he roams."[33]

"No vacation program is complete without sometime including a visit to the national parks," he concluded, "and no parks trip has yielded its best if the sight of some big game animal has not added to the thrills."[34]

The Geography of Recreation

In the summer of 1934 FDR also created the National Resources Board in order to study how best to manage the country's national resources. Wright was tagged to play a major role in this ambitious effort. His mandate was focused specifically on public lands, recreation resources, and the feasibility of Americans using and enjoying those lands. From June 20 until December 1— when the report was to be delivered to FDR—Wright's title was changed to Chief, Recreation Division, Land-Use Section, Technical Committee, National Resources Board. And he was given an office in the Architects Building in downtown Washington, DC.[35] Ben Thompson was subsequently called to Washington from Berkeley by Wright to not only help run the Wildlife Division (he was named acting chief) but also to assist with the national resources report. All the while, however, Wright was intimately engaged with his other "day job," back at Park Service headquarters. Acting Director Demaray sent out a notice to all service staff announcing Wright's temporary appointment. And, just as Albright had messaged to staff about the beginning of the wildlife survey, Demaray stated that Wright had "complete authority" to ask any member of the service to help him with information "to the fullest extent, giving precedence to his requests over all matters." Wright was also given the authority to create a team to help him with the report.[36]

FDR's executive order spelled out the overarching scope of the study in more detail, with a subsequent statement from the White House grounding it in an effort to help alleviate the continued suffering of the American people, particularly farmers.[37] "In order to grapple on a national scale with the problem of the millions of farm families now attempting unsuccessfully to wrestle a living from worn-out, eroded lands, the Board will study and plan for the better utilization of the land, water, and other national resources of the country."[38]

The group Wright gathered around him was impressive, and they brought a unique blend of experience and talent to the effort. There was Harlean James from the American Civic Association (a rare woman of authority in the field at that time); Neil M. Judd of the National Museum; leading landscape architects, city planners, and engineers; and, of course, all of the top brass of the Park Service: Thompson and Toll, for instance, were listed as staff.[39]

Wright also reached out and solicited input from Grinnell as well as from the father-son team of Loye and Alden Miller, likewise from the Museum of Vertebrate Zoology. Wright requested their input for refining a series of basic definitions—such as "leisure," "recreation," and "park." He also believed it was important that the board's research process "have the benefit of the thought and comments of conservation and recreation organizations," such as the Cooper Society, the Sierra Club, and the numerous other groups Wright was involved with.[40]

I do congratulate you on being identified with the new recreational research set-up. I, personally, can think of no one better fitted than (nor as well as) yourself to guide and direct along this important line—at a time when the use or misuse of free time on the part of the populace may have portentous significance for the future of the race.
JOSEPH GRINNELL TO GEORGE WRIGHT[41]

In late October, after almost four months of work on the report, Wright at-
tended a large conference in St. Louis, Missouri: the Twenty-Sixth National
Conference on City Planning. That year's subject, *"Planning Problems of City,
Region, State and Nation,"* worked off the National Resources Board directive.

Wright's presentation was simply titled "Recreation Areas." He argued, in
part, that the federal government should "assume certain direct responsibilities for recreational resources in addition to serving as the national planning
adviser." This entailed a wide variety of actions, including "nationalizing" all
of the country's major historical and archaeological sites; the protection of
rare and endangered species; work against a litany of "abuses" to the land;
the development of public recreational resources and opportunities; the creation of a system of coastal preserves, principally to protect beaches; and
the improvement of the "recreational values of the highway system of the
country"—namely, appropriate landscaping and the reduction of outdoor
advertising.

He then wove in two of his core goals as the chief of the Wildlife Division:
first, the preservation of wilderness in "primeval America." Citing the writings of Robert "Bob" Marshall, he urged the US government to declare "forever inviolate" all of the large remaining wilderness areas in the country. Bob
Marshall was a PhD forester from Johns Hopkins University, and he served
as Director of Forestry for the Office of Indian Affairs between 1933 and 1937.
An early and vocal advocate for wilderness preservation, he was also the
driving force behind the creation of the Wilderness Society in 1935. Wright
and Marshall were contemporaries and friends: they participated in several
conferences together over a year and a half and were both federal employees
based out of Washington, DC, who often consulted one another.[42] It is clear
that Wright was familiar with Marshall's writing and wilderness advocacy.
Wright's second goal—a huge undertaking, but only lightly mentioned at the
St. Louis venue—was "the completion of the national parks and monuments
system."[43]

Wright's program from that conference is signed not once but twice by
J. Horace McFarland—a bold cursive "*J. H. McF.*" McFarland, seventy-five
years old at the time, had managed the American Civic Association for some
twenty years, where he advocated for better living conditions for all Americans through proper planning. But he was also part of the small group of
men who first championed, then created, the National Park Service in 1916.
According to the program, Wright and McFarland shared the podium during the same session. Wright went first with his talk on recreation areas, followed by McFarland's brief but pointed "Thirty Years of Conservation and
Planning."

When at the first White House Conference on National Resources, held in 1908, conservation was mentioned, many people did not even know what the word meant. There occurred for a considerable time much "conversation," and then some of our friends who were being disturbed by the new idea, called it "confiscation," later changing the point of view to that of "consternation"! The very idea was then new, and therefore dubious![44]

As Wright sat on the stage next to McFarland, he wrote in large letters, on the back of his program: "Conservation, Conversation, Consternation."[45]

Wilderness Heritage

Wright was not the only person, by any stretch of the imagination, to be interested in, concerned with, or vocal about the future of wilderness in the United States. However, throughout the 1930s he was the primary and ascendant voice within the Park Service to advocate for preserving wilderness within the parks, and he spoke passionately on its behalf until the issue became a common topic of discussion within the service.[46] And although he stood out within the Park Service as an early supporter of wilderness, Wright learned from those who came before him as well as from his contemporaries (in and out of the service)—and through literature and his own experiences.

Wilderness, its various definitions, and its American philosophers and ardent disciples have been well documented and extensively examined.[47] For Wright, a keen student of history and his professional predecessors, his wilderness forebears likely included Henry David Thoreau and John Muir.[48] Thoreau is perhaps best known for his book *Walden* (1854), which chronicled his two years living a simple, soul-repairing, and contemplative life, close to nature at Walden Pond, just south of Concord, Massachusetts.[49] However, it is in Thoreau's 1862 essay "Walking" (published posthumously) where he truly discusses wildness, and wilderness, at length. "I wish to speak a word for Nature," he begins, "for absolute freedom and wildness, as contrasted with a freedom and culture merely civil." Later in that piece he exclaims, "Give me the ocean, the desert, or the wilderness!"[50]

Muir, who was raised in Scotland as a strict Presbyterian, unabashedly believed all of nature—raindrops, insects, plants, animals, soaring mountains—came straight from God's hands, uncorrupted by civilization and domestication.[51] His family moved to New York when he was twelve. The creative and inventive Muir variously studied, worked in factories, labored on farms, and explored. By the age of thirty-one he was in California, where he climbed into the Sierra Nevada for the first time, working as a shepherd. He soon began writing about Yosemite valley and the Sierra as a whole. Muir traveled extensively, but it was the Sierra—what he called the Range of Light—that nourished his activism, molded his conservation ethic (he cofounded the Sierra Club in 1892), and gave tenor to his call for the preservation of wilderness.[52] "In God's wildness," Muir wrote in 1890, echoing Thoreau, "lies the hope of the world—the great fresh unblighted, unredeemed wilderness."[53]

In 1916, two years after Muir's death, Grinnell and Storer discussed wilderness and national parks in an article in *Science*, though in lieu of "wilderness" they employed the terms "primeval" and "primitive," as did many of the early advocates. "As the settlement of the country progresses and the original aspect of nature is altered," the zoologists wrote, "the national parks will probably be the only areas remaining unspoiled for scientific study. Accordingly they should be left in their pristine condition as far as is compatible with the convenience of visitors."[54]

The Ecological Society of America was formed in 1915 by a who's who of American ecologists from various academic and professional backgrounds. The society was soon at the forefront of advocating for the protection of wilderness. In their expansive and detailed 761-page publication, *Naturalist's Guide to the Americas* (1926), several members argued on behalf of wilderness, including Charles Adams. "The wilderness, like the forest, was once a great hindrance to our civilization," wrote Adams, "but now the tide has turned and wildernesses and forests must be maintained, even at much expense, because human society needs them. The National Parks should remain a virgin wilderness for educational and scientific purposes. The maintenance of a virgin wilderness park is very difficult, but not a hopeless problem, if proper public sentiment is developed in its behalf."[55]

Aldo Leopold is also part of this lineage, and some would say the cause's chief and most famous advocate. Others, however, are quick to point to all of the other wilderness advocates—Leopold's predecessors and contemporaries—who remain relatively unknown for a variety of reasons.[56] In Leopold's 1925 article, "The Last Stand of the Wilderness," he argued that the American public was unaware of the dire plight of the disappearing wilderness in the United States. "This paper is a plea for a definite expression of public opinion on the question of whether a system of wilderness areas should be established in our public Forests and Parks. . . . The people in need of wilderness areas are numerous," he continued, "and the preservation of their particular kind of contact with Mother Earth is a national problem of the first magnitude."[57]

In 1928, the American Forestry and the National Parks Associations produced a report on *Recreation Resources of Federal Lands* that stated twenty-one "wilderness sites" had been identified across ten western states, where "primitive nature is modified to the least possible degree by human influence." However, they also believed that logging could continue in these areas with "careful" and "skillful" planning, an opinion Leopold agreed with early on, under certain circumstances.[58]

In 1930, Bob Marshall, often quoted by Wright, wrote "The Problem of the Wilderness," which pulled from the writings of Leopold and others to identify what wilderness was, why it was necessary, and what was needed to preserve it. He described wilderness as a region "which contains no permanent inhabitants, possesses no possibility of conveyance by any mechanical means and is sufficiently spacious that a person in crossing it must have the experience of sleeping out." He too was concerned about the lack of public support for wilderness, an issue he dedicated his young professional life attempting to fix. "There is just one hope of repulsing the tyrannical ambition of civilization to conquer every niche on the whole earth. That hope is the organization of spirited people who will fight for the freedom of the wilderness."[59]

Throughout his life, Wright was part of this continuum, this lineage, attempting to describe wilderness, advocate on its behalf, and communicate the need for its preservation to the American public. "There is another type of recreational resource of national character which can only be perpetuated through the prompt actions of the Federal Government," Wright stated at the City Planning Conference, "This resource of inestimable value is primeval *America*. . . . Primeval conditions cannot be preserved except on areas of large size. If, as Marshall states in one of his published works, only twenty primeval areas of over a million acres each, remain in the United States today, then these should be declared forever inviolate and all steps necessary to safeguard their unspoiled condition should be undertaken at once."[60]

The first section in the National Resources Board report by Wright and his team was titled "Recreational Land Requirements." This was followed by "The Development of the Nation's Recreational Resources." The two sections expanded, in detail, the issues Wright had touched upon in his St. Louis talk. A single, impressive map was included in each section. The first, labeled "Geography of Recreation," cartographically revealed what the text claimed, that "recreational resources are located without any relationship to human demands." The map highlighted massive areas in the West available for recreation, far away from most urban centers, which were still principally on the East Coast.

The second map was titled "National Park System and Some Proposed Additions." It constituted the grand wish list for Wright and his Park Service colleagues. Shown were the existing national parks, historic and military parks, battlefield sites, cemeteries, "miscellaneous memorials," and national monuments. Down the entire right-hand column, however, was a list of twenty-one "Proposed Parks," also highlighted on the map. From several suggestions on the East Coast (the White and Green Mountains), it moved south to the Okefenokee Swamp in Georgia and Florida and to the Dismal Swamp in Virginia and North Carolina. It then shifted to the Midwest to list a handful of suggested "Indian Mound" parks. In the Southwest, more suggestions were added, including what would become Big Bend in Texas. In California, the future Channel Islands and Redwood National Parks were included, as well as an impressive swath of the Sierra Nevada from Yosemite south to Kings Canyon and Sequoia National Park. In the Northwest, Wright proposed additional parks to stretch down the volcanic ridge of the Cascade Mountains. New parks were also suggested for Alaska, Hawaii, and Puerto Rico.[61]

Now Is the Time to Put Up a Fight

With his Wildlife Division hat back on at headquarters, Wright also learned how to maneuver through a large office, meet new colleagues, and negotiate within a bureaucracy he had heretofore dealt with while either on the road during the survey years or from the distant safety of Berkeley's idyllic campus. Most of the top staff at headquarters, at his level and above, had been working with New Deal funds to create park projects for over a year. The young chief had some catching up to do in order to ascertain how the new culture operated and to figure out the nature of the power hierarchy.

Two things, however, became immediately clear: With all of the CCC construction projects taking place in the parks, headquarters and the field offices were swarming with architects and engineers. Second, if Wright needed to convince anyone about expanding the Wildlife Division by placing biologists in parks, it was John D. Coffman, the Park Service's chief forester.

At fifty-one years old, Coffman was a seasoned federal employee who had worked in the Forest Service for many years before joining the Park Service. In April of 1933, Horace Albright had appointed him to oversee CCC efforts within the national parks. Conrad Wirth, assistant director and a senior Park Service landscape architect, was placed in charge of over one hundred CCC camps in state parks. Wirth reported to Coffman.[62]

Back in 1931, when Wright had presented his concept of a Wildlife Division, including his plan to train wildlife staff in each park, Harold Bryant had replied that it was impossible, for two reasons: the Biological Survey would feel that the Park Service was encroaching on its area of expertise, and also

"necessary economic measures in these days of depression" would, quite simply, prohibit it.

By mid-1933, however, conditions began to change. The Park Service was
no longer concerned about offending the Biological Survey, and funds had
been made available—for this very purpose—through the New Deal. When
Wright arrived in Washington, DC, he drafted a memo outlining the need for
CCC "wildlife technicians" in the parks.

> A trained wild life technician is requested capable of surveying conditions,
> gathering scientific data, outlining and supervising important projects, and
> formulating a wild life administration plan. He will be responsible for enforc-
> ing established national park policies relating to introduced species, protec-
> tion for predators, restoration of disappearing species, presentation of un-
> modified natural conditions, and adequate year round habitats. It is important
> that someone be provided capable of studying out the interrelations between
> plant and animal life so as to safeguard ECW [CCC] activities and provide for
> wild life management.[63]

The document was initialed by Wright and Thompson. Bryant scribbled a
line across the top, "Justification for ECW Technicians," then added his ini-
tials next to the others.[64]

Wright then laid out a staffing plan and shared it with Thompson. In
Wright's scheme, there would be a first and second technician: the head biologists below the chief. The first technician position was reserved for Thompson, and Adrey E. Borell, a Park Service staffer—and yet another student of
Grinnell's from the MVZ—was recommended for second technician. There
would also be positions for a series of naturalist technicians and naturalist
assistants. The naturalist technicians were also biologists, but typically junior
or entry-level professionals. The naturalist assistants already existed in the
national parks under the Education and Research Department, though they
were called park naturalists. Bryant and Wright agreed that the Wildlife Division could enlist these men as naturalist assistants.[65]

One of the first obstacles that Wright confronted at headquarters was the
reality that the Wildlife Division—that is, himself—was not included in park
project planning meetings. This translated into the division finding out, after the fact, that CCC projects that could be harmful had already been
approved—and, in many cases, the shovels were already in the ground. He was
not pleased.

"Dear Mr. Director," his letter of protest began. "We repeatedly find ourselves in the position where it is necessary for us to take exception, either as

a whole, or in part, to some project which is likely to affect adversely wild life values." Wright acknowledged that routing documents through yet another department would be time-consuming but, without doing so, he said, "the Wild Life Division will never be able to discharge its responsibilities until some satisfactory plan for keeping in contact with what is going on is devised."[66]

Around this same time, Thompson had been dispatched to the Grand Canyon, and he reported back to Wright that plans for a major road were in the works from Grand Canyon Village to Havasupai Point, across the relatively intact southwest section of the park. After receiving Thompson's report, Wright replied to him with his observations from a "conference on road projects" he had attended at headquarters. The note to the director had worked.

The Grand Canyon road project had come up during the conference, and it was approved without discussion. At the end of the meeting, Wright asked to revisit the project, based on Thompson's concerns. The others were, surprisingly, open to alternatives, including the director and Thomas Vint, the Park Service's chief architect. The dirt road that existed between these two points—a path that the biologists had traveled many times in the survey truck, and knew well—could be slightly improved, suggested Wright, but maintained as a "wilderness trail" for automobiles. It should be preserved, he argued, for tourists who "would like to do a little exploring on their own, as a real wild life trip."[67]

Wright further shared with Thompson that his Washington, DC, colleagues believed that the natural tendency within the service, and its preference, was to always improve roadways. However, he countered to Thompson that he believed that it was their "business to see that such a road was kept to the status which was set for it and that I thought there was a great deal of future in these wilderness trails for others."[68]

"Here is an excellent example," he continued, "of how we fail in effectiveness most of the time through being removed from the place where decisions are made. Had I not been there we would not have had opportunity to exert our influence on this particular project at least until it was already under way and of course too late for anything to be done." Wright asked Thompson to write up a report detailing his opposition to the project.[69]

Regardless of Wright's somewhat positive experience from that planning meeting, a few weeks later the relentless engineers and architects pushed back. Wright, however, was not giving in. He wrote Thompson again, urging him to finish his memorandum on the Havasupai Road. "Do not hesitate to express yourself," he said. "*Now, if ever, is the time to put up a fight for the ideals which have dominated our actions and sustained our courage these many years.*"[70]

By August, even though the proposed "first class highway" had been slightly adjusted by the engineers on paper, it was far from a "wilderness trail." Once again, Wright wrote to the director. The park, he detailed, already had over seventy miles of paved roads, with approximately forty-eight of those miles hugging the canyon's scalloped rim. The proposed road would cut directly through a remote quadrant of the park as well as a Park Service research area at Great Thumb Point. Wright personally calculated that new construction would displace some 260 acres of precious wildlife range—still overgrazed and in need of restoration. Instead, he suggested, for the second time, an alternative plan: because there were already some primitive roads in the project area, why not simply improve them, slightly, and keep them as "wilderness trails"?

"We would be grateful," Wright concluded, "had past generations not exterminated the passenger pigeon, the great auk, and numerous species of grizzly bear, or if they had not brought to the verge of extermination the bison, antelope, wolverine, fisher, trumpeter swan, whooping crane, ivory-billed woodpecker, and so on. In like manner I believe that future generations will be grateful for the tracts of primitive area, or wilderness, which we can save in our national parks without hindering our own pleasure in the least— areas which we do not stamp with our limited technique and concepts of wilderness-use."[71]

As yet another example of Wright's powers of persuasion, he prevailed. The "first class highway" was shelved. Shortly after the decision, he received a note from Bryant. "The Director wants you and me to go over six year plans and see whether there are other roads that should be disapproved before they get along as far as the Grand Canyon one."[72]

While there were, and would be, numerous additional road projects the division opposed, or wanted to significantly alter, Wright now knew how to play the game on behalf of wildlife and wilderness. In the spring of 1935, he issued a memorandum to his growing staff of wildlife technicians. "An agreement has been reached," he wrote, "between the Wildlife Division and the Branch of Plans and Design for procedures for carrying on the work that is common to both branches of the National Park Service." Working with Plans and Design, they would jointly review all park projects based on the service's master plan as well as follow mandatory procedures for both teams to ground-truth projects, then report back to headquarters.[73]

This memo was followed by a confidential note to his staff, reiterating the importance of their new obligations in the planning process, and demonstrating Wright's continued growth as a savvy team leader:

The Wildlife Division is the Baby Technical Branch of the Service. Only a short time ago, while having a right kind heart and I am sure a very decent brain, the Wildlife Division was without arms and legs. Now we have these necessary arms and legs. These are the specific agreements whereby the approval of certain activities of the Service are contingent upon approval of the Wildlife Division. We did not ask for this sort of authority but the necessity of proper consideration for wildlife has become so evident that the agreements were offered to us. Now I am most concerned, and that is the purpose of this memorandum, that we be sure not to fail on our end of it.[74]

The Everglades: Pleasure and Inspiration

In May of 1934, FDR signed the act authorizing the creation of Everglades National Park, with a maximum size of some 3,382 square miles. The establishment of the enormous park, and its boundaries, were contentious issues for years, with many competing federal, state, and local interests often at odds with one another. Additionally, national conservation groups were watching the project closely—and, at times, stepping into the fray.[75]

In November of 1930, Wright and Thompson had been sent to the Everglades by Director Albright—a trip cut short by Wright's battle with malaria. During that early trip, the young biologists had met Ernest F. Coe, executive chair and the driving force behind the 1928 creation of the Everglades National Park Association.[76]

Wright and Coe enjoyed a rich correspondence during the ensuing five years, and they worked closely to help preserve the Everglades while also developing a collegial rapport. Coe would, in fact, adopt many of Wright's positions and ideas regarding parks over time. Although Coe was a landscape architect by training, by the late 1920s he had turned all of his energies into his new passion: the Everglades. Marjory Stoneman Douglas, who became a widely recognized Everglades champion during the late 1940s, christened Coe the "Prophet" of the Everglades.[77]

On December 5, 1934, Bryant, Toll, Wright, and the Park Service Deputy Chief Engineer Oliver G. Taylor landed in Miami for an inspection tour of the Everglades. Between Wright's first sojourn to southern Florida and his second visit, three years later, numerous Park Service parties had ventured to southern Florida for similar reconnaissance trips. This contingent, sent by the director, had the express task of determining the park's boundary lines.

"I am looking forward with great anticipation to your arrival here," Coe wrote to Wright a week before the team arrived. "Everything in the power of this Association to facilitate your work will be our pleasure to extend."[78] The service personnel, often accompanied by Coe, spent eleven days talking with all of the interested parties, both in Miami and in towns surrounding the future park. They also visited at least one village of Seminole Indians south of the Tamiami Trail. Two days after arriving, the team floated above the region aboard a Goodyear blimp, with Toll taking numerous photographs of the various habitats they observed: inundated sawgrass prairies, royal and sabal palms, stands of cypress, Caribbean pine hummocks, and leggy stands of mangroves with rough, white, calcified skirts of oysters hanging below. These images were later placed in an album and presented to the director.[79]

Over the following days, the team continued their work by car and boat to explore the interior as well as numerous offshore islets and habitats. They made it as far as the Marquesas Keys, and Fort Jefferson National Monument at Dry Tortugas, beyond Key West to the far south. "As a national park of large size, there is afforded opportunity to reserve great areas and keep them undisturbed and free from human intrusion," Bryant informed the director on behalf of the team after their return. "By this means only can primeval wilderness be retained unmodified and bird and animal life afforded full opportunity for normal increase."[80]

The detailed report the team produced from their trip touched, similarly, on one of Wright's key issues with national parks: the lack of boundaries sufficient to create complete "biological units." "The proposed maximum boundary line encloses really only a minimum area necessary to carry out even reasonably the objects for which the park is to be established," the report stated. "A considerably larger area would be correspondingly much more desirable and we trust will be possible of attainment sometime in the future."[81]

During that same December trip in 1934, Wright transported his entire family to Miami while he continued to conduct research in the Everglades. He also took a brief vacation during the holidays while escaping the chill of the Washington winter. Bee, Charmaine, and Pamela—along with their longtime domestic helper and nanny, Jessie Crawford—stayed at the Ocean Towers, on the beach, for December and all of January.[82] And Bee's parents, Olive and William Ray, traveled east from Southern California to join them—and to celebrate Bee's twenty-eighth birthday in Miami on December 9.

One day in January Wright was interviewed by a reporter from the *Miami Tribune*. "An ideal location for a national park would be the Everglades," the article began, "first, because of its wild life, and second, it would be near

Wright with his daughters Pamela (left) and Sherry (right), Washington, DC, November 1935. Courtesy of Pamela Meléndez Wright Lloyd.

enough to one of the most beautiful and sophisticated cities in the United States—Miami. Believe it or not, a gentleman from California made that statement. He's George M. Wright of Berkeley, California, chief of the wild life division, National Park Service." The reporter then went on to quote Wright, who explained the investigations he was carrying out in the Everglades while extolling the impressive size and natural diversity of the future park. "But," he concluded, "unless this area is quickly established as a national park the wild life there will become extinct."[83]

Back at headquarters, Wright kept in contact with Coe, offering his assistance where needed. At Coe's request he also sent a copy of *Fauna No. 1* to Florida. Coe read it from cover to cover and immediately wrote back to Wright. "You have treated your subject fearlessly," he exclaimed. In late January, Wright sent Coe a note expressing a positive outlook on the future park—as he had to Toll in 1932, when he stated that they had an opportunity in the Everglades to do something big. "The way in which you have kept this project live and before all of us continually," Wright wrote, complimenting Coe, "is a splendid example of what intelligently directed enthusiasm can accomplish."[84]

Wright and his family returned to Washington, DC, in February 1935, where he and Bee celebrated their fourth wedding anniversary, but by mid-March, he was back in the Everglades. For this trip he served as the personal guide to Secretary of the Interior Harold Ickes and his family. John Collier, commissioner of Indian Affairs—who wanted to instill the bureau with new energy and ideas—was also present. As with previous trips, once the group gathered, it hit the ground running. They held meetings with stakeholders and traveled throughout the Everglades. Coe and his staff, once again, worked on logistics and accompanied the Park Service party.

Secretary Ickes agreed that Everglades National Park should become a reality, but he also believed a Seminole Indian Reservation should be created immediately north of the proposed park boundaries. Ickes and his wife, Anna, were early advocates for Indian rights in the United States.[85] Wright also accompanied Anna Ickes on an extended airplane trip over the park. She was taken aback by the park's beauty, stating that it was a memory that would live with her forever.[86]

Wright contacted Coe in early April and let him know he was greeted "with an exceptionally large volume of work" upon his return to headquarters. Regardless, he verified that the "certification of boundaries" had officially been submitted to Ickes; that the secretary would be in touch with Florida Governor David Sholtz promptly; that the General Lands Office had been engaged to determine the status of certain lands; and that he was working with Commissioner Collier on the project with respect to the Indian lands.

"The pleasure and inspiration of my trip will be unforgettable," Wright closed his letter. "You do not know how much the glimpse of south Florida and the happy meetings with your enthusiastic fellow workers refreshed the jaded white-collar worker from Washington."[87]

9

Outstanding Men

By mid-1935, the Wildlife Division, thanks to a continuing influx of CCC funds, consisted of at least seventeen staff members, with another seven hires pending. In addition to the core Wildlife Division team—Wright, Thompson, and Dixon—these men were soon scattered across the country in numerous parks or assigned to the Berkeley office.

In a memo to the longtime editor-in-chief and writer for the Park Service, Isabelle F. Story, Wright, no doubt angling for some mention of the division in one of the service's publications, referred to several of his key staff—Adrey E. Borell, Victor Cahalane, Adolph Murie, and E. Lowell Sumner Jr.—as "outstanding men in the field of wildlife administration."[1]

These four biologists, in particular, became strong advocates for wildlife and wilderness alongside Wright. Borell, another Grinnell student from Berkeley and now assigned to the Grand Canyon as his base of operation, became a central member of the division. He served as a "traveling technician" for part of 1934 and 1935. Cahalane, meanwhile, was hired by Wright in July 1934 and appointed to Wind Cave National Park in South Dakota. He too used the park as a springboard to travel frequently around the West on assignment. The next year he was transferred to Washington, DC, to help run the division. Murie also joined the team in summer 1934. Although ostensibly based out of the Berkeley office, he was almost always in the field. Finally, Sumner, just three years younger than Wright, was very near to completing his PhD while studying under Grinnell in 1935 when Wright offered him a position in the Wildlife Division. Sumner couldn't pass up the opportunity. He immediately left school and settled for a master's degree (though his PhD thesis was eventually published). He soon became a key itinerant biologist, whom Wright and Thompson dispatched to parks around the West to investigate management issues.[2]

Another of the division's new hires, Edward A. Kitchin, took a slightly different trajectory into the Park Service and into the lives of Wright and Thompson. Originally from the northern Scottish town of Banff, he eventually emigrated to Washington State's Puget Sound. When he wasn't working, he was birdwatching on trips that took him throughout the Northwest. In January of 1934, Kitchin published a pamphlet entitled "Distributional Check-list of the Birds of the State of Washington." That is when he appeared on Wright's radar.[3]

Thompson, on behalf of Wright, wrote Bryant to explain their interest in Kitchin and their desire to place him at Mount Rainier. "You will note that Kitchin has had only grammar school education," he wrote, "and is a man well along in years." Thompson explained that they had considered these two particulars, but that they wanted to hire the fifty-eight-year-old anyway. Rainier, Thompson explained, needed a "mature man" because the park was "somewhat nearer the frontier than other parks," and local attitudes reflected that geography.[4]

A month later, Kitchin was hired and began work at Mount Rainier as a naturalist assistant. He was informed that he had three basic tasks. First, safeguard food and cover for the park's wildlife against the potentially harmful activities of the young men in the CCC camps. Second, conduct research on the life histories of the park's animals. And third, offer recommendations for proper management and restoration programs within the park.[5] Kitchin thrived in his new role. Wright not only praised him, he tried to assist him in all aspects of his work. Wright was, in fact, so impressed with Kitchin's detailed observations and reports that he suggested the naturalist assistant publish several articles based on his reports. Wright, who encouraged all of his men to publish when possible, let him know the division was finishing guidelines for writing and placing articles as a Park Service employee, and that they would forward them to him posthaste.[6]

In order to improve Kitchin's fieldwork, Wright arranged to have an impressive list of supplies sent to the naturalist assistant. Among them were a new camera and accessories; binoculars; a thermometer; a multipart dissecting and specimen preparation kit; arsenic, formaldehyde, and other chemicals for preserving specimens; a syringe and "various needles"; three packs of notebook fillers (Wright taught the Grinnellian note taking system to division staff); two bottles of "Higgins Eternal Ink"; a plant press; twelve reference

books; periodicals covering natural history, ecology, mammalogy, and forestry; and two "special books": *Handbook of Birds of the Western United States*
and *Important Western Browse Plants*.[7]

In the spring of 1935, FDR instructed the director of the CCC, Robert Fechner, the Park Service, and all of the other bureaus and agencies with CCC programs to double the number of recruits, and they did. Soon 600,000 young
men were working in 2,916 camps. The Park Service was managing 580 of
those camps, and due to the influx of funds and concomitant management
demands, the service's staff skyrocketed from just over 4,000 in 1933 to 13,361
in 1935. (This number peaked in 1937 at 13,900.) More than half of that increase was attributed to staff directly working with CCC programs.[8]

Borell, Cahalane, Murie, and Sumner, meanwhile—along with the rest
of their division colleagues—were kept busy as the numerous CCC projects
continued to ramp up in the parks. The ever-present wildlife management
issues were often exacerbated by the construction and cleanup work of the
crews, and the wildlife team regularly had to diplomatically step in to manage
situations.[9]

Borell crisscrossed the Southwest on various assignments. At Saguaro National Monument, for example, he investigated a non-CCC-related problem:
a local rancher—who held grazing rights within the monument—maintained
that mountain lions had killed 25 percent of his calves. Borell also accompanied Dixon on several trips to Death Valley to help finalize that national monument's borders. Cahalane worked, in particular, to stem the continuing pres-
sure to control predators in and around parks. In spite of the Park Service's
official policy against such control, the practice was still in place in many
parks—with the Biological Survey, poachers, and rogue rangers to blame. Cahalane also ruffled the feathers of some architects, engineers, foresters, and
superintendents with his field reports of "nonconcurrence"—a determination
to deny a project—relative to several CCC-funded plans. One superintendent
even called Cahalane's views "not only far-fetched but picayunish."[10]

Two of Wright's most intense "outstanding men" were Adolph Murie and
Lowell Sumner. Murie was forty-six in 1935; Sumner was twenty-seven. Both
were excellent naturalists and outstanding field biologists. After extensive research in Grand Teton National Park, for example, Murie provided Wright
with a detailed map of suggested border adjustments in order to help with the
elk management issues within the park.

Murie also reviewed CCC efforts in several parks and wrote down a list
of objections and sent them to Wright. Why remove two thousand acres of

weeds in Rocky Mountain National Park, he asked, when over time, natural processes will prevail? At Grand Teton the administration wanted to place salt licks alongside the roads to attract wildlife for easy viewing. "Efforts should not be deliberately made to keep the tourists in the roads and take away any incentive for taking a look for themselves off the roads." Murie wanted to oppose this project, and Wright wholeheartedly agreed.[11]

Perhaps Murie's most eloquent statements, however, related to forests. At Mesa Verde, there was a plan to have the CCC crews plant the north rim with ponderosa pines. Wright wrote Charles Quaintance, resident wildlife technician, that the park was "one of the very outposts for this species" and that he'd rather "be inclined to favor letting nature take its course."[12] Wright asked Murie for his input.

> A natural forest has a rather definite history, it has passed through various stages, its composition is the result of intense competition between species and between individuals. It is molded by many forces, its existence, over a period of years at least, may be due to mere chance of invasion. A forest which has passed thru such a history has a meaning, a real significance. It is to preserve plant associations that have a meaning, to permit the natural forces to play on an area undisturbed, that we have National Parks. A planted forest may serve as an ornament to the landscape but during its lifetime it remains more or less an artifact with an unnatural association of plant species, lacking in true significance—*a meaningless story so far as primitiveness is concerned.* I suggest that the project of planting ponderosa pine on the North Mesa be dropped.[13]

Wright also dispatched Murie to represent the division at a large meeting in Glacier concerning the effort to cut down thousands of dead trees and standing snags after the catastrophic Half Moon Fire devastated over a hundred thousand acres in 1929. The group lobbied for a massive cleanup across an area totaling about twelve square miles. Murie disagreed. As they toured the burn site, he pointed out the profusion of regrowth and the fact that "the bird life was unusually abundant and quite varied." His memo stated, in part:

> *To those interested in preserving wilderness, destroying a natural condition in a burn is just as sacrilegious as destroying a green forest. The dead forest which it is proposed to destroy is the forest we should set out to protect.*[14]

Sumner, meanwhile, spent the 1935 field season working throughout California and other parts of the West. The Wildlife Division learned of a new road, proposed by Lassen Volcanic National Park's Superintendent L. W. Collins, to connect the park's Juniper and Summit Lakes, so he was directed to investigate. "When I arrived at Lassen," Sumner reported to Thompson, "I found a distinctly hostile feeling toward the Wildlife Division on the part of the authorities, largely engendered by the Division's stand regarding the proposed road development."

> I feel that one of the most important results of the Lassen trip has been that the authorities became decidedly friendly by the end of my stay, even after we had a long discussion regarding road construction policies in which we found ourselves on opposite sides of the issue, and even after I told them exactly what my report would be like—namely, not favorable. I think that at least the Wildlife Division has their respect.[15]

Sumner then continued on to explain his philosophy about how to approach these matters: Be even but honest, don't verbalize personal opinions, and focus on writing up the report. "However," he asked Thompson, "if you have any criticisms of this policy, I shall be more than glad to hear them. I have to live and work with these obstreperous people, and I hope to secure cooperation and avoid having to work against them any more than is necessary." Thompson appreciated his report and approved of his approach. After all, Sumner likely learned it from Wright and Thompson.[16]

Not all CCC projects potentially impacting wildlife and their habitat were declined or even adjusted by the division. In fact, at least two CCC-funded projects, spearheaded by the division, were completed in Yellowstone. The first was an effort to make bear-proof metal food and garbage containers for campgrounds—an idea Thompson had been working on for years. The other task, no doubt suggested by Wright, was the creation of artificial nesting islands for trumpeter swans at Shoshone, Swan, and Heart Lakes. The idea was to cinch logs together to form large squares, cover the platforms with soil, plant them with grasses and tule, then float them a hundred feet offshore and anchor them. "This matter has been discussed with Mr. Wright of the Wild Life Division," wrote Acting Superintendent Guy D. Edwards, "and has his concurrence."[17]

Lost Souls in the Sahara

The Wildlife Division worked alongside, but rarely agreed with, the Park Service's Forestry Division. The forestry management policies of the service, developed by Senior Naturalist and Chief Forester Ansel Hall in the 1920s, and subsequently built on by Chief Forester John Coffman, reflected traditional Forest Service views including fire control, road building, and intense management, but without the extractive economic goal of national forests.[18] Most of the young foresters hired during the New Deal to work in national parks were recent forestry school graduates with traditional views and little to no experience in the parks.

Wright, on the other hand, took a decidedly holistic view of forests as part of the biotic communities of national parks, and he championed their function as critical habitat. His beliefs came directly from Grinnell (with, no doubt, input from Mulford). In 1916, the year the National Park Service was created, Grinnell and Storer wrote that in order to maintain the "original balance" in national parks, "No trees, whether living or dead, should be cut down. Dead trees are in many respects as useful as living, and should be just as rigorously protected. No more undergrowth should be destroyed than is absolutely necessary. To many birds and mammals thickets are protective havens into which their enemies find it difficult to penetrate."[19]

In 1932, sixteen years after Grinnell and Storer's article was published, Wright stated in *Fauna No. 1* that "it is necessary that the trees be left to accumulate dead limbs and rot in the trunks; that the forest floor become littered." A year later, in an article in *The Condor*, he followed up with this: "One standing snag may be worth more than ten or a hundred living trees in supplying the peculiar habitat requirements of certain bird species."[20]

One August, Thompson traveled through the Cascade Range in Oregon and south into California, inspecting CCC roadside cleanup efforts at Mount Rainier, Crater Lake, and Lassen Volcanic National Parks. At Crater Lake he found a crew chopping down every single dead tree or snag they could find. He stopped and had a friendly talk with the young men. He realized they had no idea what they were doing or why. There were no technicians from landscape, forestry, or wildlife present—just an older man, a "straw boss" CCC contractor, who said he was told to remove everything dead and make it look "prettier."[21]

"I discovered that road-side clean-up had been so thorough," Thompson reported alarmingly, "that all forest litter had been raked from the ground as far back from the highway as one could see, and that all normal down timber, including decayed logs and old snags, which may perhaps have been there for twenty years, were completely removed."[22] Even all of the pine needles had been raked into neat piles and burned. It was façade management at its worse.

"Another instance was in Lassen Volcanic National Park," he continued, "where on the afternoon when I met Dr. Bryant, we spent some time scouting around the campground to find a comfortable log upon which to sit, meditate and discuss our various problems. Like lost souls in the Sahara, we could find no log of any description to sit on. Finally, after much aimless wandering we sat down in the dust with our knees poked up to our chins and commented on the beauties of nature."[23]

In his report, Thompson argued that the divisions needed to collaborate, agree upon management approaches, and then get that information out into the field.[24]

Fauna No. 2—Wildlife Management in the National Parks

Wright encouraged his men to read widely in the biological sciences and in natural history overall. In the Berkeley office, he would eventually assemble an impressive reference library, containing 345 books and 1,150 periodicals and pamphlets. As we've seen, he also shipped out books and pamphlets to the field naturalists for their use in the parks—in addition to other equipment. And he instilled in his staff the importance of publishing based on their fieldwork.

The Park Service had several outlets for publishing articles and park-specific "nature notes," but Wright also wanted the division's employees to author pieces in professional journals as well as in "sportsman type" periodicals in order to communicate with the "opposition" instead of always addressing those "who are already in accord with our views."[25] After reading field reports prepared by his staff, Wright sent them supportive letters to acknowledge their work, praise their observations, and make diplomatic suggestions for improving their writing or to redirect their focus to specific issues or species.

Wright was, in fact, such a believer in the dissemination of research findings that in a 1935 memo prepared for Isabelle Story, the Park Service editor and writer, he placed emphasis on the importance of one of Story's key responsibilities for the service: publishing. "In my opinion," he began, "the greatest need of the educational program in the National Park Service today is to have made available adequate funds for printing publications, both scientific and popular."[26]

Wright lobbied her to work with the Park Service's Educational Advisory Board to supplement the printing budget. Not only were his men capable of producing numerous articles and monographs, he said, but many of the wildlife technicians in the field also had specialized writing to contribute, such as annotated checklists of birds and mammals for individual parks. He thanked her for shepherding through *Fauna No. 1* in 1933, and from her limited fund then publishing a thousand copies of the second installment in the Fauna Series: *Fauna of the National Parks of the United States, Wildlife Management in the National Parks*, Fauna Series No. 2.[27]

In *Fauna No. 2*, published in the spring of 1935 and written entirely by Wright and Thompson, the authors circled back to the challenges and questions posed in *Fauna No. 1* and provided succinct updates and management suggestions.[28]

In his foreword, Director Cammerer stated that the publication "develops the idea of wilderness-use technique which was suggested in the first survey, and reports on the actual progress which has been made in wildlife administration since the establishment of the Wildlife Division. It will serve as a guide to the park administrator in his effort to accomplish the purposes for which the national parks system was established."

In Wright and Thompson's introduction to *Fauna No. 2*, they explained that Part I was "devoted to some of the phases and possibilities of national parks wilderness use as they affect wildlife." And Part II treated "specific problems according to the principles laid down in Part I" for a sampling of the parks.[29]

The articles were at once prosaic and expressive. Both Wright and Thompson had spent years exploring the West in their youth, and, more recently, working inside the national parks as biologists. So while their writing focused on presenting and framing management issues and potential solutions, their deep experiences in nature and their observations of wildlife infused their writing and elevated it beyond mere scientific or academic prose. Read today, the pieces are still relevant—and enjoyable.

Part II—"Present Status of National Parks Wildlife and the Restoration Program"—opened with an update on large mammals in the parks, then downsized to mustelids (fisher and wolverine, for example) and rodents. In "Men and Birds in Joint Occupation of National Parks" and "Men and Mammals in Joint Occupation of National Parks," Wright posed the core question he and his team had worked on for years: "How shall man and beast be reconciled in the conflicts and disturbances which inevitably arise when both occupy the same general area concurrently?"[30]

"I believe," he continued, ". . . that the more man desires to preserve the native biota, the more complex become his problems in joint occupancy."[31]

If we destroy nature blindly, it is a boomerang which will be our undoing. Consecration to the task of adjusting ourselves to the natural environment so that we secure the best values from nature without destroying it is not useless idealism; it is good hygiene for civilization. In this lies the true portent of this national parks effort. Fifty years from now we shall still be wrestling with the problems of joint occupation of national parks by men and mammals, but it is reasonable to predict that we shall have mastered some of the simplest maladjustments. It is far better to pursue such a course though success be but partial than to relax in despair and allow the destructive forces to operate unchecked.

GEORGE WRIGHT[32]

"The Primitive Persists in Bird Life of Yellowstone Park" is, perhaps, Wright at his most poetic as he celebrates the wildness of Yellowstone and takes the reader through a series of short natural history vignettes of selected birds: "Days with the birds in Yellowstone are tonic to him whose spirit is bruised by reiteration of the lament that wilderness is a dying gladiator," he wrote. "Too frequent exposure to a belief born of despair is not good for any man."[33]

Thompson's "A Wilderness-Use Technique" and "National Parks and Wilderness Use" covered challenging management and use issues, and suggested techniques for "using a wilderness without spoiling it."[34] But he too waxed poetic.

Although the overall conclusion by the authors was that "the National Park Service believes that its wildlife resources are sounder today than at any time since its establishment," there were exceptions and some dramatic management suggestions.

Their most controversial proposal, which had been discussed for at least two years, was to reduce Yellowstone's northern elk herd by 3,000 animals annually until the population stabilized. The elks' range had not improved since the biologists began their work in 1929, and they believed the herd was on the brink of disaster. "There is more certainty for the perpetuation of the elk herd if it is composed of 6,000 healthy animals on a good range than if it numbers 12,000 starving animals whose resistance to cold and disease is gone."[35] In fact, in the winter of 1934–35, the service removed 3,265 elk, and the following winter, another 3,000. This practice would continue for years.[36]

Part II then covered various management issues and ideas in Grand Canyon, Mesa Verde, Carlsbad Caverns, and Yellowstone National Parks and CCC projects relative to wildlife. Additionally, research reserves and "buffer strips" around parks were discussed. "Under this scheme," Wright explained, detailing the buffer zones, "the whole of the park becomes a primitive area" except for heavily used and developed areas. Within these undeveloped areas, research reserves were to be established where no management took place, excluding even such practices as "fish planting." This would allow for investigations in undisturbed, "pristine" areas for years to come. Then attempts would be made to create a "buffer strip of the maximum width possible" around each park in order to minimize external influences and ensure thriving and independent "biotic units." Although twenty-eight research reserves were eventually established in ten national parks, the concept never fully developed. This was due, in part, to the fact that the wildlife biologists were not initially consulted about the selection of the reserves (superintendents made most of those decisions), and eventually Wright disagreed with how and where many of the reserves were created. Plus, he was more interested in pursuing buffer zones surrounding the parks in order to minimize outside influences.[37]

Bootstraps of Wildlife Conservation

In 1935, on either side of *Fauna No. 2*'s release, Wright gave presentations at three different venues. Additionally, his 1934 radio address for National Parks Year was reprinted in the 1935 August edition of *Scientific Monthly*.

His March presentation at the San Francisco–based Bohemian Club— "The Wilderness That Did Not Vanish"—focused on the history and wildlife of Yellowstone National Park. As was tradition at the club, there was a brief but exuberant "Western" play before Wright spoke about the first white visitors to Yellowstone in the 1870s and their declaration to preserve the diverse and otherworldly landscape. He touched on the excesses of buffalo hunting by European Americans and the unfortunate era of "subduing the Indians." After highlighting the park's diverse wildlife he ended by simply stating: "The national parks today are perpetuated as wildernesses only by painstaking and scientific wildlife management."[38]

The next month, at the annual meeting of the American Society of Mammalogists at the Carnegie Museum in Pittsburgh, Pennsylvania, seven of Wright's biologists presented papers. These included details on CCC wildlife projects, updates on bighorn populations, and an analysis of the elk reduction effort in Yellowstone. Additionally, Ding Darling, now chief of the Biological Survey, presented his talk, "The Federal Duty toward Wildlife Conservation," and Bob Marshall gave an address titled "The Preservation of Our Rapidly Vanishing Wilderness."

Wright's talk, "Some Proposed National Parks in Relation to Conservation of Local Mammals," reviewed which agencies had responsibilities for specific aspects of wildlife preservation or use in the United States. Who, he asked, should be perpetuating primeval America? "Unless the Federal Government preserves the precious remains of our rich heritage of outstanding scenic, historical and floral and faunal resources they will be ground under the wheels of commercialism." Wright also discussed the need to preserve millions of acres of wilderness, something Marshall also focused on. "There is yet no Federal agency," he added, "for the single purpose of conservation of wildlife resources." Which was why, he stressed, there needed to be one. That said, however, Wright believed that, for the moment, the National Park Service was the most appropriate federal agency for "perpetuating primeval wildlife."[39]

The title of Darling's presentation echoed Wright's point. There is no question that Darling and Wright were constantly sharing ideas and strategies to create some form of national entity to oversee the country's wildlife heritage, as evidenced by their matching opinions at this conference and again two months later in New York. It was a convergence and partnership that would continue into the next year.

In the fall, at the annual convention of the National Association of Audubon Societies in New York City, Wright was happily surrounded by fellow bird aficionados, including, once again, Ding Darling. On the final evening of the four-day gathering, during a session entitled "National Conservation Program," Wright's paper, "Bootstraps of Wildlife Conservation," was interesting for several reasons.[40] He focused, once again, on his belief that there had been a recent surge in interest in "conservation programs for a number of our natural resources"—soil, forests, water—but not necessarily for wildlife. "What is the basic difficulty?" he asked. "Has wildlife conservation been trying to lift itself by its own bootstraps?" Today's common understanding of the saying is that someone who is "pulling themselves up by their own bootstraps" is to be commended and applauded. However, in the early twentieth century, it was "used to describe a quixotic attempt to achieve an impossibility, not a feat of self-reliance." In other words, Wright asks, has wildlife conservation been pursuing the unachievable?[41]

He also presented an updated vision of his philosophy on conservation and wildlife preservation. "Conservation which seeks no end other than its own existence," he stated, "is a game hardly worth playing." He further declared that, after eight years of "struggling with the wildlife administration problems of the national monuments and national parks, pure conservation theory" had proven ineffective. The national parks, he believed, had been successful in conserving wildlife for one reason: the parks were "wholly utilitarian." "If you care that the trumpeter swan has been saved and that there is still one remnant of grizzly bears," he continued, "you must recognize the recreational use of wildlife as the most important of its multiple uses." Now for Wright, human "use"— that is, people viewing and enjoying wildlife—and *not* only strict conservation, for conservation's sake, was *one* of the keys to preserving "primeval wildlife."[42]

This pivot in Wright's thinking appears like an abrupt change. However, this new phrasing and view, in fact, had been used and explained almost twenty years earlier by Wright's mentor, Grinnell, in an article entitled "Animal Life as an Asset of National Parks."[43] For Wright, it was actually more of an evolution in his beliefs, a maturation of theory born of the frustrating realities he had been struggling with both inside and outside of the government to raise the urgency of wildlife issues in the country. He wanted to educate the public, have universities establish wildlife research and conservation programs, and cultivate a vocal and dedicated constituency to help protect and restore wildlife. This broadened approach was part of his answer.

Wright once again stressed that wilderness preservation "could only be accomplished with the aid of the Federal Government." And, he emphasized, these areas "would be a form of *use*, and not a *withdrawal of use*."[44] As challenging as the task was, he told the audience, there was a group that had just formed that could help with the effort. "This is the Wilderness Society and it would be well for other conservation organizations to look to it for guidance on how and where to help." Wright fully supported the new organization; however, the founders of the Wilderness Society did not view the Park Service as a partner in the wilderness effort due to the service's years of "automobile-based tourism" and heavy emphasis on road construction at the time. In fact, the Park Service was regarded by the Wilderness Society— which placed primacy on roadless areas as the key characteristic of wilderness—as an "adversary of the very places it was legally supposed to protect."[45]

Following Wright, the final presentation of the evening was by Ding Darling, "Wanted: A National Program for Wild Life Restoration." Although the text of his presentation apparently was not archived, at the start of the convention a reporter for the *New York Times* wrote: "The formulation of ideas leading to a national wildlife conservation program will be one of the principal objects of the convention. Impetus will be given the plan when one of its chief advocates, Jay N. Darling, chief of the United States Bureau of Biological Survey, addresses the delegates on Tuesday evening."[46]

With whispers in the air about a reorganization of the Park Service, possible modifications to the CCC program, ongoing national concerns over unemployment and the economy, and problems overseas, Wright's presentations in 1935 evolved from the lyrical need to preserve wildlife, wilderness, and the beauty of nature to more serious, realistic, and policy-driven declarations: wildlife issues needed to be elevated to the national level; the public should be educated and cultivated as ambassadors for wildlife; there should be an agency or organization dedicated specifically to wildlife issues; and the Park Service, for now, was the only hope for preserving primeval wildlife and securing wilderness. His recommendations, collectively, were an urgent call to unify and collaborate before everything was "ground under the wheels of commercialism."

A Wary Eye on Europe

In FDR's inaugural address in March 1933, he set forth his Good Neighbor Policy, fashioned originally for relations with Latin America. The president, on behalf of the United States, pledged to respect the sovereignty of the countries to the south, promising not to intervene in their domestic or foreign affairs. He would, several years later, extend this policy "to our neighbors across the seas."

By 1935, however, as tensions flared between those overseas neighbors, FDR was keeping a wary eye on Europe and beyond. Adolf Hitler's Germany was on the rise, rearming, and soon Nazi troops would begin their spread across Europe. In September of that year, the Nazi Party instituted the Nuremberg Race Laws, stripping German Jews of their citizenship. Benito Mussolini's fascist Italy invaded Ethiopia in October, thus beginning a bloody occupation that lasted several years. Japan, meanwhile, had invaded and occupied the Chinese territory of Manchuria in 1931. The small island nation, ruled by Emperor Hirohito, became increasingly militaristic and vocal in its aggressive, expansionist desires. And, waiting in the wings, Spain's Generalíssimo Francisco Franco engineered plans to roll out a brutal civil war across the Iberian Peninsula.

On August 31, 1935, with those conflicts brewing, FDR signed the Neutrality Act. He then released a statement in which he called the act an "expression of the fixed desire of the Government and the people of the United States to avoid any action which might involve us in war." The next year, at a talk in Chautauqua, New York, FDR famously stated, "We are not isolationists except in so far as we seek to isolate ourselves completely from war. Yet we must remember that so long as war exists on earth there will be some danger that even the Nation which most ardently desires peace may be drawn into war. I have seen war. . . . I hate war."[47]

It Is Good to Be Here, Is It Not?

Wright, Thompson, and Ding Darling developed a close working relationship after Darling took over the Biological Survey in early 1934. Because of this, in part, relations between the Biological Survey and the Park Service improved. In February of 1935, for example, Darling sent Arno Cammerer a letter praising the Wildlife Division staff and offering his bureau's personnel to assist with "wildlife problems." The director thanked him in return. "With this basis of mutual confidence," wrote Cammerer, "coupled with the methods of cooperative consultation which you suggest, much will be accomplished in wildlife conservation."[48]

In the fall of 1934, while Wright was finishing up his report for the National Resources Board, he, Darling, Thompson, and Toll had lunch at the esteemed Cosmos Club in Washington, DC. Wright had a proposal for Darling.

Wright regaled Darling with stories about Montana's spectacular Centennial Valley. He talked of the region's lakes and marshes filled with waterfowl, and especially the recent discovery of a healthy population of trumpeter swans on the valley's Red Rock Lakes. "George said he would put up $500 for land acquisition there," Thompson recalled. "Roger Toll said he would match that, then Ding said, 'Wait a minute, I have some emergency money to buy refuge lands and I will have it looked at.'"[49] Soon thereafter, Darling started the process to secure a wildlife refuge in the region.

The following spring, after Wright received the winter census report on Yellowstone's trumpeter swan population from Frank W. Childs, assistant chief ranger, he wrote to Childs, copying eleven others, including the director, Darling, Toll, Grinnell, and Isabelle Story:

> There is little doubt in our minds but that all swans present in this region in mid-winter are trumpeters. The total of 96 trumpeter swans, even allowing for possible duplications, leads me to conclude that the National Park Service is seeing the reward of long anxious years of endeavor to bring the trumpeter swan back from the extreme vanishing point. . . . However, the efforts of those who are concerned for the safety of this largest and finest of all North American wildfowl, must not be relaxed, until Yellowstone and the adjacent region can boast, not one or two hundred, but several thousand trumpeter swans.[50]

In April of 1935, FDR created Red Rock Lakes Migratory Waterfowl Refuge by executive order. Two weeks after the refuge was created, Wright, Darling, and Thompson gave an NBC radio presentation entitled "The National Parks Program!" They discussed a variety of topics, including swans and Red Rock Lakes, then Wright wrapped up the half-hour presentation on a unifying note. "Let's get together often, Ding, and work out our mutual problems. If our two Services work jointly on wildlife conservation we can help to put that national program into effect and do a big, constructive thing for our country."[51]

About a week later Wright wrote a letter to Grinnell:

> In the summer of 1929 I had the great privilege of an introduction to Mr. and Mrs. Trumpeter Swan, aristocratic survivors of a once great race. On April 22 of this year, President Roosevelt signed the Executive Order establishing Red Rock Lakes Migratory Bird Refuge. This action . . . means that all the nesting grounds of the trumpeter swans in the United States and most of their winter habitats are under Federal jurisdiction. Recently, Mr. Darling told me of his feeling that if he accomplished nothing else during his administration, this one project would have made it all worth while. It is good to be here, is it not?[52]

The Last Wilderness

George Wright's declared first love was Yosemite. In Yellowstone, mean-while, he reveled in the wildlife, especially the trumpeter swans, the forests, the mountains, and the high and open vistas of America's senior park. Yet it was the southern Sierra Nevada, the "Kings and Kern country," that truly forged Wright's destiny as a young man. That landscape imprinted on every fiber of his being during each pack trip he undertook; it constantly pulled him back. He knew that wilderness intimately: deep and yawning canyons, smooth green streams and wild foaming rivers; turquoise-blue alpine lakes, excellent fly-fishing, and sharp-edged granitic peaks soaring to over fourteen thousand feet.

As early as 1933, in lieu of fieldwork at Crater Lake, Wright lobbied Bryant to let his team conduct an extensive faunal survey of California's Sequoia Na-tional Park and the Kings River drainage immediately to the north. "Sequoia," he wrote, "is a park concerning which we should have full wild life knowledge in order that we may properly develop the biotic reasons for the addition of the south and possibly middle forks of the King's River drainage to its total. If we could but do this and also secure the Mineral King area, which is tremen-dously valuable faunistically, we would have here one of the finest wild life parks in the whole system."[53]

The addition of the Kings River Canyon (as Wright often called it) to Se-quoia National Park had been discussed for many years. And for many years it had been shot down by San Joaquin Valley agricultural interests. In 1935, the campaign to preserve Kings Canyon—and the steadily lifting landscape reaching eastward into high country—began to heat up again with pending legislation. Yosemite's Superintendent Thomson, whose park was just north of Kings Canyon, wrote the director to implore the service to get more pre-pared for the fight, and he copied Wright, Sequoia's Superintendent White, and the Sierra Club's William E. Colby.[54]

"The opponents of national park status have been organized excellently all through these years," wrote Thomson, "whenever such status is proposed, those who head up the opposition merely press the button—and up pop the cattlemen's association, the wool growers' association, a portion of the irri-gationists, so-called sportsmen's organizations, etc." Each time, he wrote, the Park Service had been on the defensive. The western office and "friends in the fight" needed to be on the same page. They required a plan, a public relations campaign, and a program to reach out to the communities in the valley.[55]

Director Cammerer turned to Wright for guidance. In a note to Francis Farquhar, president of the Sierra Club, the director apologized for not traveling west personally to work on Kings Canyon, explaining that the "pyramiding of urgent projects on all fronts" related to CCC programs had made it impossible. "Mr. George M. Wright," he continued, "Chief of our Wildlife Division, has just returned recently to Berkeley from a year's assignment in the Washington office, and I am delegating him as my personal representative on the Kings Canyon project. He is fully informed of the past history of this project and will be able to give you the information which I would like to give if there were opportunity for us to discuss it." Cammerer sent a similar note to Colby, the longtime secretary of the Sierra Club and organizer of the club's annual High Country Trip into the Sierra.[56]

If Sequoia is to save a sample of the Sierra and Sierran life for all time, it should include the Kings River country immediately adjacent to the north, sufficient territory for deer winter range on the west, the Mineral King country on the south, and enough of the east side of the Sierra to provide for the few remaining mountain sheep and high-mountain fur-bearers. Especially is the Kings River country necessary, because it would provide the solid block of protected territory sufficient to maintain normal wild-life conditions.

FAUNA NO. 1[57]

One of the first actions Wright took was to request a legislative update from headquarters and copies of several park bills, in order to share the information with allies. Without them he felt "handicapped" and unable to make complete arguments for support. He cited his recent presentation to the board of governors of his beloved Cooper Ornithological Society, of which he was a recent regional president, and their logical reluctance to support bills they could not read. He was also to attend the Sierra Club's executive council meeting in San Francisco for the same purpose, and he wanted to prevent a similar reaction, as unlikely as that might be. In early July, Wright took another action and called on his old friend, Ansel Adams, to work on a campaign to educate the public and politicians about the potential Kings Canyon National Park.

Wright and Adams met in Yosemite Valley during early July to discuss strategy. They agreed that Wright should attend the Sierra Club's annual "encampment" that gathered prior to each High Country Trip. That year, the club planned another outing into Kings Canyon, so they met in Big Meadow (on Forest Service land downslope from the canyon) a week or so after talking in Yosemite. Adams and Wright continued their planning at Big Meadow, along with most of the club's senior staff and board members. It was a prolonged and informal conversation, mixed in with hikes, meals, and the traditional

Wright talking strategy with past Sierra Club president Philip Bernays (left) and acting club president Ernest Dawson (right) during a July 1935 High Country Trip to Kings Canyon, California. Proof print by Ansel Adams. © The Ansel Adams Publishing Rights Trust.

nightly campfire. Wright brought Lowell Sumner with him, and the two stayed with the outing for at least three days after leaving Big Meadow. They lingered at Horse Corral Meadows, up and into the canyon, settling a "quarter of a mile or so below Kanawyers." "While here," wrote Robert Lipman in the *Sierra Club Bulletin*, "we were fortunate indeed in having Mr. George Wright tell us of the proposed new Kings River National Park and Lowell Sumner, also of the National Park Service, give us an account of the predatory animals in this region."[58]

The two biologists turned around the next morning, no doubt reluctantly, and hiked down-canyon, as the group, including Adams, continued upward for several weeks of high-elevation adventure, an experience Wright knew well. Wright, however, was leaving with a plan. "As part of our program to stimulate national interest in Kings Canyon National Park," he wrote Cammerer upon his return to Berkeley, "it is proposed that the National Park Service shall sponsor a traveling exhibit of Ansel Adams' photographs of the southern Sierra. The key thought here is that Mr. Adams' work has such outstanding artistic quality that opportunity to display his pictures will be welcomed merely because of their craftsmanship, the subject matter being a mere incidental. He will, I feel sure, upon your invitation be willing to make and loan a collection of enlargements to us. It would be expected, of course, that the National Park Service would arrange all incidental expenses."[59]

In August of 1935, the Wright family repacked their household items and moved back to Washington, DC. "In the interests of good administration," Cammerer wrote Secretary Ickes, "it is desired to move Mr. Wright's headquarters from Berkeley, California to Washington, DC. His recent detail to the Washington Office has proved of immeasurable value."[60] This also meant that the Wildlife Division's office on the Berkeley campus was moving to the Underwood Building in San Francisco, to join other "technical branches" of the Park Service which were part of the Park Service's western office.

Wright felt obliged to write Grinnell. "I do deeply regret the necessity of putting the San Francisco Bay between our group and yours, but I am optimistic that this is not going to lessen the valuable and happy contacts we have enjoyed in the past. The Wildlife Division is not yet so big and strong that it can get along without your paternal and friendly eye, and I hope it never will be."[61]

As soon as he settled in back into Washington, Wright picked up the Kings Canyon conversation with Adams. Wright let Adams know that Acting Director Demaray approved the plan for financing the proposed traveling exhibit. "Dear Ansel," he wrote. "I am still very eager to get this project under way because of my belief that its effect will be beneficial to the establishment of Kings Canyon National Park."[62]

In addition to the traveling exhibit project, Wright also encouraged Adams to come to Washington the following January to lobby on behalf of the Sierra Club; to bring some of his prints to show politicians; and also to give a presentation at a conference on the National Park Service that Wright was organizing. At the same time, Wright asked Farquhar if the club could print some "attractive bulletins" that could be distributed in the spring during discussions of the park bill. The ground work had been done. Although Wright was now physically far away from the southern Sierra, that wilderness informed his every move.

I do not know that there is a particle of use in crying about it, but I cannot let your press clipping for the Director on the subject of Horse Corral Meadow development go by without registering my wail of dismay. The thought of automobiles in Horse Corral Meadow is truly heart-breaking to me. Sometimes I am sure that we lovers of the wilderness are fighting an absolutely losing battle. In fact I am always sure of it in my more sensible moments. The Kings River country is to me, personally, the last wilderness.

GEORGE WRIGHT TO SUPERINTENDENT JOHN H. WHITE[63]

It Looks Like a Resurrection

By January 1936, at the age of thirty-one, Wright had already made a significant impact within the Park Service, and his influence on national conservation issues was growing. With a trusted handful of colleagues he had created the wildlife survey while still just a fledgling ranger in Yosemite. He then personally funded the groundbreaking project as he further explored the western national parks with his two partners and friends, Ben Thompson and Joseph Dixon. With his emphasis on talking to "old-timers," coupled with disciplined and extensive fieldwork documented with detailed notes, Wright set a high bar for research. He created a professional and well-equipped core of biologists and wildlife technicians in the parks—now numbering twenty-seven staff—taught them the Grinnellian field note system, and encouragingly insisted on regular field reports.[1] He transformed the findings of this novel undertaking into two visionary publications, of which he was the principal author: *Fauna No. 1* and *Fauna No. 2*.

Wright became the primary researcher and advocate for saving the endangered trumpeter swan, while also initiating the much-needed reduction of Yellowstone's northern elk herd. And throughout the 1930s he doggedly worked to change first the service's views and then its policy regarding the indiscriminate slaughter of predators. The young biologist also moved to end the western parks' bear shows and to study the ongoing management issues created by humans and wildlife in "joint occupation of national parks." He believed that shipping animals between parks or to other locales was completely unnatural and harmful. Equally unnatural, to Wright's mind, were the artificial boundaries of many of the parks, which severely impacted the natural movement of species and the overall health of parks' wildlife and ecosystems.

The "jaded white-collar worker from Washington"—and loving husband and father—slowly adapted to his new role in Washington, DC. He expanded his thinking around the best ways to educate the public about wildlife in parks, and he widened his perspective on how to preserve that "resource." His shift from field biologist to a national-level conservation leader is evidenced by his work on the National Resources Board; he increasingly emphasized the need to preserve wilderness, with frequent references to Aldo Leopold and especially Bob Marshall, with whom he attended many of the same conferences. Wright was also tasked with leading the effort to create Kings Canyon National Park, and he teamed up with Ansel Adams and the Sierra Club to lay the groundwork for its eventual establishment. Wright's numerous publications and radio and conference presentations throughout 1934 and 1935, and his collaboration with Ding Darling to design a national organization to focus solely on America's wildlife, demonstrate a broadening of his views on wildlife, wilderness, and conservation. These beliefs and accomplishments would all come together and be on display during the first very busy two months of 1936.

That January, Beatrice Newcomer, Wright's trusted secretary, responded on his behalf to a letter from his sister-in-law, Bee's sister Jane, about the possibilities of a secretarial job in the Park Service's San Francisco office. "Mr. Wright will do his darndest—and you know that is a darn good darndest."[2] Jane was more than qualified for any administrative job with the service. Not only did she receive a master's degree in history from Berkeley, but she also earned her pilot's license at the age of twenty-three, becoming the sixty-sixth woman in the United States to do so.[3]

Newcomer's letter contained much more than a job update for Jane—it also provided a concise snapshot of Wright's work schedule and challenges for the first two months of the year. "I don't know how much you may have heard out there of ECW reorganization as it may affect our own situation," Newcomer offered, referring to the CCC. "No one seems yet to be very sure here, either, but there are all kinds of speculations."[4]

In fact, the previous year there had been discussions about having Assistant Director Conrad Wirth, who was in charge of the extensive state parks CCC program, absorb John Coffman's national park CCC responsibilities and his staff, in order to run the entire program under one administrator. Director Cammerer believed the management of two distinct CCC programs was proving wasteful, and Coffman wanted to concentrate exclusively on forest issues.[5] Wright believed, according to Newcomer, that instead of being reduced, "The division may in fact be increased. And when the fog clears, after that merger, we may be able to see more clearly just what positions are left filled and to be filled."[6]

In addition to major changes taking place with the CCC program, the entire National Park Service itself was undergoing a long-anticipated reorganization, which Wright was involved in. Some advocated for simply taking the regional CCC offices, increasing their bureaucratic footprint, and declaring a reimagined Park Service. Instead, the reorganization revolved around dividing the country into distinct sections, to be managed somewhat autonomously but with ultimate oversight and direction from Washington headquarters.[7]

The effort took months to finalize and even longer to implement. However, in the interim, former director Albright, as he was wont to do, penned a private note to Cammerer with his own detailed restructuring ideas. Albright believed two regions should be created, east and west. "I would put a man like Wright at San Francisco," Albright suggested. Make him an assistant director, he recommended, and let Wright manage the entire western United States. For the east, he wanted to see Wirth in charge, preferably based out of headquarters. "Both have traveled extensively," Albright opined, "make contacts easily, are thoroughly familiar with Washington policy and know the parks. Both have had some business experience."[8]

The other news item that Newcomer shared with Jane Ray was how incredibly busy Wright was. "In these rather wild moments," she wrote, "he is trying to hold quietly in his lap: the North American Wildlife Conference, the conference of the American Planning and Civic Association, the program for the assembled wild-life technicians, and the reorganization of the Wildlife Division itself under the new ECW set-up. You may imagine, it's an armful."[9]

Wright was instrumental in organizing the National Park Service's conference in late January, hosted by his colleagues at the American Planning and Civic Association and the Board of Directors of the National Conference on State Parks. The meeting was attended by Albright; Park Service brass; Henry Wallace, Secretary of Agriculture; Harold Ickes, Secretary of the Interior; Ding Darling; and the superintendents from Yosemite, Sequoia, Glacier, and Yellowstone National Parks, among many others.

The conference began with "Standards and Policies Applied in National Parks," and Director Cammerer kicked off the session with an address of the same title. The speech was a rather dry historical review of how national park standards and ideals were originally conceived, how they evolved over time, and their application for determining new parks, extensions to existing parks, and development within parks. However, because the predominant thread weaving through the conference was wilderness—What was it? Why was it needed? And how to preserve it?—the director eventually leaned in to take a jab at the Forest Service and attempt to clarify, once again, the Park Service's stance on wilderness preservation.

He brought up the Forest Service's primitive and recreation areas because, he stated, they did not exclude the very activities that would destroy their primeval character. "That is," he continued, "grazing, hunting, and mining are permitted, and logging and power developments will be permitted if and when they are economically feasible." The Park Service, he explained, needs to build roads and develop some portions of parks for visitors, and if done properly, "roads may be used as an implement of wilderness conservation." That is, leaning on his predecessors' explanations of wilderness in National Parks, everywhere you don't build a road in a park is default wilderness. "We do not want primeval areas modified; we do not want the parks tamed and gardened. A wilderness cannot be 'improved,' because its unimproved state is what we are trying to preserve."[10]

Wright followed Cammerer's presentation with "The Philosophy of Standards for National Parks," which took on a slightly different tone than the director's presentation.[11] "Human use," he began, "is predicated upon human need, and the term natural resource has no meaning whatsoever except as it relates to human use either present or future." Wright and Thompson had long written about the recreational and scientific value to humans of wildlife and wilderness as well as potential conflicts, as in *Fauna No. 1* and *Fauna No. 2*. However, after his experience on the National Resources Committee, Wright pivoted in his thinking to propose a more specific view: human needs had to be considered and incorporated in order to save wildlife and wilderness. The recreational needs of people, in *all* of their forms, must be of primary concern, as long as they didn't impair those natural resources and create conflicts with "joint occupation" inside national parks. There was a critical need, he believed, to not only educate Americans about wildlife and wilderness, but, more importantly, to cultivate a strong and dedicated constituency in order to protect those resources, as he had stated several months before in New York City.

He then shifted to wilderness preservation. Wright chastised those who wasted time arguing over which mountain was best, this one or that, while "echoes of the axes" ate into the hearts of "four-hundred-year-old monarch trees" on their slopes and made the argument moot. "Clearly enough," he proclaimed once again, "the remaining primeval areas of 1,000,000 acres or more should receive a unanimous vote."[12]

If we must in this century develop the last twenty million acres of a two-billion-acre
wilderness in order to sustain our civilization, then that civilization will surely crumble
in the succeeding century.

GEORGE WRIGHT[13]

The evening session on the same day was themed "Wilderness and Wildlife
in National Parks." Thompson gave an impressive talk simply called "Wilderness."[14] He opened by asking the essential question: What is wilderness? "It
generally means," he answered himself succinctly, "a large area without roads
or human habitations. It also means an area in biologically primeval condition." He then explained how nature and wilderness can be inexorably altered,
and ruined, "bit by bit." The incremental improvements in a park, created
for the benefit of humans, spun "an ever-tightening web" of roads, trails, and
campgrounds "through which the wilderness could not penetrate."[15]

Roger Toll emphasized that there was a "keener appreciation of the value
of Wilderness," as well as an acknowledgment that "what we call civilization
is steadily advancing into the wilderness." He explained that there were seven
large, roadless wilderness areas in Yellowstone, the smallest comprising two
hundred square miles; the two largest took in over six hundred square miles.
They should all be preserved, he argued, for wildlife as well as humans. "The
wilderness is there. Those who leave their automobile and go in search of the
primitive always find it." Yosemite's Superintendent Thomson and Sequoia's
Superintendent White mentioned how wilderness areas in parks "increasingly
attract" visitors, and yet threats remained from outside interests who wanted
to "open up" the parks further, principally by road building.[16]

Wright then gave his second talk of the day, "Wildlife in National Parks."
He lamented the "plight" of wildlife in the country as being "the most miser-
able of any of our resources, unless it be the soil itself." Wright admitted they'd
come a long way in the understanding of basic wildlife ecology over the past
thirty years, but, he stated candidly, "Wildlife management is a virgin field in
the United States. There is no one who knows much about it. The business
of wildlife management and wildlife administration is in its infancy." He believed the remedy was training more biologists and basic research.[17]

"An apathetic national consciousness condemned wildlife to walk the
plank. If there is to be a reprieve I, for one, firmly believe it is due to the heroic pleadings of our good friend who is a director of the American Planning
and Civic Association, Mr. Jay N. Darling," Wright stated, on an upbeat note.
"Darling's dramatic appeals have made willing listeners of the people of the

Nation. Our President, a good conservationist, giving heed to the wakening consciousness—I might say frankly, listening to Mr. Darling—has consented to call a North American Wildlife Conference in this city which will be held in about two weeks, from the third to the seventh of February."[18]

The NPS conference wrapped up the following morning with a session on pending national park legislation. It was there that thirty-four-year-old Ansel Adams, on a rare East Coast trip, would present what was likely his first major address on the national stage. The previous year, Wright had convinced the Sierra Club Board and Adams himself (who joined the club board in 1932) that attending the conference would be a strategic lobbying opportunity on behalf of Kings Canyon, because there was a park bill working its way through Congress.

Adams took advantage of the club-sponsored Washington trip to first board a train to New York City with a portfolio of his photographs. His goal was to meet with Alfred Stieglitz, one of the country's most influential living photographers and a fine-arts supporter, before swinging down to Washington, DC. It was a monumental few days in New York for Adams. His audience with Stieglitz, which took place in his studio—named *An American Place*—was a success. He was bestowed with a fall exhibit in the studio—a monumental achievement for a young photographer. And after meeting with the US representative of the Germany-based Zeiss camera company, he was gifted a treasure trove of equipment. While there, Adams also spent time with the artist Georgia O'Keefe, who was then married to Stieglitz; writer and critic Dorothy Parker; and several other well-known artists and benefactors. However, his mind soon turned to Washington, DC, and the Kings Canyon project.

On January 17, Adams wrote an ecstatic letter to his wife Virginia, back in San Francisco, with all of the details of his fruitful visit. He closed out the note with "Tell Francis [Farquhar] . . . I have done a lot of heavy research on the Kings' matter. Will stay with George Wright in Washington for a few days at least."[19] In another note, he let her know he had been "constantly working on the Kings' project; while I am to get a lot of immediate data from George in Washington, I feel that I have a full knowledge of the Sierra Club's past in relation to the matter. Tell Francis and Wm. E. [Colby] that I will do my durndest to put it over right."[20]

Adams's conference presentation, "Kings River Canyon Qualifies as a National Park," was impressive. Not only was it the longest lecture of the three-day meeting, but it was filled with new and dramatic information for the East Coast audience. It was truly eye-opening—in no small part because of his spectacular photographs that were on display while he talked. It is unclear exactly which Kings Canyon images he brought with him, but in the conference's published proceedings, at least two, *Mount Clarence King* and *Deadman Canyon–Roaring River*, are nicely reproduced. Another image, *Peak above Woods Lake*, was also part of the lobbying effort.[21]

Adams smartly opened with an explanation of the Sierra Club. "A lot of people," he stated, "think that we are something else than what we really are. We have a position in conservation which is much more important than the position we hold as a hiking or outdoor club." Offering up a good dose of club history, the Sierra Nevada in general, and Kings Canyon in particular, Adams spoke from years of experience exploring the mountains. "As a Nation," he said, "we are not sensitive to qualities of the more subtle variety such as the mood of the wilderness or the simple unmechanized existence offered us in the high places of the earth. In this as yet unspoiled wilderness may be found the very essence of the majesty and beauty of the Sierra Nevadas." And yet, he detailed, there was a long list of threats to the region.

The Forest Service claimed it could take on the Kings Canyon project and manage it well. But the Park Service disagreed, as did Adams: "We feel . . . that in an area such as the proposed Kings River National Park, it is the National Park Service's special responsibility to operate the protective and recreational phases of development, and to relate them to national park standards." Adams ended his speech with a call for cooperation between all the parties involved in the project, and, on behalf of the Sierra Club, he urged the government to create a national park there immediately. That night he wrote to Virginia again, from the Wright's house on O Street: "Everything went exceedingly well. The Conference was most successful and I am sure my Kings' River paper went over well. Tomorrow I am having breakfast with Albright, seeing Senator Johnson at 11, and having lunch with Eugene Meyer at 12. Cocktail party here at the Wrights at 6, and a big evening somewhere about town." Although the park bill failed that year (it would go on to succeed in 1940), Adams, the photographer *and* environmental activist, had emerged, with an assist from Wright's determined yet invisible hand.[22]

The Unflagging Energy of Jay Darling

The North American Wildlife Conference held its initial meeting during the first week of February 1936, in Washington, DC, just two weeks after the National Parks conference. The gathering, building on twenty-two years of previous meetings in New York City—which had focused primarily on game breeding, hunting, and fishing—was made possible by the transformation in

1935 of the American Game Association into the American Wildlife Institute, and the latter's focus on wildlife management. President Roosevelt worked with this new organization to announce the 1936 conference.

"My hope is that through this conference new cooperation between public and private interests, and between Canada, Mexico, and this country, will be developed," the president explained in a written greeting to the attendees. "It has long been my feeling that there has been lack of a full and complete public realization of our wildlife plight, of the urgency of it, and of the many social and economic values that wildlife has to our people."[23]

As Wright had alluded to two weeks before, it was Ding Darling who convinced FDR that such a conference was necessary—no doubt with help from Wright and many others. Throughout the previous year, both Darling and Wright had been declaring the need for an organization that focused solely on wildlife, and now they had their opportunity. The concept of the conference was unique. All state governors were invited, and each state was allowed twice as many delegates as they had senators and representatives. State fish and game agencies were summoned as well as a wide range of traditionally antagonistic interest groups representing hunting, fishing, farming, forestry, conservation, environmental concerns, and overall outdoor enthusiasts. Federal agencies were present as well as politicians. It was truly a public-private sector undertaking. And, because the conference was convened by the president, it wasn't surprising that, in the end, some 1,200 men and women delegates crammed into the Connecting Wing Auditorium on Constitution Avenue between Twelfth and Fourteenth Streets for opening remarks.

After introductory comments from the chair, F. A. Silcox, chief of the Forest Service, representatives from both Mexico and Canada—Juan Zinser and Hoyes Lloyd—spoke of their countries' enthusiasm for the international meeting. Darling also talked. "When I look across this surprisingly large audience and the great breadth of interests [that] have come to this conference, instead of being a crisis it looks like a resurrection to me," he paused, as the crowd reportedly applauded loudly.[24]

Over a four-day period, a who's who of wildlife experts, politicians, and private citizens presented an array of papers.[25] Secretary Ickes, Gifford Pinchot, Biological Survey chief Ira N. Gabrielson, Aldo Leopold, and Bob Marshall were there. Additionally, from the Wildlife Division, Thompson, Dixon, and George Baggley also participated and gave papers on trumpeter swans, Sierra Nevada bighorn, and the status of American grizzlies, respectively.

Wright's talk, "The National Park System in Relation to National Wildlife Restoration," began with more praise for Darling and what he had accomplished. "Spurred on by the unflagging energy of Jay Darling, the conference has painted the wildlife crisis in one and one-half days; brought lifelong foes together into a general federation of wildlife interests in one day; and now has us working frantically to complete the solution of the national wildlife restoration problem." Wright emphasized his recurring themes of the past year, stressing that the success of national parks to protect and manage wildlife depended on an effective national program of wildlife restoration, and vice versa.[26]

Let no man say to the other, "We will let you have your parks, your sanctuaries, and your refuges for sentimental enjoyment if you will just let us do as we please about the rest of the wildlife." Actually the shoe is on the other foot. Unless there can be a national program of wildlife restoration and conservation, then eventually the parks and sanctuaries will become drained of their wildlife and will become part of the growing biological desert of America.

GEORGE WRIGHT[27]

The delegates finally arrived at the central purpose of the meeting, which was to create a new organization: the General Wildlife Federation. By unanimous consent, they did so, and elected Darling as its first chair. A *New York Times* article proclaimed that "a new era in wild life conservation dawned today as 1,200 men and women from the forty-eight States forgot past differences and joined forces in a common cause." Another columnist wrote of "momentous events at the North American wildlife conference."[28]

The name quickly changed to the National Wildlife Federation, but the basic organizational premise carried through, as it does to this day: Local representatives from the public and private sectors gather to discuss regional wildlife issues and policy. Then, once a year, they convene to set policies and agendas they work on locally and nationally. Darling's and Wright's desired organization, focused solely on wildlife, had been created.

Chapo

The Chisos Mountains, roughly cradled by the meandering Rio Grande, rise 7,800 feet over the arid terrain of southern Texas. They are the rugged yet vibrant heart of Big Bend country. Further south, beyond the tapering range and the river, Mexico's expansive Chihuahuan Desert spreads out beyond the hazy tan horizon, and the peaks of the spectacular Sierra Del Carmen, southeast of the border town Boquillas, soar almost nine thousand feet above the pine-topped limestone cliffs and parched sand below. Considered as a whole and disregarding the international boundary that is the Rio Grande, it is a harsh and difficult landscape, yet biologically rich and expansively beautiful. Native peoples lived here for thousands of years: the Chisos, Mescalero Apache, and Comanche, among others. Álvar Nuñez Cabeza de Vaca, the wayward early sixteenth-century Spanish explorer, was the first of several Europeans who stumbled through the region in search of conquest and riches. Mexican revolutionary and guerrilla fighter Pancho Villa hid in the sinuous remote canyons here in the early twentieth century, evading the US Army. Big Bend's rich human history is only surpassed by its ecological wonders.[1]

Big Bend National Park had been planned for a handful of years in the 1930s and discussed by local boosters for many more than that—principally by Everett E. Townsend: native son, Texas Ranger, sheriff, and eventually, in 1932, a Texas state representative. Along with fellow representative Robert Wagstaff, legislation was introduced in early 1933 to create Big Bend State Park—the impetus for the eventual national park of the same name.[2]

In March of 1933, FDR's new government wrestled with the growing maelstrom of the failing US economy, skyrocketing unemployment, and natural disasters. The president pressed his staff and career federal employees to be imaginative, to think big, and to be aggressive, as long as it helped the American

people. That effort produced, in brief, the New Deal. Soil and water conservation, forests, and parks were part of that program. Texas's park advocates took
note and began lobbying the Park Service to consider Big Bend for national
park status.

The Park Service's first move was to dispatch Roger Toll, its senior in-
vestigator for potential new parks. In January 1934, he traveled to southern
Texas. After meeting Townsend and three others in the small town of Alpine,
he spent the next four days touring the northern shore of the Rio Grande
and exploring the Chisos, including a horseback ride, then hike, to the top of
7,832-foot Emory Peak. He delivered a report to the director stating that
"the Big Bend Country seems to be decidedly the outstanding scenic area of
Texas." He described the views from the south rim of the Chisos as "highly
spectacular," and Santa Elena, Mariscal, and Boquillas canyons—ranging from
1,000 to 1,500 feet deep—as "the chief scenic features of the area."[3]

Just as a matter of personal preference I wish that our proposed national park in Texas
would be called Rio Grande National Park rather than Big Bend National Park. The
western half of the United States is replete with places called Big Bend. If the park were
to be called Rio Grande National Park it would have a very euphonious and beautiful
name conveying not only some ideas as to its geographic location, but also calling to
mind colorful history and the relation to Mexico which it is hoped that the area will
have some day as part of an international park.

                    GEORGE WRIGHT[4]

Three months after Toll's reconnaissance, Wright sent Thompson to Big
Bend to survey the wildlife and flora. Thompson put in long days accompanied by local representatives, all the while discussing wildlife. He also kept a
detailed list of birds and plants. Upon his return to headquarters, he wrote an
upbeat preliminary report: "The fauna and flora of the region is extremely
interesting and the region picturesque. It is suggested from the wild life point
of view that the area is of national parks caliber and that the boundaries proposed by Superintendent Toll in his report are adequate to protect the wild
life of the area."[5]

The following year, the Park Service, with the help of the State Department, was in conversation with Mexico about organizing a joint expedition
to Big Bend in order to discuss an international park along the border as well
as parks and wildlife refuges to the west, in southern New Mexico and Arizona. It was an innovative concept but not unprecedented. In 1932, the United
States and Canada had created Waterton-Glacier International Peace Park,

straddling Montana and Alberta. It was the first of its kind, and Wright was a big fan after visiting in 1933.

Finally, in June 1935, the creation of Big Bend National Park was authorized, and activities intensified. Wirth telegrammed Toll and instructed him to organize a field party consisting of Toll, Wright, and several others, and to travel south quickly.[6] That trip never occurred, for unknown reasons, however a US-Mexico commission gathered in November to make plans for a joint expedition in February 1936.

The day after the North American Wildlife Conference, Wright received a letter from the secretary of state's office: "The President has approved your designation as a member of a Commission to represent the United States in conferences with a Mexican Commission to formulate policies and plans for the establishment and development of international parks, forest reserves and wild life refuges along the international boundary between Mexico and the United States."[7]

Wright, Toll, Wirth, and most of the US contingent rolled into Alpine, Texas, on a Southern Pacific train at 2:55 a.m. on February 17, 1936. A few hours later they were met by their Mexican counterparts, arriving from El Paso. The contingent from Mexico included three senior government representatives: Daniel F. Galicia, Juan F. Treviño, and Raúl Santos Ibarra. All three were from the Forestry, Game and Fisheries Department (where parks resided administratively). Galicia was the special deputy officer for the trip. He and Treviño were based in Mexico City. Ibarra worked out of Chihuahua City. They all hopped into cars, drove south through the gathering light to the CCC camp that had been established in the Chisos Mountains. They ate breakfast, then saddled up horses for a ride to the south rim of the mountains.[8]

Two key NPS staff who had also joined the trip were geologist Carroll H. Wegemann and chief photographer George A. Grant. Wegemann wrote an account of the outing: "Diary of a Trip from Alpine, Texas to the Big Bend and Old Mexico with the International Park Commission."[9] Though understandably filled with details of the stark and fascinating geology and landscape they traversed, he also included the group's basic itinerary and threw in a few nongeologic observations. Grant, meanwhile, recorded a treasure trove of impressive images.[10]

"Our party climbed the steep trail slowly," wrote Wegemann on their first day, "stopping frequently to breath the horses and to enjoy the view of the valley below and the glimpses of the desert which lies beyond the mountains." They stopped for lunch in Boot Springs Canyon, and after a full afternoon of additional exploring, including a ride along the southeast rim of the Chisos, they returned to the CCC camp for the evening.

Commission studying international parks and wildlife refuges along the US and Mexico border, Santa Elena Canyon, Big Bend, Texas, February 18, 1936. Wright is in the center, Roger Toll (hat off) is kneeling in front of Wright. Photograph by George Grant. Courtesy of NPS History Collection.

The next morning, they drove around the north side of the Chisos to the mouth of Santa Elena Canyon. They paused there, and Grant lined up everyone for an impressive group photograph.

After lunch in the small riverside community of Castolon, they proceeded to the Johnson Ranch. This remote outpost had been the Army Air Corps' base and landing field since the days of Pancho Villa's raids. The Johnsons maintained the field, put up the airmen when they arrived, and fed them.[11]

At Johnson's, the group waited for the arrival of two Vought Corsair Army biplanes. While doing so, it was decided that Toll, Wright, Galicia, and Ibarra should make the flights. The rest of the contingent drove on to the small settlement of Boquillas on the Rio Grande, to Juan and Chata Sada's well-known establishment. "We enjoyed an excellent dinner at the road ranch and store kept by Juan Sada at Boquillas on the American side," noted Wegemann. "The fliers joined us later and reported that they had seen most interesting country." Toll recorded that the group "Slept on dirt floor of a house without window glass. Rooster in same room."[12]

Wright in flight suit, Johnson's Field, Big Bend, Texas, February 18, 1936. Photograph by George Grant. Courtesy of Pamela Meléndez Wright Lloyd.

Crossing the Rio Grande near Boquillas, Big Bend, Texas, February 19, 1936. Photograph by George Grant. Courtesy of NPS History Collection.

The next morning, after a "good breakfast," the party took their four cars to the water's edge and drove into the Rio Grande at a known crossing point, purportedly shallow enough for automobiles. They wanted to reach the other half of Boquillas, on the Mexican side, in the state of Coahuila, and the territory beyond. One after another, all of the vehicles got stuck or slowly drifted sideways. They had to be towed across by a helpful group of Mexicans with horses, mules, and strong ropes. After they reached the Mexican side of the river and dried off, Toll records that they had to drain the oil from each vehicle because it was mixed with water, then refill the crankcases, and only then were they able to start their cars. They visited Boquillas before motoring south across a broad flat expanse with the Del Carmine range jutting up out of the desert to the east.[13]

They continued south, then east toward the Carmens, and continued on into the afternoon. Eventually they entered Cañon de Los Alamos, toward the southern tip of the range. "We followed the mountain canyon for some six miles," recorded Wegemann, "and finally reached a ranch house and four or five huts nearby. This was to be our headquarters for our stay in the Frontera."[14]

The commission members mounted horses the next morning and climbed into the Carmens with the goal of reaching Picacho Vaca, the range's second-highest peak—one that the geologist estimated to stretch up to ten thousand feet. By noon they had climbed up to timberline, then continued to Picacho Vaca. Standing among pines atop an ancient lava flow capping a sheer cliff, dropping about a quarter of a mile, the members spread out maps, gathered around, and oriented themselves. "The view," stated Wegemann, "was magnificent."[15]

The group eventually maneuvered their horses down off the mountain and spent the evening back at the ranch. In the morning, they said goodbye to their hosts, motored back down the canyon, then turned north toward the Rio Grande. Again, they experienced a troublesome crossing, which was only softened by yet another memorable meal at the Sada establishment. That evening they returned to the CCC camp.

On Saturday, February 22, they visited a quicksilver mining camp at Terlingua, crossed the Rio Grande at Lajitas—again with the aid of helpful Mexicans—and moved slowly, in the dark, up a dry streambed, attempting to reach the small town of San Carlos, in the state of Chihuahua.[16] "The sand was cut up by the passage of cars ahead of us," wrote Wegemann. "We were assisted by two Mexicans on saddle horses, a bottle of toquilla [sic] which they carried, increasing their good nature but hardly their efficiency." When they arrived, the entire town turned out to greet them, and then prepared a notable meal for the travelers. Toll records another night on a dirt floor, and in the morning the travelers "washed in street in front of 'hotel' with audience of 75 men."[17]

The next day was slightly less hectic. It was Sunday, so they visited the old church in town before driving northwest through the Sierra Rica, arriving in the pueblo of Ojinaga on the riverine border late in the afternoon, about forty miles northwest of Lajitas. They crossed over to the hamlet of Presidio, on the American side. After yet another celebratory dinner, this time put on jointly by the chambers of commerce of the two small towns, the commissioners slowly dispersed. Wegemann, Trevino, and Galicia left that night for Alpine to catch trains. Toll and Wright likely stayed in Presidio for the night, then drove north to Alpine in the morning.

For Wright, after a few hectic months in DC, the Big Bend trip was the perfect wilderness elixir he needed to refresh the spirit of the "jaded white-collar worker from Washington" he'd become, as he had written Ernest Coe after his Everglades trip. He enjoyed the Big Bend trip to the fullest—a fact that is abundantly clear in the images Grant captured of the men.

The next day in Alpine, Toll and Wright joined W. B. Bell (of the Biological Survey, who had been on the trip), and Walter B. McDougall (an NPS botanist, who had not joined them at Big Bend). The plan was for the foursome to continue west to the Hatchet Mountains in western New Mexico and eastern Arizona and then travel south over the border. From there, it was on to the Ajo Mountains of Arizona and the adjacent Mexican territory in order to assess those landscapes as potential parks or wildlife refuges. Many of the

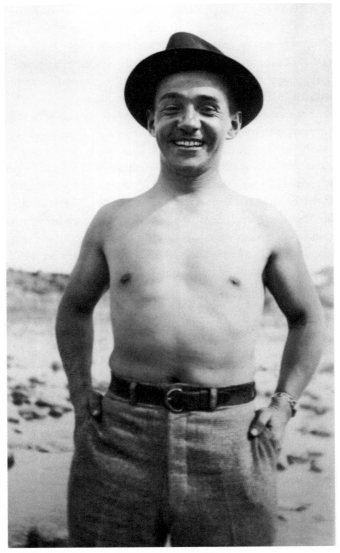

Last known photograph of Wright, Big Bend, Texas, February 23, 1936. Photograph by Roger Toll. Courtesy of Pamela Meléndez Wright Lloyd.

individuals on the Big Bend trip, particularly the Mexican contingent, were to follow and rendezvous in Tucson. From Alpine to El Paso, some two hundred miles, Wright and McDougall rode in one car, and Toll and Bell in another.[18]

The next morning, a Tuesday, Toll scribbled a quick note to his eldest child. "Hi Don! How's everything? We've a new name for George, 'Chappo,' meaning shorty. Leaving now."[19] Before departing for Tucson, they all agreed that Toll and Wright would drive in the lead car. Toll was behind the wheel.

At 10:55 a.m., Toll recorded a note in his travel log, "Las Cruces, N.M., turn west." They headed west on Highway 10, cutting through a flat landscape punctuated by the occasional low dry mountain range, on the northern edge of the Chihuahuan Desert. About two hours into their drive, seven miles outside of Deming, New Mexico, an oncoming car's tire blew out. In an instant, the vehicle swerved directly in front of Toll and Wright. Toll died upon impact, as did the teenager, Thomas Ohmar, driving the other car. Wright, fatally injured, fell unconscious. Ohmar's parents and two siblings were only slightly injured. McDougall and Bell, who had witnessed the entire horrific event, frantically extracted the three bodies from the mangled wreckage and transported them to a hospital in Deming. Doctors confirmed Toll and the boy were dead. Wright passed away at 1:30 in the afternoon.

In a daze, McDougall wired Herbert Maier, the regional NPS director, who was back in El Paso, and informed him about the accident. Maier immediately drove to Deming. "When the preliminaries were all worked out," McDougall recalled, "Herb Maier accompanied Roger Toll's body to Denver, which was his home, and I accompanied George Wright's body to Washington. Then I went to his house and talked to his wife."[20]

As Director Cammerer wrote to his staff, "There was nothing that Toll could do. The crash was upon them before he had time to think." In an instant, the National Park Service had lost two of its most important men.[21]

Everyone Is Inarticulate and Very Much Alone in the Face of Tragedy

Separated by half the country, a parallel grieving process unfolded for both families. Bee received countless letters, including personal notes from Eleanor Roosevelt and many politicians; biologists far and wide; the directors of natural history museums; the numerous conservation organizations Wright either belonged to or had worked with; and even a few people he had met only briefly, but who had been impacted deeply by the young biologist.

My Dear Mrs. Wright, I was terribly shocked when I learned of the sudden death of Mr. Wright. Officially he will be greatly missed because he brought to his work not only unusual qualifications but a sustained enthusiasm which is not attained by many of us. His personal qualities also were unusual and it was always a pleasure for me when our paths crossed officially. I shall miss him greatly.
HAROLD L. ICKES, SECRETARY OF THE INTERIOR[22]

Between his former colleagues, the correspondence was heart-wrenching. Joseph Dixon wrote Ding Darling two weeks after the accident. "The untimely and tragic death of our mutual friend George M. Wright, has left a vacancy in our ranks which will be exceedingly difficult or even impossible to fill. . . . I feel as though I had lost my own son."[23]

H. C. Bryant sent a letter to Joseph Grinnell. "We have been crushed by the tragic deaths of Roger Toll and George Wright. No two men have contributed more to high ideals than these two men! Where I shall turn to find a man to replace George Wright, I do not know."[24]

Carl Russell also wrote a letter to Wright's mentor at the Museum of Vertebrate Zoology:

> I feel an urge to write a note of sympathy to you, for I know that you are deeply affected by his untimely death. . . . George was at once my greatest inspiration and best sustaining friend in the office. I feel we have lost the conservationists in our official ranks who really combined understanding with action. I can think of no one who can replace George. I wish to join those many conservationists who are grateful to you for having shaped George Wright's early plans in such manner as to prepare him for the important part he has played in National Parks work and in American conservation in general. His period of activity was brief, but his contribution was exceedingly full and important. His regard for you was such that I believe your influences upon him meant much. I hope he expressed to you some of the sentiment and affection for you that I have heard him reveal.[25]

Bee and Marguerite Toll knew each other well and had always been very supportive of one another and their children. Their bond, however, was deeply strengthened after the tragedy. Bee wrote Marguerite about meeting Toll at the train station, with Wright and Thompson, before Toll and Wright left for their Big Bend trip.

> I can still see him sauntering down toward us, the "big boy," so remarkably fine—George, Ben, and I stood watching him and all said "Roger and you will have a glorious time." They were together. I find myself happy about yesterday—such a completely full and beautiful life as we four knew—not a regret and in our years together, we all found that which most never find—love. George and Roger shall continue on together, and we shall in this world. Very devoted love, Bee.[26]

Thompson also received many comforting letters and cards, in recognition of his deep bond and working relationship with Wright. "I find myself in no way capable of writing or saying what I feel about it," Ansel Adams offered to Thompson, "but I just wanted you to know I am thinking about you and wishing there was something in my power to do to help at this time." He then asked Thompson to contact him if there was anything he could do for Bee. "Everyone is inarticulate and very much alone in the face of tragedy."[27]

Thompson was very protective of Bee after the accident. She was reported to be tired, but calm and courageous. He spent little time in the office in those early months of grieving: he was making sure Bee was left undisturbed, except by those she wanted to see. He even took care of some of her correspondence and other logistics and spent time with the children, Sherry (as Charmaine was known) and Pam.[28] Bee's sister Jane Ray soon arrived from California, and their other sister Roberta reached the capital from Philadelphia. Shortly thereafter, their parents came from Southern California. And with Jessie Crawford's help, they slowly made it through, day by day.

Wright had requested to be cremated in his will. There was also to be no funeral and no flowers. Instead, the Sunday after his death, Bee invited close friends to their house on O Street. They played some of George's favorite music and celebrated his life. During the next few months, a quiet joy grew out of the deep sorrow: Thompson and Jane Ray began courting.

I think the only tribute worth paying is to try to make as much of life as they did. Roger and Togo left so much in all of us, and so much to do, perhaps that is the only answer.
BEN THOMPSON TO MRS. TOLL[29]

One important letter Bee asked Thompson to write on her behalf was to F. M. MacFarland at Stanford University. A renowned expert on marine mollusks, MacFarland was also the president of the San Francisco–based California Academy of Sciences from 1934 to 1946 and a longtime fellow of the esteemed institution. In the fall of 1935, he had traveled to Washington, DC, and met with Wright. Before leaving for Big Bend, Wright started a letter to MacFarland but never completed it. "Your visit of last fall found me as unprepared as I could probably be for consideration of your suggestion of the opportunities which would be those of the Director of the California Academy of Sciences or of the honor which would be mine. My chief interest, apart from my family, lies in giving such . . ."[30]

Thompson included a transcription of Wright's unfinished letter and informed MacFarland that the Wrights "had given careful consideration to the matter and, of course, were very happy with it." He continued that he didn't want to guess what Wright would have written, "but I know that his heart was always in conservation and scientific work for public benefit. We who knew him intimately will always be glad that he had the pleasure of that discussion with you."[31]

Bee, the girls, Jane, and Jessie stayed in Washington, DC, through the spring and early summer. Roberta returned to Philadelphia and her family, while the Rays continued to New York City for a few weeks. Bee organized the family's belongings and had them crated and transported to San Francisco; she had decided not to move back into the Berkeley house on Thousand Oaks. She tied up loose ends, said goodbye to her national parks friends, then all five of them traveled to New York City. From there, they boarded a steamer and sailed south to the Panama Canal, then north to California and a new life.

Shortly after arriving and settling into their new San Francisco home, Bee drove to the city of Colma, just south of San Francisco, and the Cypress Lawn Memorial Park. She found the grave of Cordelia Wright and scattered George Wright's ashes across Auntie's grave.

Two months later, Ben Thompson and Jane Ray got married. When their first son was born, they named him George Wright Thompson.

Probably more than any one person, George Wright was responsible for bringing about the healthy change in the general attitude toward the wild life problem which has recently developed. . . . George Wright was one of the most ardent advocates in the country for the preservation of the primitive outdoor values. Unlike so many primitive advocates, he did not think merely in terms of keeping out roads or preventing lumbering or stopping hunting. He thought in terms of the primitive whole, just as he thought in terms of wild life as a whole. . . . No one could ever ask for a better friend.

BOB MARSHALL[32]

Legacy

In any assessment of Wright's life, one thing is clear: his successes were the result of objectively excellent work, both in the field and within the bureaucracy—the impact of which was magnified and extended by his personal characteristics. His solid and extensive fieldwork, backed by the acuity and vision of his thinking as well as the persuasiveness of his personality, gave him a foundation of credibility even among those, including his Park Service peers, who disagreed with his recommendations.

George Wright was a most unusual and unforgettable personality. He was so sunny in disposition and so considerate of other people. He had a special knack for winning over people both inside and outside the National Park Service who were inclined at first to be skeptical of his goals and his program.

LOWELL SUMNER[1]

Having carefully laid this professional and political groundwork, Wright was able to convince Director Horace Albright of the importance of "scientific wildlife management," that it should be the primary focus for overall park management, and that the Park Service needed a professionally staffed Wildlife Division. With that done, he was, at the time of his death, well on his way to institutionalizing this ambitious program into all corners of the service while also advocating for wilderness protection. This is why Wright is universally acknowledged as the father of scientific research and resource management in the National Park Service.

As impressive as these accomplishments were, however, they only hint at the full significance of Wright's work. More broadly, the young biologist's fundamental achievement was to introduce new possibilities for how the National Park Service could conceptualize itself as well as the places under its care. Wright not only looked at specific wildlife problems in new and innovative ways, he also reimagined what wildlife meant in the context of the national parks, all the while attempting to improve relations between the Park Service, the Biological Survey, and the Forest Service. For Wright, wildlife and wilderness were integral parts of the larger ecological systems that extended beyond park boundaries, and that were themselves connected to and influenced by human society. This kind of broad systems thinking had simply never been broached by anyone involved with the national parks—and by very few others in the wider world of American conservation.

In hindsight, Wright's untimely death is made even more tragic in light of where his innovative thinking might have taken us. His friendship and support for many of the service's earliest female botanists and naturalists suggest a path he might have helped shape, one that respected women's rights and roles in the Park Service and biological work in general. Likewise his sensitivity to the cultural and material importance of bison to the Blackfeet tribe anticipates the recognition of the importance of Indigenous Peoples in the comanaging of wildlife in and around the parks.

After Wright's death the Wildlife Division was never the same. The staff attempted to carry on, but many of the deep-rooted cultural traditions within the Park Service that Wright had been able to keep in check reemerged and found new strength. Lowell Sumner confirmed this slow, if partial, return of old habits and beliefs: "No one else had George Wright's ability to placate and win over the opposing school of thought which, increasingly, was coming to feel that biologists were impractical, were unaware that 'parks are for people,' and were a hindrance to large scale plans for park development."[2] Historian Sellars agreed. "They were insurgents in a tradition-bound realm," he writes.[3] Wright signaled this early on in his 1929 letter to Dixon detailing the concept of the Wildlife Survey, while asking if he was visionary or crazy—he signed off with "More power to our side."

Still, as Sellars notes, it would be difficult to impossible "to trace all of the reasons" for the decline of the Wildlife Division and the diminished role of biologists in the National Park Service for decades to come. The New Deal and CCC efforts had emphasized the recreational and utilitarian aspects of the service's original mandate: in essence, roads and facilities for tourists. In other words: the exact opposite of the biologists' vision for the parks (though they, too, benefited from CCC funding). With Wright gone, that momentum, after years of New Deal infrastructure improvements, grew and the importance of the biologists and their emphasis on research and ecological considerations waned. Budgets adjusted accordingly and landscape architects, planners, and foresters ascended.

By 1939, only eleven biologists remained in the Park Service, down from a high of twenty-seven at the time of Wright's death.[4] Additionally, after a departmental reorganization, these remaining biologists, though they continued to work on park-related issues, were transferred to the Biological Survey. The following year, the Biological Survey and the Bureau of Fisheries combined to create the Fish and Wildlife Service. By the time the United States entered World War II in December 1941, only Victor Cahalane (then chief of the Wildlife Division), Joseph Dixon, Adolph Murie, and Lowell Sumner remained as active biologists in the Park Service. Ben Thompson had been promoted to special assistant to the director. With all resources focused on the war effort, CCC funding evaporated. And while *Fauna No. 1* remained the "working bible" for Park Service biologists at the time, soon after the war it went out of print, thereby slipping out of the collective consciousness of the next generation of biologists.

The war, stated Sumner, marked the end of an era.[5]

And yet Wright's rich legacy survived throughout the decades—manifested and referenced in varied ways. After the war, two mountains were named in his honor: one in Denali National Park, where he had ventured with Dixon at the age of twenty-two and discovered the surfbird nest; and the other, in Big Bend National Park, where he worked on an international park with colleagues from Mexico and spent his final days. Not far away from Wright Mountain in Big Bend is Toll Mountain, named after Wright's dear friend and colleague.

In the early 1960s, due to both internal and external pressures, the Park Service began to rethink the role and importance of biologists. Two committees were formed to focus on science and research in the parks: the Special Advisory Board on Wildlife Management and the Advisory Committee to the National Park Service on Research by the National Academy of Sciences–National Research Council. Lowell Sumner was chief adviser to the director at the time, and he insisted, time and again (as his wife and colleagues recall), that these committees just needed to read *Fauna No. 1* and *Fauna No. 2* because "George Wright had all this figured out years ago."[6]

The concerns and recommendations delivered by the first committee—known as the Leopold Report—are strikingly similar to those of *Fauna No. 1* and *Fauna No. 2*. Titled "Wildlife Management in the National Parks," the brief report discussed how parks should represent "a vignette of primitive

America"; emphasized the importance of predators and endangered species; warned of excessive ungulate populations and overgrazing issues; the need for natural fires in the parks; that zoos and fenced enclosures for park animals should be forbidden; that roads and developments need to be limited; that wilderness areas should be "permanently zoned"; and more.[7]

The second committee, chaired by William J. Robbins, echoed many of the points of the Leopold Report but was more detailed and far more critical of the Park Service and its almost total abandonment of research and science. "Research by the National Park Service has lacked continuity, coordination, and depth. It has been marked by expediency rather than by long-term considerations." After a brief but concise review of Wright's contributions in the 1930s, the report offered a series of recommendations, including the need to create a "research unit" in the Park Service to "serve as consultant on natural history problems for the entire National Park System." A research program was necessary for each park, the reported continued, and all findings should be published.[8]

Other committees with a national focus on predators and pesticides formed during this period, and they included parks as well as other federal lands in their investigation. Combined, all of these reports provided tangible evidence for Sumner's claim: Wright had, in fact, figured it all out—decades before.[9]

The number of biologists in the Park Service increased with time, but slowly. What is more, these new service biologists often found themselves facing the very same issues Wright and his colleagues had battled in the 1930s, as Jonathan Jarvis discussed in his foreword. In 1980, this realization led two of the Park Service's top scientists, Bob Linn and Ted Sudia, to reach back some fifty years for inspiration from Wright and his work to create the George Wright Society, a nonprofit organization designed "to promote research, the synthesis of information, and the useful dissemination of results to management, policy-makers and the public in whose hands the ultimate fate of parks, historic sites and reserves will rest."[10]

Twenty years later, in 2010, the Park Service created the George Meléndez Wright climate internship and fellowship initiatives. The programs, stated NPS Director Jarvis, were "named in honor of the early 20th-century National Park Service biologist who promoted the idea of science-based research as central to preservation of national parks and who envisioned a system of protected areas to promote ecosystem health and resilience."[11]

The next year, the Schoodic Institute at Acadia National Park dedicated the George M. Wright Hall on its campus as the "epicenter for research" for staff scientists, educators, and field technicians. And in 2020, after a decade of work, the Park Service adopted the "RAD (Resist-Accept-Direct) decision framework" to assess and make management decisions about rapid ecosystem changes within parks impacted by climate change. Wright is quoted and referenced throughout the framework, including his "prescient statement" that "protection, far from being the magic touch which healed all wounds, was unconsciously just the first step on a long road winding through years of endeavor toward a goal too far to reach, yet always shining ahead as a magnificent ideal."[12]

In 2021, after more than a year of work under pandemic protocols, over 4,600 images from the Wildlife Division's relatively unknown archive of some 11,000 photographs were made available for the first time through NPS's History Collection website—with plans to publish the entire collection at a later date. The images—many captured by Dixon, Wright, and Thompson—are an invaluable resource for the NPS; other federal, state, and tribal land managers; academics and other researchers; and the general public. Their potential use for biological inventories, ecological studies, and new photographic surveys is enormous.[13]

Perhaps the most meaningful and fitting testament to Wright's legacy, however, is an ongoing collaborative effort to name a large and beautifully rugged landscape within Big Bend National Park the George Meléndez Wright Wilderness Area.[14]

I believe that future generations will be grateful for the tracts of primitive area, or wilderness, which we can save in our national parks without hindering our own pleasure in the least.

GEORGE WRIGHT[15]

These are all developments that prove scientific research and informed resource management in the parks, though they have at times proceeded fitfully since Wright's death, are now, in the third decade of the twenty-first century, indispensable core elements of an agency that is staring down the existential threat of climate change, among other serious ecological and administrative challenges.

When looking back at the figure of this young, visionary biologist, there is both much to celebrate and much to wish for. His was a life that was at once full to the brim—maybe as full as one could ever hope for—yet cut short by that tragic accident on a lonely stretch of New Mexico highway. We can never know how George Meléndez Wright might have changed the future of wild-life, wilderness, and the National Parks—but his legacy is one that will surely continue for decades to come.

———————

Once I heard the "chiming" song of the Mearns Quail. The several notes, all of the same quality and equally spaced are silvery clear and totally sweet, soft and yet penetrating. The song came from no direction. It was just on the air. About it there was a timeless quality. There was no beginning and never an end, just the voice of eternity in the wind on the desert.

GEORGE WRIGHT[16]

———————

On a Good Day

In October of 1987, my wife Jeannie and I traveled to Glenwood, New Mexico, to visit with Ben and Jane Thompson—or Snook, as she was also known to the family. Bee, the grandmother who left Jeannie with many memories, had died the year before. Jeannie resembles her grandmother Bee, and although the Thompsons had known Jeannie since childhood, it was no doubt both fun and nostalgic for Ben and Snook to spend time with her. The weather was spectacular at that time of year—cool clear nights gave way to warm dry days. It was an unforgettable time, going for drives through the spectacular landscape of southwestern New Mexico, sharing meals, and talking—lots and lots of talking. Ben and Jane were quiet, gentle, humble, and caring people. It was obvious to us that they enjoyed each other's company, that they could still laugh at each other, and that they were still very much in love after fifty-one years of marriage.

On the last evening of our stay, Snook and Jeannie were in the kitchen talking, while Ben and I were in the living room. I was taping another brief interview with him about the early days of the wildlife survey with George and Joe.

Why was George special, and how was he different, I asked? Ben, who was eighty-three at the time, paused, then said:

> People reacted positively to him. I don't think he had any enemies. Wherever he went, very quickly he was welcomed. And, I think that had something to do with it. Also, going ahead with his ideas, they weren't universally accepted in the parks at that time. There were a number of longtime employees, super-intendents, chief rangers, and others, who liked the good 'ol days of predatory animal control, and corralling the ungulates so the public could see them, like the buffalo, and feeding the elk so they'd concentrate for viewing, feeding the

bears at feeding stations and making a big show of it. There was all of that to overcome. And, to make progress with that, and have them still like you, was quite an accomplishment. Joe and I didn't have that kind of personality. And, we knew it. But George did have it. It was a gift of his character.[1]

Finally, I asked, if George had lived, how might he have continued to impact the Park Service and wildlife conservation in the United States? "I've thought about that myself many times," replied Ben, slowly, "and I have no way of measuring it." He paused for a while, looking off to the side. "As somebody else has said, history does not reveal her alternatives. I think it could have been different had he lived. I think so. But I have no way of knowing."

It was obvious to me, as I asked Ben these questions, and as he methodically and thoughtfully responded, that he still missed his friend George, after all those years. His memories evoked feelings that were at once proud, happy, and melancholic. A few times, he had no answer, and simply smiled, saying, "Sorry, the memory is a bit fuzzy. You'll have to ask Lowell about that." Lowell Sumner and his wife lived just up the valley from the Thompsons.

There were several long, yet comfortable, pauses in our conversation. As the cheerful sounds of Snook and Jeannie floated down the hallway, Ben, slightly bent over in his chair—his bolo tie hanging, just off his chest, pendulum-like— worked his gnarled and weathered hands in his lap, one over another, as if trying to conjure memories from a distant time. The call to dinner reached our ears, but the two of us continued sitting easily for a while, facing each other. A hint of a smile rose across his face, like a gradual winter sunrise. It brightened. He straightened and shifted to his right, pointing a slightly bent index finger out a large window overlooking the San Francisco River and the juniper-covered mountains rising toward Webster Mesa in the distance. A pair of seasoned binoculars lay below the window, resting on a bed of well-used and neatly stacked books.

"On a good day," he said, turning back to me, his smile now complete, "you can see bighorns over there."

Forever the field man.

Acknowledgments

This book is dedicated to my mother-in-law, Pamela Meléndez Wright Lloyd. However, my daughter Sami comes in a very close second. From her home in Berlin, where she is a writer, she listened to every word I spoke and read every word I wrote. I could not have finished this book without her insightful edits and suggestions. The encouraging support of my wife Jeannie Lloyd and our eldest daughter Sarah (from distant Copenhagen) also powered me through. Jeannie and her mother Pam (who also read the manuscript) accompanied me down many "rabbit holes," researching countless bits of information to our delight, edification, and frustration. And I would be remiss if I didn't mention our dear crazy deaf dog Tula, who spent many long days keeping me company in my office.

David Harmon, executive director of the George Wright Society, was a constant source of support and information. He also reviewed the manuscript and suggested excellent edits and additions to the text. I met Karen Bodding, a Wright family historian, when I started writing in earnest in 2019, thanks to my sister Robin Emory who is a passionate amateur genealogist. Karen had an amazing ability to track down the most minute but critical tidbits about George Wright's extended family—and anyone else I wanted to know about. Her research was invaluable. The staff of UC Berkeley's Museum of Vertebrate Zoology—Carla Cicero, Christina Velazquez Fidler (now with the Bancroft Library), Michelle Koo, and James Patton, professor emeritus—helped me for years. They have been patient and generous with their time and information.

Jonathan Jarvis, former director of the National Park Service, was not only supportive of my work but also introduced me to Joe Calamia at the University of Chicago Press and wrote the foreword to this book. I'm forever in his debt. Dayton Duncan, an award-winning writer and documentary filmmaker, first "met" Wright when he worked with Ken Burns to write and coproduce *The National Parks: America's Best Idea*. He too would occasionally check in with encouraging nudges, asking how the biography was developing. In his own quiet way, the late historian Richard West Sellars pushed me to write this book, strategically sending me enticing Wright-related documents he discovered as he researched *Preserving Nature in the National Parks: A History*. I hope I came even somewhat close to how Dick would have shined in writing about Wright. Copy editor Susan Olin improved this work by performing a detailed and precise review of the manuscript and notes. In the 1980s, when I was attempting to become a full-time writer, the work of the late Barry Lopez was inspirational. He became a distant mentor of mine—our few conversations and his brief letters and postcards of kind and gentle encouragement over the years kept hope alive.

I have been thinking about this book for over thirty years, and I worked on it in fits and starts, here and there. When I started getting serious about my research in 2014, I was introduced to Janet A. McDonnell, who carried out research for me at the National Archives in College Park, Maryland. She did an amazing job, particularly regarding Big Bend. I went back to her in 2018 but she was busy with other projects, so she introduced me to Joan Zenzen. Joan, an independent public historian with deep knowledge of the NPS, struck gold for me several times. Their expertise, time, and discoveries were invaluable. My neighbor, author, and friend Dr. Thomas Singer took great interest in the project. Our end-of-driveway conversations were fortifying—particularly his thoughts on what it means for someone to be a visionary.

Wright's mother, Mercedes Meléndez Ramírez, came from a very large family in El Salvador. Wright had many relatives there, including his brother Juan's family. Through family connections (and one chance encounter) I met several of Wright's relatives and corresponded with others. Amalia Trigueros, a cousin of Pam Lloyd, was extremely helpful with information and connections to other Meléndez family members, including Carlos Borja. Julio Rank Wright introduced me to his uncle and cousin in El Salvador, Juan T. Wright Castro and Johnny T. Wright Sol, the grandson and great-grandson of George Wright's brother. They provided me with copies of invaluable family correspondence and documents. Their contribution to the book was vital.

Relatives of Wright's Park Service partners, Ben Thompson and Joseph Dixon, also provided key information for this biography. Ben's son, the late Howie Thompson (retired from the NPS) gave me a copy of his father's field notes from the wildlife survey and answered numerous questions about his parents' lives. Howie's daughter, Kathleen Graham, also helped with family documents. I interviewed two of Dixon's children in 2000, Mary Dixon Rhyne and the David Dixon (now both deceased). Mary's son, Weaver, shared unique information about his grandfather, and David's son Paul also helped.

And I'd like to thank the following archivists, researchers, librarians, specialists, and experts for answering my questions and helping me obtain documents and publications: Pattie Apple; Bancroft Library staff, UC Berkeley; Robert W. Blythe; David E. Brown; Bonnie Ciolino, Everglades National Park; Daniel Davis, Utah State University; Ren and Helen Davis; Therese Dunn, Sierra Club; Ward Eldredge, Sequoia and Kings Canyon National Parks; Alaska geographer Thom Eley; Claudia Eshoo, Jonathan Jones, Mark Budak, Lowell High School; Anne Foster, Yellowstone Heritage and Research Center; Jamie Henderson, California Historical Society; Steve Henrikson, Alaska State Museum; Laurel Kearns, Drew Theological School; John LaMont, Seattle Public Library; David Landow and Jeff Brashares, Buick Heritage Alliance; David Larson, professor emeritus, California State University, East Bay; James G. Lewis, Forest History Society; Ariel Lugo and Sylvia Zavala Trías, International Institute of Tropical Forestry; Rob Malone; Tom McAnear, National Archives and Records Administration; Meredith Mann, New York Public Library; Becky Miller, Natural Resources and Environmental Sciences Librarian, UC Berkeley; Charles Miller, National Archives and Records Administration; Lindsay Moen and Jenna Silver, University of Iowa; Wade V. Myers, NPS, Harpers Ferry Center for Media Services; Ernesto Ortega, retired NPS; David Parsons; Claudia Rice, Trustee and General Manager, The Ansel Adams Publishing Rights Trust; Paul Rogers and Amy McKinney, Yosemite National Park; Nancy Russell, NPS, Harpers Ferry Center for Media Services; Virginia Sanchez, Yosemite National Park; Society of American Foresters staff; Stuart Schwartz and the Image Flow staff; Alan Stangenberger, UC Berkeley Forestry, retired; Paul Starrs, professor emeritus, University of Nevada, Reno; Leslie Squyres, Ansel Adams Archive, University of Arizona, retired; Shelley Tanenbaum, Quaker Earthcare Witness; Robert Timm, American Association of Mammalogists; Jeremiah Trimble, Harvard Museum of Comparative Zoology; Robert D. Turner, curator emeritus, Royal BC Museum; Emily Wakild, Boise State University; Liz Williams, cultural anthropologist/tribal liaison, Yosemite National Park; Theresa Wolner, indexer.

Notes

Prologue

1. Ben H. Thompson, interview with the author, Glenwood, New Mexico, October 17, 1987; all quotes within this prologue are from this interview.

Chapter One

1. George M. Wright, "The Magic Window," *The Gull: Journal of the Audubon Society of the Pacific* 16, no. 7 (July 1934): 1–2.

2. His older brother John, thirteen, is not mentioned.

3. George M. Wright, letter received, *The Gull: Journal of the Audubon Society of the Pacific* 14, no. 11 (November 1933): 2. Wright wrote a letter to his friends at the San Francisco–based Audubon Association of the Pacific in 1932, two years before he wrote "The Magic Window," stating, "Most of my early recollections of bird life are centered around the happy days spent in the field with members of the Audubon Society. In going over my early records, I find a list of birds seen from my home at 2617 Laguna Street, San Francisco. This list was compiled during the years of 1916–19 inclusive. In view of the rapidly changing conditions affecting bird life in San Francisco, it seems to me that this list already has an historical value and that your organization above any other, should be the repository of the record." This is followed by his list of birds. *The Gull: Journal of the Audubon Society of the Pacific* 14, no. 11 (November 1932). The Audubon Association of the Pacific was the precursor to today's Golden Gate Audubon Society, now based out of Berkeley.

4. The Wright and Meléndez families demonstrate a common if somewhat confusing tendency to have many of the same names passed down over generations. John Tennant Wright (1801–68), the great-grandfather of George Meléndez Wright, sailed to New York City from Darlington, England, working on a boat at the age of ten. He had ten children. The Wright Line of steamships was created by his sons John Tennant Wright Jr. (1826–1911); Thomas Wright (1828–95); and George Sutton Wright (1832–1905). George Sutton Wright named his son John Tennant Wright (1857–1912)—he was George Meléndez Wright's father—who, in turn, named his eldest son John Tennant Wright (1896–1952)—George Meléndez Wright's older brother. George's older brother married in El Salvador, and his living grandson and great-grandson are, respectively, John Wright Castro and Johnny Wright Sol, of San Salvador.

5. *Lewis & Dryden's Marine History of the Pacific Northwest* (Portland, OR: Lewis and Dryden Printing, 1895), 66, https://archive.org/details/bub_gb_seRDAAAAYAAJ; Erik Heyl, *Early American Steamers*, vol. 1, *1888–1973* (Buffalo, NY: 1953), 64, 209, 210, 415, https://hdl.handle.net/2027/mdp.39015024193131; *Seattle Post-Intelligencer*, November 19, 1895, 8. In an obituary for Captain Thomas Wright in the *Seattle Post-Intelligencer*, it is noted that he was the son of Captain John T. Wright, "a well-known sea captain," and was known as "Old Capt. Bully Wright." And, like his father, Thomas Wright "made at least two fortunes in his lifetime and lost them."

6. Port of San Francisco, "Port History," https://sfport.com/port-history; James P. Delgado, *Gold Rush Port: The Maritime Archeology of San Francisco's Waterfront* (Berkeley: University of California Press, 2009), 52–53, 60–77, 37.

7. That is the rough equivalent of $150,000 a month in 2022 dollars. It is not clear if all of the Wright Line ships were idled or for how many years. John T. Wright, "Early Navigation in California Waters," 1826, Oral History [ca. 1887], Bancroft Library, Hubert Howe Bancroft collection.

8. "Presidents of El Salvador," https://en.wikipedia.org; see also "La Madre de la Dinastía, Mercedes R. De Meléndez," *La Prensa Gráfica*, San Salvador, El Salvador, May 12, 2002.

9. B. Olney Hough, *American Exporter's Trade Directory* (New York: Johnston Export Publishing, 1915), 199, https://hdl.handle.net/2027/nyp.33433016908067.

10. *Morning Call* (San Francisco), January 20, 1892, 3. Chronicling America: Historic American Newspapers, Library of Congress, https://chroniclingamerica.loc.gov/lccn/sn94052989/1892-01-20/ed-1/seq-3/.

11. Port of San Francisco, 173.

12. *Morning Call*, 3. The *Morning Call*'s social column throughout the 1890s references the Wrights' activities, including trips to Cazadero on the Russian River in Northern California, musical events where the younger Meléndez girls performed, and other outings.

13. The Wright brothers were also often referred to in correspondence by their Spanish names: Juan Tennant Wright, Jorge Meléndez Wright, and Carlos Antonio Wright.

14. George Sutton Wright, John T. Wright's father, died in June 1905 in San Francisco. When his first wife, Louise Ward Wright, had died in 1860, he married her sister, Cordelia Ward. They had no children together. Cordelia Ward Wright was technically George Meléndez Wright's step-grandmother, but she was commonly referred to as a great aunt and therefore Auntie.

15. 1910 United States Federal Census. San Francisco Assembly District 41, San Francisco, California, roll T624_101; page 2A; enumeration district: 0275; FHL microfilm: 1374114. National Archives and Records Administration (hereafter NARA), Washington, DC; roll 105; roll 0105—certificates: 23575–24474, April 5, 1910–April 13, 1910, Selected Passports. National Archives, Washington, DC.

16. John T. Wright to Carmen de Letona, March 24, 1912, letter held by Carlos Borja, San Salvador, El Salvador. Carlos Borja is Carmen de Letona's grandson. John T. Wright to Carmen de Letona, May 26, 1912, letter held by John Wright Castro and Johnny Wright Sol, San Salvador, El Salvador. John and Johnny are respectively the grandson and great-grandson of George Wright's brother, John T. Wright.

17. National Resources Board, *A Report on National Planning and Public Works in Relation to Natural Resources and Including Land Use and Water Resources with Findings and Recommendations*, December 1, 1934, Submitted to the President in Accordance with Executive Order No. 6777, June 30, 1934 (Washington, DC: Government Printing Office, 1934), 144, https://archive.org/details/reportonnational1934unitrich. All quotes from government reports have been reproduced exactly, including the original spelling and punctuation.

18. National Park Service, "The Panama-Pacific International Exhibition," https://www.nps .gov/articles/the-panama-pacific-international-exhibition.htm; California Historical Society, "National Parks at the PPIE," https://ppie100.org/parks-and-the-ppie/.

19. Ben H. Thompson, interview with the author, Glenwood, New Mexico, October 17, 1987.

20. George M. Wright, "The Lowell High Audubon Society," *The Lowell*, Lowell High School, San Francisco, vol. 36, no. 1, August 17, 1920, 2.

21. For a brief biography of Bryant, see https://www.nps.gov/parkhistory/online_books/son tag/bryant.htm.

22. H. C. Bryant, "With Opened Eyes," *The Spokesman*, University of California Extension Division, vol. 2, no. 2, December 1923, 28.

23. San Francisco Bay Area Council, "Camp Dimond History 1919–1948," http://www.sfbac -history.org/Dimond-History.html; Oakland Wiki, "Camp Dimond, Boy Scouts of America," https://localwiki.org/oakland/Camp_Dimond%2C_Boy_Scouts_of_America.

24. George M. Wright, Application for promotion, National Park Service, 1933. This document, along with numerous other personnel documents, was obtained through a Freedom of Information/Privacy Act request in 1985 by George Wright's eldest daughter, Sherry Wright Brichetto (deceased). Documents held by Pamela Meléndez Wright Lloyd.

25. George M. Wright, "Cougar Surprised at Well-Stocked Larder," *Journal of Mammalogy* 15, no. 4 (November 1934): 321, https://doi.org/10.1093/jmammal/15.4.321.

26. Wright, "Cougar Surprised," 321.

27. Wright, "Magic Window," 1–2.

Chapter Two

1. Ben H. Thompson, interview with the author, Glenwood, New Mexico, October 17, 1987.

2. *Delta Upsilon Quarterly*, official organ of the fraternity, vol. 41, no. 3 (July 1928): 294.

3. Gareth Kellam to Frederick Kellam, June 10, 1926. Letter held by Pamela Meléndez Wright Lloyd.

4. National Park Service, "Togo," November 28, 2017, https://www.nps.gov/people/togo.htm.

5. James G. Lewis, Forest History Association, email to the author, August 5, 2019.

6. The author is indebted to Dr. James Lewis, historian at the Forest History Society in Durham, North Carolina, for his insights and suggested readings on the nexus between forestry and conservation in the early twentieth century. This section of Forest Service history relied on the following sources: James G. Lewis, *The Forest Service and the Greatest Good: A Centennial History* (Durham, NC: Forest History Society, 2005), 24–55; Samuel P. Hays, *Conservation and the Gospel of Efficiency: The Progressive Conservation Movement, 1890–1920* (Cambridge, MA: Harvard University Press, 1959), 27–48; Harold K. Steen, *The US Forest Service: A History*, Centennial Edition (Seattle: Forest History Society in association with University of Washington Press, 2004), 69–102; Gerald W. Williams, *The USDA Forest Service—The First Century* (FS-650; Washington, DC: USDA Forest Service, Office of Communications, 2005), https://www.fs.fed .us/sites/default/files/media/2015/06/The_USDA_Forest_Service_TheFirstCentury.pdf.

7. John C. Miles, *Wilderness in National Parks: Playground or Preserve* (Seattle: University of Washington Press, 2009), 18–26.

8. Douglas W. MacCleery, *American Forests: A History of Resiliency and Recovery*, Issues Series (Durham, NC: Forest History Society, 2011), 31–53.

9. James G. Lewis, "April 15, 1920: Greeley Named Forest Service Chief," April 15, 2009, https://foresthistory.org/april-15-1920-new-forest-service-chief-named/.

10. John A. Ford, "Here Is Colonel W. B. Greeley, the Government's Chief Forester, Who Has Risen from the Ranks, He Wants to Make the Nation's Forests Serve You Better," US Department of Agriculture, Division of Publications Office of Information, news release, October 11, 1920, 6. https://foresthistory.org/wp-content/uploads/2017/01/Greeley_pressrelease.pdf.

11. A. E. Wieslander, *University of California Journal of Agriculture* 1, no. 10 (May 1914): 10.

12. Paul Casamajor, ed., *Forestry Education at the University of California, Berkeley: The First Fifty Years* , (Berkeley: California Alumni Foresters, 1965), 3.

13. When Wright was at Berkeley, the mandatory summer session was called Camp Califor-est. "Sierra Nevada" is Spanish for, literally and aptly, a snow-covered saw.

14. *Journal of Forestry* 53, no. 11 (November 1955): 852.

15. Casamajor, 42. There are no known collected papers of Mulford. It is known that Mulford lost personal belongings and some papers in a 1923 Berkeley fire, but that does not account for his remaining years at the university. In comparison, the Museum of Vertebrate Zoology safe-guards a robust set of original correspondence from Grinnell, Dixon, Thompson, and Wright, and some from Mulford as well as many others associated with the museum. In 1946, a year before Mulford's retirement, the Division of Forestry was elevated to a full department, and the University of California, Berkeley School of Forestry was created, followed quickly by the con-struction of a new forestry building, appropriately named Mulford Hall.

16. Hilda W. Grinnell, "Joseph Grinnell: 1877-1939," *The Condor* 42, no. 1 (January–February 1940): 4, https://www.mammalogy.org/uploads/HGrinnell1940.pdf.

17. As cited in Barbara R. Stein, *On Her Own Terms: Annie Montague Alexander and the Rise of Science in the American West* (Berkeley: University of California Press, 2001), 64.

18. Annie Alexander was extremely important to scientific expeditions and the creation of both the Museum of Vertebrate Zoology and the Museum of Paleontology at Berkeley, among many other achievements, including her own extensive fieldwork, collections, and sponsorships. In addition to paying for the MVZ and Joseph Grinnell's salary, she also financially assisted Joseph Dixon throughout the years.

19. Kenneth Brower, "Disturbing Yosemite," *California Magazine*, Cal Alumni Association, UCBerkeley,(May–June2006),https://alumni.berkeley.edu/california-magazine/may-june-2006 -whats-happened-animals-yosemite/disturbing-yosemite; a description of the Yosemite tran-sect survey can be found at http://mvz.berkeley.edu/Grinnell/yosemite/index.html.

20. James L. Patton, curator and professor emeritus, Museum of Vertebrate Zoology, Uni-versity of California, Berkeley, interview with the author, September 4, 2019.

21. Ben H. Thompson, interview with the author, Glenwood, New Mexico, October 17, 1987.

22. As cited in Stein, 77. Grinnell also believed that the true value of the Museum of Verte-brate Zoology would not prove itself for years to come. "I wish to emphasize what I believe will ultimately prove to be the greatest value of our museum. This value will not, however, be realized until the lapse of many years, possibly a century, assuming that our material is safely preserved. And this is that the student of the future will have access to the original record of faunal condi-tions in California and the west wherever we now work." Joseph Grinnell, "The Methods and Uses of a Research Museum," *Popular Science Monthly* 77 (August 1910): 166, http://ia800204 .us.archive.org/18/items/popularsciencemo77newy/popularsciencemo77newy.pdf.

23. John D. Perrine and James L. Patton, "Letters to the Future," as cited in *Field Notes on Science & Nature*, ed. Michael R. Canfield (Cambridge, MA: Harvard University Press, 2011),

219. Another very detailed remembrance of Grinnell by a former student turned colleague is E. Raymond Hall, "Joseph Grinnell (1877 to 1939)," *Journal of Mammalogy* 20, no. 4 (1939): 411, http://www.jstor.org/stable/1374589.

24. For a precise discussion of why and how specimens were collected in the early twentieth century, see Grinnell, "Methods and Uses of a Research Museum."

25. Joseph S. Dixon, field notes, Off Point Humphreys, Arctic Ocean, Alaska, September 3–30, 1913, 4, Museum of Vertebrate Zoology Archives, University of California, Berkeley. All quotes from field notes have been reproduced exactly, including the original spelling and punctuation.

26. T. J. Eley, email to the author, August 27, 2019. Professor Thomas Eley (retired), University of Alaska, is a biogeographer and ornithologist with a keen penchant for history. Dixon referred to the local inhabitants that helped them as Eskimos. Today they are recognized as the Inupiaq people who speak the Inupiat language.

27. Joseph S. Dixon, "Birds Observed between Point Barrow and Herschel Island on the Arctic Coast of Alaska," *The Condor* 45, no. 2 (1943): 49, https://sora.unm.edu/sites/default/files /journals/condor/v045n02/p0049-p0057.pdf.

28. Dixon, "Birds Observed between Point Barrow and Herschel Island," 51.

29. James L. Patton, curator and professor emeritus, Museum of Vertebrate Zoology, University of California, Berkeley, interview with the author, January 13, 2015.

30. Craig L. Shafer, "Conservation Biology Trailblazers: George Wright, Ben Thompson, and Joseph Dixon," *Conservation Biology* 15, no. 2 (2001): 332–44.

31. Between 1905 and 1940 Dixon wrote approximately ninety publications. These included circulars, bulletins, booklets, nature notes, books and coauthored books, with the vast majority consisting of articles in professional journals and some popular magazines. His hand-typed "Personal Bibliography," dated September 27, 1940, is held by his grandson, Weaver Rhyne. Weaver's mother, Mary Dixon Rhyne was Dixon's youngest child.

32. For a sampling of over three thousand of his images, see Museum of Vertebrate Zoology Archives, University of California, Berkeley, https://calphotos.berkeley.edu/mvz.html; Joseph S. Dixon Collection 1909–1948, 1–39.

33. Laurel Kearns, email to the author, August 6, 2019; Quaker Information Center, Earlham School of Religion, Richmond, IN, http://www.quakerinfo.org/quakerism/branches/index. The author would also like to thank genealogist Karen Bodding for providing me with a detailed Dixon family history.

34. Laurel Kearns, "Quaker Ecological Foundations and the Universe Story," in *Quakers, Creation Care, and Sustainability, Quakers and the Disciplines*, vol. 6, ed. C. Bock and S. Pottoff (Longmeadow, MA: Full Media Services, 2019), 176; Mary M. Ross, "The Solace of History: Reflections on Quakers and the Environment," *Friends Journal* (February 17, 2012), https://www .friendsjournal.org/the-solace-of-history-reflections-on-quakers-and-the-environment/.

35. Mary Dixon Rhyne, letter to the author, November 19, 2000.

Chapter Three

1. Wright's academic records were destroyed, along with those of all students from that period, due to concerns stemming from the Family Educational Rights and Privacy Act; Department of Forestry, UC Berkeley, email to the author, April 24, 2019. Lowell High School in San Francisco maintains impressive archives. The author was able to view Wright's "Scholarship Record" as well as clippings from the school newspaper, *The Lowell*.

2. The US census records Alaska boasting some fifty-five thousand residents in 1920, an actual decline from the previous two census periods. By comparison, New York state had over ten million residents. Statistical Abstract of the United States, 1921, https://www2.census.gov/prod2/statcomp/documents/1921-02.pdf.

3. Images held by Pamela Meléndez Wright Lloyd.

4. White was born in England, attended Oxford University, and eventually joined the US Army and commanded in the Philippines. He also fought in the First World War, eventually retiring in 1919. NPS director Stephen Mather hired him the next year to manage Sequoia National Park, where he stayed until 1947. Lary M. Dilsaver and William C. Tweed, *Challenge of the Big Trees: A Resource History of Sequoia and Kings Canyon National Parks* (Three Rivers, CA: Sequoia Natural History Association, 1990), chap. 5, https://www.nps.gov/parkhistory/online_books/dilsaver-tweed/chap5.htm. Eight years after this initial meeting with the Sierra Club, Superintendent White and George Wright became colleagues and good friends, though there was a large age difference between the two men.

5. Alice Kahler Marshall, *Pen Names of Women Writers* (Camp Hill, PA: Alice Kahler Marshall, 1985), 113; a members' list of the 1922 outing shows the writer using Allen Chaffee as a pen name to register. This list was provided to the author by Therese Dunn, librarian, William E. Colby Memorial Library, Sierra Club, Oakland, California.

6. Hardtack is a simple and durable biscuit, made of flour, water, and salt.

7. Allen Chaffee, *Adventures on The High Trail* (Springfield, MA: Milton Bradley, 1923), 203–13.

8. All quotes from this section are from "The Perils of Ponderous Peter." Diary held by Pamela Meléndez Wright Lloyd.

9. George Wright, field notes, Cracker Lake, Glacier National Park, September 1, 1931, 332, Museum of Vertebrate Zoology Archives, University of California, Berkeley.

10. Spellings, punctuation, and emphasis (underlining or italics) from these notebooks and other documents have been reproduced per the originals throughout this book.

11. David Leroy Harmon, "American Camp Culture: A History of Recreational Vehicle Development and Leisure Camping in the United States, 1890–1960," Retrospective Theses and Dissertations, 2001, https://lib.dr.iastate.edu/rtd/433; Sarah Laskow, "How America Joined Its Two Great Loves, Cars and the Outdoors: Auto Camps Were All the Rage in the 1920s," Atlas Obscura, July 5, 2016, https://www.atlasobscura.com/articles/how-america-joined-its-two-great-loves-cars-and-the-outdoors.

12. Several years Wright's senior, Robert (Bob) Sibley was another Delta Upsilon member, and he went on to manage Berkeley's office of Alumni Affairs for many years. Sibley was a keen naturalist and hiking enthusiast. He would eventually be a cofounder of the renowned East Bay Regional Park District in California and to have a park named after him. Sibley and Wright were good friends for many years and often hiked in the East Bay.

13. George M. Wright, to Joseph Dixon, April 26, 1926, Museum of Vertebrate Zoology Archives, University of California, Berkeley.

14. Jeremiah Trimble, email to the author, April 22, 2019. Jeremiah Trimble is a curatorial associate and collections manager, ornithology, Museum of Comparative Zoology, Harvard University, Cambridge, Massachusetts.

15. It is now known they reach southern Chile during those winter months: their migration is some eleven thousand long miles, one way; Cornell Lab of Ornithology, All About Birds, Surfbird, https://www.allaboutbirds.org/guide/surfbird.

16. John E. Thayer to Joseph Dixon, January 15, 1926, Museum of Vertebrate Zoology Archives, University of California, Berkeley.

17. Joseph Grinnell to John E. Thayer, January 20, 1926, Museum of Vertebrate Zoology Archives, University of California, Berkeley. It is not known what Wright did during the summer months of 1925. However, throughout the year, he was very active with his fellow forestry students and traveled throughout the greater San Francisco Bay Area on field trips. Approximately a dozen photographs of the class have survived, and they were all taken by Woodbridge Metcalf, a professor of silviculture and dendrology at Berkeley. Metcalf had joined the faculty the same year Walter Mulford was hired, in 1914. His images can be found by entering his name on UC Berkeley's Digital Collections site, https://digicoll.lib.berkeley.edu.

18. Dixon, field notes, May 19, 1926, 1934, Museum of Vertebrate Zoology Archives, University of California, Berkeley.

19. Wright, field notes, May 28, 1926, 29–34, Museum of Vertebrate Zoology Archives, University of California, Berkeley. The Museum of Vertebrate Zoology at the University of California, Berkeley, as well as the library in Yosemite National Park both have complete sets of notes from Wright's expedition with Joseph Dixon to Mount McKinley National Park (May 19, 1926–July 27, 1926, pages 1–145) and his time in Yosemite (November 15, 1927–June 10, 1929, pages 1–74), as well as his extensive notes from the wildlife survey with the National Park Service (February 28, 1930–September 24, 1933, pages 77–542). The author and his wife, Jeannie Lloyd, facilitated this arrangement.

20. Dixon, field notes, 1926, 1963.

21. Wright, field notes, 1926, 35–36; in his early field notes, Wright switched back and forth between the Spanish spelling *cañon* and the English *canyon*. With time, he eventually settled on the English spelling, unless *cañon* was part of a formal place name.

22. Wright, field notes, 1926, 39.

23. Joseph Grinnell to John E. Thayer, March 8, 1926. Museum of Vertebrate Zoology Archives, University of California, Berkeley.

24. Wright, field notes, 1926, 58.

25. Joseph Dixon, *Birds & Mammals of Mount McKinley National Park, Alaska*, Fauna Series no. 3 (Washington, DC: United States Government Printing Office, 1938), x–xi.

26. Roger W. Toll, *Mountaineering in the Rocky Mountain National Park*, Department of the Interior, National Park Service (Washington, DC: Government Printing Office, 1919), 10, https://archive.org/details/mountaineeringin00toll.

27. Joseph Dixon to John E. Thayer, August 19, 1926. Museum of Vertebrate Zoology Archives, University of California, Berkeley; Joseph Dixon, "The Surf-Bird's Secret," *The Condor*, Cooper Ornithological Club, vol. 29, no. 1 (January–February 1927), 3–4, https://sora.unm.edu/node/97210.

28. John E. Thayer to Joseph Dixon, December 16, 1926, Museum of Vertebrate Zoology Archives, University of California, Berkeley.

29. Jeremiah Trimble, email to the author, April 22, 2019.

30. Joseph Grinnell to George M. Wright, February 7, 1927, Museum of Vertebrate Zoology Archives, University of California, Berkeley.

31. T. I. Storer, "Annual Meeting," *The Condor*, 29, no. 4 (1927): 212, https://sora.unm.edu/node/97327. Two years later, Wright hosted 110 guests during their annual meeting. Grinnell was particularly happy about that. "My Dear George. I am more than pleased, personally, that you, rather than someone else, should have undertaken to serve as host. . . . I am now sure that

the occasion will be the very last word in quiet good taste." Joseph Grinnell to George Wright, April 12, 1929, Museum of Vertebrate Zoology Archives, University of California, Berkeley.

32. George Scott to George M. Wright, October 17, 1927. Letter held by Pamela Meléndez Wright Lloyd.

Chapter Four

1. For a thorough discussion on the evolution of Yosemite National Park, see chaps. 2–4 of Alfred Runte's comprehensive book, *Yosemite: The Embattled Wilderness* (Lincoln: University of Nebraska Press, 1990).

2. Runte, 161; Washington B. Lewis was superintendent of Yosemite National Park from April 3, 1916, until July 3, 1928.

3. George Wright, field notes, Yosemite Valley, November 15, 1927, 1, Museum of Vertebrate Zoology Archives, University of California, Berkeley.

4. George M. Wright, Joseph S. Dixon, and Ben H. Thompson, *Fauna of the National Parks of the United States: A Preliminary Survey of Faunal Relations in National Parks*, Contribution of Wild Life Survey, Fauna Series No. 1 (Washington, DC: Government Printing Office, May 1933) [*Fauna No. 1*], 20.

5. As early as 1886 the US Cavalry rode into Yellowstone to relieve the civilian park managers. Lawlessness reigned; poaching and the theft of artifacts were rampant. The military presence was seen as temporary, but they stayed for thirty-two years. The cavalry also seasonally patrolled Yosemite, Sequoia, and General Grant National Parks. Yosemite and Sequoia National Parks were annually patrolled from 1891 to 1914, including by the famous Buffalo Soldiers, the African American cavalry unit based out of the Presidio of San Francisco. See Duane H. Hampton, *How the US Cavalry Saved Our National Parks* (Bloomington: University of Indiana Press, 1971); Shelton Johnson, "Preserving Yosemite's Cultural Past," *Yosemite Conservancy Magazine* 4, no. 1 (Spring/Summer 2013): 10–11; and https://www.nps.gov/yose/learn/historyculture/buffalo-soldiers.htm; Jim Morrison, "How the US Army Saved Our National Parks," *Smithsonian Magazine*, October 8, 2015, https://www.smithsonianmag.com/history/how-army-saved-our-national-parks-180956840/; John Muir, *Our National Parks* (Boston: Houghton, Mifflin, 1901).

6. Wallace Stegner, *Beyond the Hundredth Meridian: John Wesley Powell and the Second Opening of the West* (Boston: Houghton Mifflin, 1954).

7. United States Department of the Interior, Extract from the Annual Report of the Secretary of the Interior, Relating to the National Park Service, Fiscal Year 1928 (Washington: United States Government Printing Office, 1928), 21–24, https://hdl.handle.net/2027/mdp.39015006870888.

8. Horace M. Albright and Marian Albright Schenck, *Creating the National Park Service—The Missing Years* (Norman: University of Oklahoma Press, 1999), 39–40.

9. Manic depression is more commonly referred to today as bipolar disorder. Mather left office in January 1929 after suffering a stroke. He died one year later.

10. Albright's stationery from that time clearly stated his title as "Assistant Director (Field)," even though Arno Cammerer was officially the assistant director based out of the DC headquarters.

11. Two books about Steven Mather and Horace Albright are noted for further reading: Robert Shankland, *Steve Mather of the National Parks* (New York: Alfred A. Knopf, 1954); and Albright and Schenck, *Creating the National Park Service*.

12. Stephen T. Mather, *Progress in the Development of the National Parks*, Department of the Interior, Office of the Secretary (Washington, DC: Government Printing Office, 1916), 4–5, https://archive.org/details/progressindevelo00unit/mode/2up.

13. Stephen T. Mather, *Extracts from the Annual Report of the Secretary of the Interior Fiscal Year 1927* (Washington, DC: Government Printing Office, 1927), 6–7, 22, http://npshistory.com /publications/annual_reports/director/1927.pdf.

14. Yosemite Valley Grant Act, appendix A, "Legislation about the Yosemite," https://vault .sierraclub.org/john_muir_exhibit/writings/the_yosemite/appendix_a.aspx.

15. The Traditionally Associated Tribes of Yosemite National Park, *Voices of the People* (National Park Service in collaboration with Yosemite Conservancy, 2019), 25.

16. The author would like to thank Liz Williams, cultural anthropologist/tribal liaison at Yosemite National Park, for providing American Indian information for the park and for reviewing portions of the manuscript discussing Indians, specifically at Yosemite. Personal communication, May 2021. See also Runte, 10–12; Mark Spence, "Dispossessing the Wilderness: Yosemite Indians and the National Park Ideal, 1864–1930," *Pacific Historical Review* 65, no. 1 (February 1996): 27–59. In the Yosemite region, tribal groups have historically been described as *Ahwahnechee*, people of the Ahwahnee. This term is frequently used to collectively describe the different American Indian groups who either lived in, near, or seasonally visited Yosemite Valley and what is known today as the Mariposa Grove of Giant Sequoias for countless generations, prior to the arrival of the Euro-Americans. Ahwahnechee may represent American Indians of multiple tribal affiliations who now refer to themselves as the Traditionally Associated Tribes of Yosemite and are self-identified as American Indian Council of Mariposa County, Bishop Paiute Tribe, Bridgeport Indian Colony, Mono Lake Kutzadika'a Tribe, North Fork Rancheria of Mono Indians of California, Picayune Rancheria of Chukchansi Indians, and the Tuolumne Band of Me-Wuk Indians. See *Voices of the People*, and "Surviving Communities, Yosemite National Park," https://www.nps.gov/yose/learn/historyculture/surviving-communities.htm.

17. Wright, field notes, Yosemite Valley, November 15, 1927, 14–15.

18. In a 1940 article author Hugh M. Miller states that, at that time, the civil service requirement for a ranger's height was 5′ 7″. See Hugh M. Miller, "Park Service Rangers," United States Department of the Interior, National Park Service, *Region III Quarterly* 2, no. 4 (October 1940), https://www.nps.gov/parkhistory/online_books/region_111/vol2-4g.htm.

19. Horace M. Albright, to the director, March 1, 1928. Document held by Pamela Meléndez Wright Lloyd.

20. Horace M. Albright to the director, April 17, 1928. Document held by Pamela Meléndez Wright Lloyd.

21. Stephen T. Mather, memorandum for the secretary, April 20, 1928. Document held by Pamela Meléndez Wright Lloyd.

22. Years later, two people confirmed that Wright was on both Albright and Mather's radars as a rising star in the National Park Service. "He was unmistakably a Mather man—built in Mather's image, it used to be said around the parks—and was looked upon as a future director of the Service," Shankland, 275; "George Wright, Ben Thompson and I were all youngsters at the same time in school. I was the oldest. Togo, as we called him, was a rare and beautiful human being. Mr. Mather and Mr. Albright induced him into the National Park Service," George L. Collins to Gracie Wellman, December 2, 1975. Copy of letter held by Pamela Meléndez Wright Lloyd. Collins entered the Park Service in 1929 and held various positions until his retirement in 1960.

23. Wright, field notes, Yosemite Valley, November 15, 1927, 11–12.

24. For an excellent reference on the early role of women in the conservation and park movement, see Polly Welts Kaufman, *National Parks and the Woman's Voice: A History* (Albuquerque: University of New Mexico Press, 1996). For brief biographies of Michaels and Baggley, see http://www.yosemite.ca.us/library/yosemite_nature_notes/46/2/enid_michael.html and https://www.nps.gov/parkhistory/online_books/sontag/baggley.htm.

25. W. B. Lewis, Annual Report, Yosemite National Park, 1927, https://calisphere.org/item/6ad b943ef4ddbddc23d94336b0167de6/; E. P. Leavitt, Superintendent's Annual Report, Yosemite National Park, 1928, https://npgallery.nps.gov/AssetDetail/d98b24918075416e909578976cac751c.

26. Both Jorgensen and Widforss gave Wright paintings that are still held by the family.

27. Ansel Adams, *Ansel Adams, Our National Parks*, ed. Andrea G. Stillman and William A. Turnage (Boston: Little, Brown and Company, 1992), 8.

28. The business eventually became the Ansel Adams Gallery and helped launch his career; see the Ansel Adams Gallery, https://www.anseladams.com/.

29. George M. Wright, "Fare of the Golden Eagle," *Yosemite Nature Notes* 7, no. 4 (1928): 29.

30. George M. Wright to Joseph S. Dixon, December 10, 1928, Museum of Vertebrate Zoology Archives, University of California, Berkeley.

31. Mrs. H. J. Taylor, "Maria Lebrado Is a Guest at Museum," *Yosemite Nature Notes* 8, no. 9 (September 1929): 85−86.

32. Colonel Charles Goff Thomson took over from E. P. Leavitt as Yosemite National Park Superintendent in February 1929 and was in that position until March 1937, when he died of a heart attack in the park's hospital. Wright and Thomson formed an excellent working relationship, even though they didn't always see eye to eye on management issues.

33. George Crow to George Wright, March 13, 1931, RG 79 NPS, Region IV, Regional Wildlife Technician, Wildlife Reports, 1929−1941, accn: 82-001 (FRC 51-0102B), container #6, Yosemite National Park, 1930−34.

34. Yosemite's Indian Village was home to American Indians who today are the Traditionally Associated Tribes of Yosemite. They were skilled laborers in the park, and many of the women were master basket makers and sold their goods to tourists. They also participated in "Indian Field Days" in the early twentieth century (see *Voices of the People*, 71−72). The village had a long, and ultimately unfortunate, history, recounted by many authors (see below). During Wright's almost two years working in the valley, Superintendent Thomson proclaimed that the resident Indians had no legal rights to live in the valley, but they did have a "moral right that must be zealously respected." This may appear as an advanced and liberal attitude for the time, however Thomson considered the village "atrocious" and "squalid." He had the village, "one of Yosemite's worst eyesores," "completely eliminated," and the Park Service built small cabins at another location in the early 1930s, the "New Indian Village." He also used this process to remove some individuals he deemed to not be true Yosemite Indians. C. G. Thomson, Yosemite National Park Superintendent's Annual Report, 1929, 15, https://npgallery.nps.gov/AssetDetail/66dcf88ae 6e7411885e11350239dd9cd; C. G. Thomson, Yosemite National Park Superintendent's Annual Report, 1930−31, https://npgallery.nps.gov/AssetDetail/36bf4cc752214c8e879a0c965e67825b; C. G. Thomson, Yosemite National Park Superintendent's Annual Report, 1933, https://npgallery.nps.gov/AssetDetail/11f5b9bb24cc4124bf1aa8086cc79911. For detailed information about both the old and new Indian Villages, see *Voices of the People*, and Linda Wedel Greene, *Yosemite: The Park and Its Resources: A History of the Discovery, Management, and Physical Development of Yosemite National Park, California*, vols. 1 and 2, (U.S. Department of the Interior, National Park Service, September 1987), https://archive.org/details/historicresource00yose.

Chapter Five

1. Historian Richard West Sellars describes how Director Mather encouraged the parks in the early 1920s to create small zoos in order for people to be able to see a few typical park animals up close. Throughout the 1930s these zoos were closed, thanks to the work of Wright and others. Richard West Sellars, *Preserving Nature in the National Parks: A History* (New Haven, CT: Yale University Press, 1997), 78.

2. National Park Service, Organic Act of 1916, https://www.nps.gov/grba/learn/management /organic-act-of-1916.htm.

3. Sellars, 4–5.

4. "This objective is to restore and perpetuate the fauna in its pristine state by combating the harmful effects of human influence." George M. Wright, Joseph S. Dixon, and Ben H. Thompson, *Fauna of the National Parks of the United States: A Preliminary Survey of Faunal Relations in National Parks*, Contribution of Wild Life Survey, Fauna Series No. 1 (Washington, DC: Government Printing Office, May 1933) [*Fauna No. 1*], 4.

5. George Wright, field notes, 1928, 47. Museum of Vertebrate Zoology Archives, University of California, Berkeley. For details on how tule elk came to Yosemite National Park, see Alfred Runte, *Yosemite: The Embattled Wilderness* (Lincoln: University of Nebraska Press, 1990), 130–34.

6. Wright, Dixon, and Thompson, *Fauna No. 1*, 15.

7. Daniil Nikolaevich Kashkarov (1878–1941) was a pioneering Soviet zoologist. Douglas R. Weiner, *Models of Nature, Ecology, Conservation and Cultural Revolution in Soviet Russia* (Pittsburgh: University of Pittsburgh Press, 1988), and *the Great Soviet Encyclopedia, 3rd ed., s.v.* "Kashkarov, Daniil Nikolaevich," https://encyclopedia2.thefreedictionary.com/Kashkarov%2c +Daniil+Nikolaevich.

8. George Wright to Joseph Grinnell, September 20, 1928, Museum of Vertebrate Zoology Archives, University of California, Berkeley. This letter could be the first of Wright's that was actually typed by a secretary. The bottom left of the letter shows "GMW:RN." Many of the letters also have noted, in the bottom left corner, "(Dictated, but not read)." This process would continue throughout his career: the use—and dependence on—secretaries to type letters he either dictated or wrote out ahead of time in longhand. But his correspondence also includes handwritten notes and some letters obviously typed by himself, which he admits and apologizes for due to the typos.

9. George Wright to Joseph Dixon, October 11, 1928, Museum of Vertebrate Zoology Archives, University of California, Berkeley.

10. George Wright to Joseph Dixon, February 25, 1929. A copy of this letter was given to the author in January 2000, by David Dixon, Joseph Dixon's youngest son. The author interviewed David Dixon and his sister, Mary Dixon Rhyne, in Oakland, California.

11. Joseph Dixon to Horace Albright, March 7, 1929, Museum of Vertebrate Zoology Archives, University of California, Berkeley.

12. Joseph Dixon to Harold Bryant, March 7, 1929, Museum of Vertebrate Zoology Archives, University of California, Berkeley. The secretary of the interior appointed the Educational Advisory Board in 1928 to write a report on the educational issues facing parks. The board consisted of Bryant, Merriam, and Hermon C. Bumpus, as well as Dr. Vernon Kellogg, secretary of the National Research Council, and Dr. Frank R. Oastler of New York. Before their final report was submitted, the secretary appointed an "informal board" to directly advise the National Park Service director on educational matters. Again Merriam, Bumpus, Kellogg, and Oastler participated. They were joined by Dr. Wallace W. Atwood, president of Clark University; Dr. Clark

Wissler, curator of the American Museum of Natural History; and Dr. Isaiah Bowman, president of the American Geographic Society. Wright and his team would have interactions with these board members in the field for several years.

13. George Wright to Horace Albright, March 27, 1929, RG 79 NPS, Region IV, Regional Naturalist, Wildlife Files, 1929–1940, accn: 82-001 (FRC 52-0235B), General Program and Pest Control Files, container #1.

14. Included with letter, Wright to Albright, March 27, 1929.

15. Wright's donation of $10,000 is roughly equivalent to $150,000 in today's dollars.

16. Horace Albright to George Wright, March 29, 1929, RG 79 NPS, Region IV, Regional Naturalist Wildlife Files, 1929–1940, accn: 82-001 (FRC 52-0235B), General Program and Pest Control Files, container #1.

17. Oath of Office, National Park Service, August 26, 1929. Document held by Pamela Meléndez Wright Lloyd.

18. Joseph Grinnell to George Wright, May 21, 1929. Document held by Pamela Meléndez Wright Lloyd.

19. The American Trust Building, completed in 1927, is still standing and occupied to this day. It is included in the National Register of Historic Places.

20. Joseph S. Dixon, field notes, August 7, 1930, 213, Yosemite, California, Park Service History Collection, HFCA-01113.

21. Runte, 140–42.

22. Dixon, field notes, September 11–12, 1929, 113–16.

23. There are two species of North American bears, *Ursus americanus* and *Ursus arctos*. The common name for *U. americanus* is black bear (regardless if it is black, brown, cinnamon, or even white). The general common name for *U. arctos* is brown bear, and it is found throughout the portions of all northern continents. Several of the North American *U. arctos* subspecies are also called grizzly bears, as they are in the Yellowstone ecosystem. But in some regions of North American they are referred to as brown bears, as in the Alaskan brown bear of southeast Alaska. And, to add to the confusion, there is a plethora of regional usages, but they are all *U. arctos*. Thanks to James Patton, curator and professor emeritus, Berkeley's Museum of Vertebrate Zoology for clarifying the distinctions between the two species.

24. Dixon, field notes, 1929, 116.

25. George Wright to the director, August, 25, 1931, Museum of Vertebrate Zoology Archives, University of California, Berkeley.

26. Winston E. Banko, "The Trumpeter Swan, Its History, Habits, and Population in the United States," *North American Fauna*, no. 63 (1960): 26.

27. Wright, Dixon, and Thompson, 28.

28. Banko, 11–12. Powder puffs were used to apply perfumed powder to women's faces.

29. John Kenneth Galbraith, *The Great Crash 1929* (Boston: Mariner Books, Houghton Mifflin Harcourt, 2009).

Chapter Six

1. Ben H. Thompson in George M. Wright and Ben H. Thompson, *Fauna of the National Parks of the United States, Wildlife Management in the National Parks*, Contribution of Wildlife Division, Fauna Series No. 2 (Washington, DC: Government Printing Office, July 1935) [*Fauna No. 2*], 55.

2. George Wright, field notes, Yosemite Valley, March 27, 1930, 81. Museum of Vertebrate Zoology Archives, University of California, Berkeley.

3. The author would like to thank David M. Landow, historian, Buick Heritage Alliance, and Jeffrey R. Brashares, president of the alliance, for identifying the wildlife survey team's vehicle. Ben Thompson confirmed it was roadster, but Landow and Brashares added: "The truck is definitely a highly modified 1930 Buick (Buick did not build a pick-up truck model in 1930)." David M. Landow, email to the author, April 5, 2019.

4. Ben H. Thompson, interview with the author, Glenwood, New Mexico, October 17, 1987.

5. George Wright to C. A. Harwell, May 15, 1930, RG 79 NPS, Region IV, Regional Wildlife Technician, Wildlife Reports, 1929–1941, accn: 82-001 (FRC 51-0102B), National parks & monuments: Yosemite to Wind Cave, container #6.

6. King City (not Kings) is located approximately 150 miles south of Berkeley.

7. The wildlife team referred to the plateaus on either side of the Grand Canyon as the Kaibab Plateau (north) and the Southern Kaibab. However, today, it is more common that the Kaibab Plateau refers solely to the northern plateau and forest, and the southern plateau is known physiographically as the Coconino Plateau.

8. Wright, field notes, VT Ranch, 8800 ft. Kaibab National Forest, Arizona, June 1, 1930, 90.

9. Michael F. Anderson, *Polishing the Jewel: An Administrative History of Grand Canyon National Park* (Grand Canyon, AZ: Grand Canyon Association, 2000), 7–8.

10. Richard West Sellars, *Preserving Nature in the National Parks: A History* (New Haven, CT: Yale University Press, 1997), 78.

11. Numerous publications have dealt with the Kaibab deer herd die off. Here are three: Binkley et al., "Was Aldo Leopold Right about the Kaibab Deer Herd?" *Ecosystems* 9, no. 2 (2006): 227–41, http://www.jstor.org/stable/25470332; Sellars, 77–78; Christian C. Young, *In the Absence of Predators: Conservation and Controversy on the Kaibab Plateau* (Lincoln: University of Nebraska Press, 2002).

12. Wright, field notes, Grand Cañon to Coconino Basin, November 5, 1930, 188.

13. Wright, field notes, November 5, 1930, 189. Wright's "Sublime Spectacle" is a subtle but important reference to one of the region's most famous American explorers of the river, John Wesley Powell, and a phrase he made famous. In 1895, the one-armed Civil War veteran wrote a book detailing his amazing trip. When describing the Grand Canyon, he makes the point that it is made up of many smaller canyons. "Yet all these canyons unite to form one grand canyon," he wrote, "the most sublime spectacle on earth." J. W. Powell, *The Exploration of the Colorado River and Its Canyons* (1895; New York: Dover Publications, 1961), 390.

14. Wright, field notes, VT Ranch, 8800 ft, Kaibab National Forest, Arizona, June 1, 1930, 91; underlining per original.

15. Wright, field notes, June 1, 1930, 90–91.

16. Anderson, 25–40.

17. Anderson, 25.

18. Horace Albright to Joseph Dixon, March 21, 1930, RG 79 NPS, Region IV, Regional Wildlife Technician, Wildlife Reports, 1929–1941, accn: 82-001 (FRC 51-0102B), National parks & monuments: Grand Canyon to Kings Canyon, container #2.

19. It is important to realize that Dixon's statement regarding the pre-European American conditions of the parks is based on no knowledge of those conditions. At that time, researchers had no sense of how native people managed, and changed, what were thought to be pristine landscapes. And they wouldn't for many decades; Sellars, 23.

20. Joseph Dixon to Horace Albright, March 31, 193, RG 79 NPS, Region IV, Regional Wildlife Technician, Wildlife Reports, 1929–1941, accn: 82-001 (FRC 51-0102B), National parks & monuments: Grand Canyon to Kings Canyon, container #2.

21. George M. Wright, Joseph S. Dixon, and Ben H. Thompson, *Fauna of the National Parks of the United States: A Preliminary Survey of Faunal Relations in National Parks*, Contribution of Wild Life Survey, Fauna Series No. 1 (Washington, DC: Government Printing Office, May 1933) [*Fauna No. 1*], 37.

22. Anderson, 61.

23. Anderson, 37.

24. C. Hart Merriam, "Revision of the North American Pocket Mice," *North American Fauna*, no. 1, US Department of Agriculture, Division of Ornithology and Mammalogy (Washington, DC: Government Printing Office, 1889): 7, https://archive.org/details/northamericanfau14unit.

25. Wright used the name "white-faced glossy ibis" in his field notes. Today it is recognized that there are three ibis found in North America: the white-faced ibis (*Plegadis chihi*), common in the western United States, and what Wright saw in the Bear Marsh; the glossy ibis (*P. falcinellus*) on the East Coast and south; and the white ibis (*Eudocimus albus*), whose range overlaps that of the glossy ibis; Cornell Lab of Ornithology, https://www.allaboutbirds.org/news/search/?q=ibis.

26. Wright, field notes, Bear River Marshes, Birgham, Utah, June 6–7, 1930, 93.

27. Wright, field notes, Trumpeter Lake, Yellowstone, Wyoming, June 2, 1931, 256.

28. Fifty-four pages are missing from Ben Thompson's 1930 notes. They don't begin again until September 29, at Mount Rainier National Park.

29. Arthur C. Bent, *Life Histories of North American Wild Fowl, Order Anseres*, Smithsonian Institution, Bulletin 130 (Washington, DC: Government Printing Office, 1925), 293–301.

30. Wright, Dixon, and Thompson, *Fauna No. 1*, 28–31; Winston E. Banko, "*The Trumpeter Swan, Its History, Habits, and Population in the United States*," *North American Fauna*, no. 63 (1960): 14–25.

31. Today biologists know a lot more about this largest waterfowl in North America—for example, that they tend to stay together for life and nest in the same area—therefore, it was likely the same pair from the previous year.

32. Joseph Dixon, field notes, Lamar River, Yellowstone, June 9-23, 1930, 127–59. Park Service History Collection, HFCA-01113.

33. Dixon, field notes, 1930, 130.

34. Dixon, field notes, 1930, 135.

35. Dixon, field notes, 1930, 144.

36. Joseph Dixon, "Save the Trumpeter Swan," *American Forests* (August 1931): 454.

37. Dixon, field notes, 1930, 150.

38. Wright, field notes, Tern Lake, Yellowstone, June 11, 1930, 113.

39. Wright, field notes, Lamar River, Yellowstone, June 9, 1930, 109.

40. Wright, field notes, Tern Lake, Yellowstone, June 11, 1930, 117.

41. Wright, field notes, Tern Lake, Yellowstone, June 12, 1930, 122.

42. Wright, field notes, Lamar River, Yellowstone, June 28, 1930, 138.

43. Carl P. Russell, *A Concise History of Scientists and Scientific Investigations in Yellowstone National Park* (Department of the Interior, January 1934), 9, http://npshistory.com/publications/yell/scientists.pdf.

44. George Wright to C. G. Thomson, June 26, 1930, RG 79 NPS, Region IV, Regional Wildlife

Technician, Wildlife Reports, 1929–1941, accn: 82-001 (FRC 51-0102B), National parks & monuments: Yosemite to Wind Cave, container #6.

45. Wright to Thomson, June 26, 1930.

46. Wright to Thomson, June 26, 1930.

47. Wright, field notes, Yellowstone, June 30–July 1, 1930, 140.

48. T. H. Beck, J. N. Darling, A. Leopold, *Report of the President's Committee on Wild Life* (Washington, DC: Government Printing Office, 1934), 15, https://archive.org/details/CAT311 26980.

49. E. W. Nelson, *Status of the Pronghorned Antelope, 1922–1924*, United States Department of Agriculture, Bulletin No. 1346 (Washington, DC: Government Printing Office, 1925), https://archive.org/details/statusofpronghor1346nels/mode/2up.

50. David Brown, email to the author, June 5, 2020. Professor Brown is a leading pronghorn expert.

51. Lloyd K. Musselman, *Rocky Mountain National Park Administrative History, 1915–1965* (Washington, DC: National Park Service, 1971), 76, https://www.nps.gov/romo/learn/history culture/administrative-history.htm.

52. Musselman, 75.

53. Wright, field notes, Estes Park Colorado, July 7, 1930, 148.

54. Dixon, field notes, 1930, 82.

55. George Wright to Dr. E. Raymond Hall, California, July 11, 1930, Museum of Vertebrate Zoology Archives, University of California, Berkeley.

56. Joseph Grinnell to George Wright, July 22, 1930, Museum of Vertebrate Zoology Archives, University of California, Berkeley.

57. Horace M. Albright, "Memorandum for Park Superintendents, Managers of Park Operations—Hotels, Lodges, Stores, Etc.," Berkeley, California, August 17, 1930. Letter held by Pamela Meléndez Wright Lloyd.

58. George Wright to C. Frank Brockman, March 11, 1930, RG 79 NPS, Region IV, Regional Wildlife Technician, Wildlife Reports, 1929–1941, accn: 82-001 (FRC 51-0102B), National parks & monuments: Rocky Mountain to Shenandoah, container #4.

59. Foundation Document, Mount Rainier National Park, National Park Service, Department of the Interior, 2015, 5, https://www.nps.gov/mora/learn/management/upload/MORA_FD _Signatures_emailsize_10-2017_v2.pdf.

60. Theodore Catton, *Wonderland: An Administrative History of Mt. Rainer National Park* (National Park Service, 1996), chap. 3, http://npshistory.com/publications/mora/adhi/chap3.htm.

61. Wright, field notes, Longmire Springs, Washington, September 28, 1930, 152.

62. Dixon, field notes, Paradise Park, Mount Rainier, 1930, 69.

63. Ben H. Thompson, field notes, Mount Rainier, October 6, 1930, 66, Museum of Vertebrate Zoology Archives, University of California, Berkeley.

64. Thompson, field notes, 1930, 56.

65. Wright, field notes, Lewis to Ohanapecosh Hot Springs, Washington, September 30, 1930, 158.

66. Paul Schullery, *A History of Native Elk in Mt. Rainier National Park* (Yellowstone Park, WY: Yellowstone Center for Resources, October 2004), http://npshistory.com/publications/mora /elk-studies/elkstudy-84a.htm.

67. Thompson, field notes, 1930, 56.

68. Wright, field notes, 1930, 156.

69. Wright, field notes, 1930, 160; Thompson, field notes, 1930, 60.

70. Thompson, field notes, 1930, 66.

71. Wright, field notes, Seattle, Washington, October 7, 1930, 168.

72. Bab Godfrey and Bill Godfrey to George Wright, May 6, 1930, RG 79 NPS, Region IV, Regional Wildlife Technician, Wildlife Reports, 1929–1941, accn: 82-001 (FRC 51-0102B), National parks & monuments: General to Glacier, container #1.

73. Douglas Deur, "A Most Sacred Place: The Significance of Crater Lake among the Indians of Southern Oregon," *Oregon Historical Quarterly* 103, no. 1 (2002), 18–49, http://www.jstor.org /stable/20615207.

74. Thompson, field notes, 1930, 68.

75. Dixon, field notes, October 15, 1930, 14, Crater Lake, Oregon, Park Service History Collection, HFCA-01113. According to the following document, the net area of Forest Service lands in 1935 totaled 167,248,072 acres (mostly in the western United States). Of that, game refuges existed on 25,245,612 acres, broken down into federal game refuges (4,002,071) and game refuges on Forest Service land managed by states (21,243,541). Land Planning Committee to the National Resources Board, *Planning for Wildlife in the United States*, Part IX of the Supplementary Report of the Land Planning Committee to the National Resources Board, M. L. Wilson, Chairman (Washington, DC: United States Government Printing Office, 1935), https://archive.org/details /planningforwildlife1935rich.

76. Dixon, field notes, 1930, 3.

77. Boyd E. Wickman, *The Battle against Bark Beetles in Crater Lake National Park, 1925– 34*, United States Department of Agriculture, Forest Service, General Technical Report PNW-GTR-259, 1990, 9–13, https://www.fs.fed.us/pnw/pubs/pnw_gtr259.pdf. For information on similar drastic measures in Yellowstone National Park at the same time, plus the use of chemicals, see Malcolm M. Furniss and Roy Renkin, "Forest Entomology in Yellowstone National Park, 1923–1957: A Time of Discovery and Learning to Let Live," *American Entomologist* 49, no. 4 (Winter 2003): 198–209, https://doi.org/10.1093/ae/49.4.198.

78. Wright, field notes, Grand Cañon, Arizona, October 29, 1930, 175.

79. Nelson, 10.

80. Thompson, field notes, 1930, 80.

81. Thompson, field notes, 1930, 84.

82. It is unclear where the team learned of the herd of a thousand pronghorn. In Nelson's report on antelope, based on research six years earlier, he estimated the total state population to be 650, widely scattered across the state in eighteen groups; Nelson, 24.

83. Report of the Director of the National Park Service to the Secretary of the Interior for the Fiscal Year Ended June 30, 1930 and the Travel Season, Department of the Interior (Washington, DC: United States Government Printing Office, 1929), 105, http://npshistory.com/publications /annual_reports/director/1930.pdf. The "House Rock" bison herd also roamed across the southern part of the Kaibab, but their numbers were so low that they were basically left alone. National Park Service, Bison Bellows: Grand Canyon National Park, https://www.nps.gov/articles/bison -bellows-4-21-16.htm.

84. Wright, Dixon, and Thompson, 93. Grinnell wrote his PhD dissertation on this very topic: the separation of species by a physical barrier and its influence on otherwise similar species. The barrier was the lower Colorado River. Joseph Grinnell, *An Account of the Mammals and Birds of the Lower Colorado Valley with Especial Reference to the Distributional Problems Presented*, University of California Publications in Zoology 12, no. 4 (1914): 51–52.

85. Wright, field notes, Grand Cañon, Arizona, November 1, 1930, 182.

86. Wright, field notes, VT Ranch, 8800 ft., Kaibab National Forest, Arizona, June 1, 1930, back of page 91.

87. Horace M. Albright and Frank J. Taylor, *"Oh, Ranger!" A Book about the National Parks* (Stanford, CA: Stanford University Press, 1929), 3. See also *Proceedings of the National Park Conference Held at Berkeley, California, March 11, 12, and 13, 1915*, 44, https://archive.org/details/proceedingsofnat15nati.

88. Timothy R. Manns, "History of the Park Ranger in Yellowstone National Park," April 18, 1980, http://www.npshistory.com/publications/yell/ranger-history.pdf.

89. George Wright, Statistics from Grand Canyon National Park Office File, 1930, RG 79 NPS, Region IV, Regional Naturalist, Wildlife Files, 1929–1940, accn: 82-001 (FRC 52-0235B), Program—General, container #1.

90. Wright, field notes, Mammoth to Buffalo Ranch, Yellowstone, November 16, 1932, 483.

91. Vernon Bailey, *Destruction of Wolves and Coyotes: Results Obtained during 1907.* Bureau of Biological Survey, C. Hart Merriam, Chief of Bureau, circular no. 63, United States Department of Agriculture. April 29, 1908, 5, https://archive.org/details/CAT31414423.

92. Henry W. Henshaw, Report of Chief of Bureau of Biological Survey, United States Department of Agriculture, Washington, DC, August 31, 1916, 3, https://archive.org/details/reportofchiefofb1916unit.

93. E. W. Nelson, Report of Chief of Bureau of Biological Survey, United Stated Department of Agriculture, Washington, DC, June 30, 1923, 2, https://archive.org/details/reportofchiefof1923unit_0/.

94. Statistics from the annual reports of the chief of the Bureau of the Biological Survey from 1915 to 1930.

95. Joseph Dixon to Horace Albright, October 16, 1929, RG 79 NPS, Region IV, Regional Naturalist, Wildlife Files, 1929–1940, accn: 82-001 (FRC 52-0235B), Program—General, container #1.

96. Horace Albright to Joseph Dixon, October 25, 1929, RG 79 NPS, Region IV, Regional Naturalist, Wildlife Files, 1929–1940, accn: 82-001 (FRC 52-0235B), Program—General, container #1.

97. Joseph Grinnell, *Personal Statement concerning the Use of Poison against Vertebrate Animal Life*, October 29, 1932, RG 79 NPS, Region IV, Regional Naturalist, Wildlife Files, 1929–1940, accn: 82-001 (FRC 52-0235B), General Program and Pest Control Files, container #1.

98. Joseph Grinnell and Tracy I. Storer, "Animal Life as an Asset of National Parks," *Science* 44, no. 1133 (September 15, 1916): 378, http://www.jstor.org/stable/1643783.

99. Lee R. Dice, "Scientific Value of Predatory Mammals," *Journal of Mammalogy* 6, no. 1 (1925): 25, http://www.jstor.org/stable/1373466.

100. Dice, 25; Joseph Dixon, "Food Predilections of Predatory and Fur-Bearing Mammals," *Journal of Mammalogy* 6, no. 1 (1925): 46, http://www.jstor.org/stable/1373468; E. A. Goldman, "Predatory Mammal Problem and the Balance of Nature," *Journal of Mammalogy* 6, no. 1 (1925): 28–33, http://www.jstor.org/stable/1373467.

101. "A Protest," 1930, RG 79, I, Region IV, Regional Naturalist, Wildlife Files, 1929–1940, accn: 82-001 (FRC 52-0235B), I—General, container #1.

102. Wright, field notes, Mesa Verde to the Kaibab Plateau, November 11–14, 1930, 202.

103. Joseph Dixon to Frank Been, November 25, 1930, RG 79, Regional Wildlife Technician, Wildlife Reports, 1929–1941, accn: 82-001 (FRC 51-0102B), National parks & monuments: Yellowstone to Yosemite, container #5.

104. George Wright to E. C. Solinsky, November 26, 1930, RG 79 NPS, Region IV, Regional Wildlife Technician, Wildlife Reports, 1929–1941, accn: 82-001 (FRC 51-0102B), National parks & monuments: General to Glacier, container #1.

Chapter Seven

1. Richard West Sellars, *Preserving Nature in the National Parks: A History* (New Haven, CT: Yale University Press, 1997), 96.

2. Robert W. Blythe, *Wilderness on the Edge: A History of Everglades National Park* (Chicago: National Park Service/Organization of American Historians, 2017), 81, https://evergladeswilder nessontheedge.com.

3. Malaria in Florida and the southeast was a scourge for generations around the turn of the nineteenth century. In the early 1930s, some five thousand people died annually across the United States from this mosquito-borne disease. The advent of window screens, targeted insecticides, and the draining of wetlands among other measures began to contain the disease. Florida Department of Health, http://www.floridahealth.gov/diseases-and-conditions/mosquito-borne-diseases/_doc uments/guidebook-chapter-eight.pdf; Ernest Carroll Faust, "The History of Malaria in the United States," *American Scientist* 39, no. 1 (1951): 124, http://www.jstor.org/stable/27826354.

4. There are no family stories or written accounts about their decision to marry in the hospital.

5. Wright to A. E. Demaray, March 12, 1931, RG 79 NPS, Region IV, Regional Naturalist, Wildlife Files, 1929–1940, accn: 82-001 (FRC 52-0235B), General Program and Pest Control Files, container #1.

6. Ben H. Thompson, "Brief Note on Mrs. J. Robert Shuman (formerly Mrs. George M. Wright)," *George Wright Forum* 5, no. 1 (1986): 27.

7. George Wright, field notes, Trumpeter Lake, Yellowstone, Wyoming, June 6, 1931, 266. Museum of Vertebrate Zoology Archives, University of California, Berkeley.

8. Mercedes Quiñónez, letter to George Wright, October 4, 1930. Document held by Pamela Meléndez Wright Lloyd.

9. Mercedes Quiñónez, letter to George Wright, November 27, 1932. Document held by Pamela Meléndez Wright Lloyd.

10. Wright, field notes, Yellowstone National Park, May 16, 1932, 416.

11. George Wright to the director, August, 25, 1931, Museum of Vertebrate Zoology Archives, University of California, Berkeley.

12. Wright to the director, August, 25, 1931.

13. Joseph Dixon, "Save the Trumpeter Swan," *American Forests* 37, no. 8 (1931): 492.

14. Wright discovered that the Canadian Government had been tracking trumpeters in southern British Columbia that reportedly nested to the north. Wright requested more information, but J. B. Harkin, of the National Parks of Canada, diplomatically informed Wright they were still analyzing the information and that in the best interest of the swan population's security, he was unwilling to share the information. J. B. Harkin to George Wright, September 23, 1931, Museum of Vertebrate Zoology Archives, University of California, Berkeley. James Bernard Harkin is considered the Stephen Mather of Parks Canada (as the agency is known today). It was founded in 1911, five years prior to the creation of the National Park Service.

15. George Baggley was married to Herma Albertson Baggley, the first woman to be appointed to a year-round naturalist position in the National Park Service, based out of Yellowstone.

Wright was very close to both of them, and he was always supportive of Herma's work, as was Joseph Dixon. In her classic botany guide—*Plants of Yellowstone National Park*—published in 1936 with Dr. Walter B. McDougall, many of the photographs were taken by Dixon.

16. George Wright to George F. Baggley, January 20, 1933, RG 79 NPS, Region IV, Regional Wildlife Technician, Wildlife Reports, 1929–1941, accn: 82-001 (FRC 51-0102B), National parks & monuments: Yellowstone to Yosemite, container #5; at least two Yellowstone district rangers, Allyn F. Hanks and Curtis K. Skinner, sent detailed swan observations to Wright.

17. Wright, field notes, Tern Lake, Yellowstone, Wyoming, June 14, 1931, 281.

18. Wright, field notes, Red Rock Lake, Montana, June 11, 1932, 442.

19. By late 1933, Director Albright, writing about research in the National Parks, highlights the work of Wright, Dixon, and Thompson, while calling attention to trumpeter swans. "It has been found that in the Yellowstone region these birds are making a last stand, and the Wild Life Division, with the cooperation of Yellowstone National Park officials, is bending every effort toward affording the necessary conditions in the park to permit the rehabilitation . . . of this magnificent species of bird." Horace M. Albright, "Research in the National Parks," *Scientific Monthly* 36, no. 6 (1933): 497, http://www.jstor.org/stable/15421.

20. Ben H. Thompson, "Brief Note on Mrs. J. Robert Shuman (formerly Mrs. George M. Wright)," *George Wright Forum* 5, no. 1 (1986): 27.

21. Wright, field notes, West Yellowstone to Old Faithful, Yellowstone, November 11, 1932, 474.

22. George Wright to Joseph Grinnell, September 2, 1933, Museum of Vertebrate Zoology Archives, University of California, Berkeley.

23. George Wright to Mr. and Mrs. William E. Branch, November 15, 1933, RG 79 NPS, Region IV, Regional Wildlife Technician, Wildlife Reports, 1929–1941, accn: 82-001 (FRC 51-0102B), National parks & monuments: Rocky Mountain to Shenandoah, container 4. The elk herd, introduced to Platt in the 1920s, was unhealthy and not thriving. The five bison at the park (introduced in 1920), on the other hand, appeared healthy to Wright and were enjoying a new fenced-in pasture exhibit. Platt, officially established in 1906 as a national park in order to protect its mineral-rich springs for the public, was one of the rare parks that was "demoted" to a different, supposedly lesser, designation. In 1976 it was expanded slightly and renamed the Chickasaw National Recreation Area; it is still part of the National Park System.

24. George Wright to Carl P. Russell, August 9, 1932. Letter held by Pamela Meléndez Wright Lloyd.

25. Ben H. Thompson, field notes, Zion National Park, East Rim, 1931, 138. Museum of Vertebrate Zoology Archives, University of California, Berkeley.

26. Joseph Dixon, field notes, Bryce National Park, Utah, 1931, 7, 10. Park Service History Collection, HFCA-01113.

27. Dixon, field notes, Bryce National Park, May 31, 1933, 3040. Catalog #4852, held at Sequoia Kings Canyon National Parks Museum Facility, Ash Mountain, California.

28. George M. Wright and Ben H. Thompson, *Fauna of the National Parks of the United States, Wildlife Management in the National Parks*, Contribution of Wildlife Division, Fauna Series No. 2 (Washington, DC: Government Printing Office, July 1935) [*Fauna No. 2*], 67.

29. Yellowstone National Park, *Yellowstone's Northern Range: Complexity and Change in a Wildland Ecosystem* (Mammoth Hot Springs, WY: National Park Service, 1997), 53–54, http://npshistory.com/publications/yell/northern_range.pdf.

30. Numerous herds of elk live within and adjacent to Yellowstone National Park. The northern herd and the herd within the National Elk Refuge are two of the largest. Within the park there may be six to seven distinct herds that spend part of the year there. Yellowstone National Park, *Yellowstone's Northern Range*, 71.

31. Wright, field notes, Mammoth Hot Springs, Yellowstone, April 12, 1932, 373. Wright also expressed serious concern for bird and small mammal species that would rely on these trees and ground cover for nesting and food.

32. Milton P. Skinner, "Predatory and Fur-Bearing Animals of the Yellowstone National Park," *Roosevelt Wild Life Bulletin* 4, no. 2 (1927), http://digitalcommons.esf.edu/rwlsbulletin/21; W. M. Rush, "Northern Yellowstone Elk Study," Montana Fish and Game Commission, 1933, https://archive.org/details/northernyellowst1933rush. Rush's study was initiated by Albright when the latter was Yellowstone's superintendent. The study was then cooperatively supported by the Forest Service, Park Service, Biological Survey, and the Montana Fish and Game Commission. Horace M. Albright, "Research in the National Parks," *Scientific Monthly* 36, no. 6 (1933): 497, https://archive.org/details/in.ernet.dli.2015.25859.

33. O. J. Murie, "Big Game Range," *Transactions of the Eighteenth American Game Conference*, New York City (December 1931).

34. Adolph Murie, *Ecology of the Coyote in the Yellowstone*, Fauna Series No. 4, Conservation Bulletin no. 4, United States Department of the Interior, National Park Service (Washington, DC: Government Printing Office, 1940), 15.

35. Environmental Protection Agency, "Climate Change Indicators: Drought, Average Drought Conditions in the Contiguous 48 States, 1895–2015," https://www.epa.gov/climate-indicators /climate-change-indicators-drought#ref5.

36. Wright and Thompson, 79.

37. Wright, field notes, Gallatin Station, Yellowstone, November 13, 1932, 477–80.

38. Rush, 80–81.

39. A. E. Demaray to Roger Toll, December 9, 1932, RG 79 NPS, Region IV, Regional Naturalist, Wildlife Files, 1929–1940, accn: 82-001 (FRC 52-0235B), Wildlife Files, container #7.

40. George M. Wright, handwritten note, July 16, 1932, RG 79 NPS, Region IV, Regional Naturalist, Wildlife Files, 1929–1940, accn: 82-001 (FRC 52-0235B), Wildlife Files, container #7.

41. Thompson, field notes, 1932, 214–15.

42. Although a precise number would have been impossible to establish, various authors agree that it was between twenty and forty individuals that survived. The story of how outside buffalo were brought in to create a new herd, and some of the concerns around that, has also been covered by many publications: Wright and Thompson, 59; Rush, 41; Margaret Mary Meagher, *Bison of Yellowstone National Park*, National Park Service, Scientific Monograph Series no. 1 (1973), 17, https://archive.org/details/bisonofyellowsto00meag.

43. Wright participated in a November roundup of bison in 1932. Ten riders started out at dawn in zero-degree weather. They rode to the top of the snow-covered Absarokas in search of the animals lingering on their winter grounds in order to drive them downslope and back to the ranch. Wright, field notes, Buffalo Ranch, Yellowstone, November 23, 1932, 490–92.

44. Wright and Thompson give a concise but thorough description of the bison program in *Fauna No. 2*, 59–61. In Wright's field notes from November 16, 1932, 484, he records the following: "Buffalo Management. Within a week the round up starts. It may last a month. A minimum of 150 all ages from 2 years on will be slaughtered and disposed of at a cost of 2¢ per pound delivered at the railroad. Indian Service will pay this price for those that go to the Blackfeet." There is

also an excellent historical summary of bison and Yellowstone in P. J. White, Rick L. Wallen, and David E. Hallac, eds., *Yellowstone Bison: Conserving an American Icon in Modern Society* (Yellowstone Association, 2015), https://www.nps.gov/yell/learn/management/bison-resources.htm.

45. Wright and Thompson, 60.

46. Wright, field notes, Buffalo Ranch, Yellowstone, bison roundup, November 23, 1932, 492.

47. O. J. Murie to George Wright, November 14, 1933, RG 79 NPS, Region IV, Regional Naturalist, Wildlife Files, 1929–1940, accn: 82-001 (FRC 52-0235B), Wildlife Files, container #7.

48. George M. Wright, Joseph S. Dixon, and Ben H. Thompson, *Fauna of the National Parks of the United States: A Preliminary Survey of Faunal Relations in National Parks*, Contribution of Wild Life Survey, Fauna Series No. 1 (Washington, DC: Government Printing Office, May 1933) [*Fauna No. 1*], 94; Ricardo Torres-Reyes sums up the Wildlife Division's goals at Mesa Verde in his study *Mesa Verde National Park, An Administrative History, 1906–1970*, United States Department of the Interior, National Park Service, Office of History and Historic Architecture (Washington, DC: Eastern Service Center, 1970), http://npshistory.com/publications/meve/adhi/chap9.htm.

49. Although Carlsbad Caverns was originally added to the national park system in 1923 to preserve over 120 impressive limestone caves, including Lechuguilla Cave, "the nation's second deepest limestone cave at 1,604 feet and the world's seventh longest cave," it also harbored not only unique cave fauna but also species of the surrounding Chihuahuan Desert. Wright believed it had potential for the reintroduction of species recently eliminated from the park, or rare species, such as the Merriam turkey, Texas bighorn, collared peccary, and the Mearns quail. National Park Service, Department of the Interior, *Foundation Document Overview, Carlsbad Caverns National Park*, New Mexico, http://npshistory.com/publications/foundation-documents /cave-fd-overview.pdf; Wright, Dixon, and Thompson, 102–3.

50. Horace Albright to George Wright, November 6, 1931, RG 79 NPS, Region IV, Regional Wildlife Technician, Wildlife Reports, 1929–1941, accn: 82-001 (FRC 51-0102B), National parks & monuments: General to Glacier, container #1.

51. Thompson, field notes, April 25, 1931, 115.

52. For a brief biography of Toll, see https://www.nps.gov/parkhistory/online_books/son tag/toll.htm.

53. George Wright to Roger Toll, January 26, 1932, RG 79 NPS, Region IV, Regional Wildlife Technician, Wildlife Reports, 1929–1941, accn: 82-001 (FRC 51-0102B), Proposed parks: General to White Mountain, container #8.

54. The list included Death Valley, Carlsbad Caverns extension, Everglades, proposed Navajo National Park (northeastern Arizona), proposed Virgin National Park (northwestern Arizona, southwestern Utah, and southeastern Nevada), proposed Redwood National Park, proposed Grand Teton National Park enlargement, and Pyramid and Winnemucca Lakes. National Monuments, existing and proposed, included Great Sand Dunes (Colorado), White Sands (New Mexico), Indian Mound Monument (Iowa), Meteor Crater (Arizona), and Bandelier National Monument (New Mexico). Some of these place names have changed with time. Roger W. Toll to George Wright, February 4, 1932, RG 79 NPS, Region IV, Regional Wildlife Technician, Wildlife Reports, 1929–1941, accn: 82-001 (FRC 51-0102B), Proposed parks: General to White Mountain, container #8.

55. George Wright to Roger Toll, February 10, 1932, RG 79 NPS, Region IV, Regional Wildlife Technician, Wildlife Reports, 1929–1941, accn: 82-001 (FRC 51-0102B), Proposed parks: General to White Mountain, container #8.

56. Wright to Toll, February 10, 1932.

57. Wright to Toll, February 10, 1932.

58. The General Land Office, part of the Department of the Interior, was responsible for public domain lands in the United States. In 1949 it merged with the Grazing Service to form the Bureau of Land Management. Department of the Interior, Bureau of Land Management, History, https://www.blm.gov/about/history/timeline.

59. George Wright to the director, March 7, 1933, RG 79 NPS, Region IV, Regional Wildlife Technician, Wildlife Reports, 1929–1941, accn: 82-001 (FRC 51-0102B), Proposed Everglades National Park, container #8.

60. Although President Roosevelt signed enabling legislation for the creation of Everglades National Park in 1934, it did not become a reality until 1947. Blythe, 130; Harold Bryant to George Wright, March 20, 1933, RG 79 NPS, Region IV, Regional Wildlife Technician, Wildlife Reports, 1929–1941, accn: 82-001 (FRC 51-0102B), Proposed parks: General to White Mountain, container #8.

61. Historian Blythe notes that the report produced by the group concluded that "only an approximation of the maximum boundary as set can fulfill conservation requirements and consequently approval of any material reduction in size must be avoided" (99).

62. Wright, Dixon, and Thompson, *Fauna No. 1*, 37.

63. George Wright to Harold Bryant, National Park Service, Department of the Interior, Washington, DC, March 10, 1931, RG 79 NPS, Region IV, Regional Naturalist, Wildlife Files, 1929–1940, accn: 82-001 (FRC 52-0235B), Program—General, container #1.

64. National Park Service, National Park Service Policy on Predatory Mammals, May 1931, RG 79 NPS, Region IV, Regional Naturalist, Wildlife Files, 1929–1940, accn: 82-001 (FRC 52-0235B), Program—General, container #1; Horace M. Albright, "Comment and News," *Journal of Mammalogy* 12, no. 2 (1931): 185–86. http://www.jstor.org/stable/1373920.

65. National Park Service, Policy on Predatory Mammals, 186.

66. M. R. Tillotson to the director, June 26, 1931, RG 79 NPS, Region IV, Regional Naturalist, Wildlife Files, 1929–1940, accn: 82-001 (FRC 52-0235B), General Program and Pest Control Files, container #1.

67. George Wright to E. T. Scoyen, September 17, 1931, RG 79 NPS, Region IV, Regional Naturalist, Wildlife Files, 1929–1940, accn: 82-001 (FRC 52-0235B), Program-General, container #1. Wright also copied David Madsen, a longtime biologist with the Park Service. During and beyond the wildlife survey years , Madsen was the supervisor of Fish Resources. A devout Mormon, Madsen was based out of Salt Lake City, Utah, but traveled throughout the West.

68. Wright to Scoyen, September 17, 1931.

69. Wright, field notes, Mammoth Springs, Yellowstone, April 28, 1932, 385.

70. For a detailed explanation of the white pelican controversy in Yellowstone, which was surprisingly complicated, see James A. Pritchard, *Preserving Yellowstone's Natural Conditions—Science and the Perception of Nature* (Lincoln: University of Nebraska Press, 1999).

71. Thompson's master's thesis can be found at http://npshistory.com/publications/wildlife/white-pelican-status.pdf.

72. Joseph Grinnell to Horace Albright, August 18, 1932, Museum of Vertebrate Zoology Archives, University of California, Berkeley. A few days before, Albright had visited with Grinnell on the Berkeley campus to discuss a variety of Park Service issues.

73. Arno B. Cammerer, acting director, memo to all superintendents and custodians, September 10, 1931, RG 79 NPS, Region IV, Regional Naturalist, Wildlife Files, 1929–1940, accn: 82-001 (FRC 52-0235B), Program—General, container #1.

74. Harold Bryant to George Wright, September 29, 1931, RG 79 NPS, Region IV, Regional Naturalist, Wildlife Files, 1929–1940, accn: 82-001 (FRC 52-0235B), Program—General, container #1.

75. George Wright to the director, February 1, 1932, RG 79 NPS, Region IV, Regional Wildlife Technician, Wildlife Reports, 1929–1941, accn: 82-001 (FRC 51-0102B), National parks & monuments: Yellowstone to Yosemite, container #5.

76. Colonel C. G. Thomson, Superintendent, memorandum for Chief Ranger Townsley, November 1, 1932, RG 79 NPS, Region IV, Regional Wildlife Technician, Wildlife Reports, 1929–1941, accn: 82-001 (FRC 51-0102B), National parks & monuments: Yosemite to Wind Cave, container #6.

77. Wright and Thompson, 17.

78. As cited in Pritchard, 108.

79. Roger W. Toll, Annual Report for Yellowstone National Park, 1929, 33, https://archive
.org/details/annualreportsofs001929; Roger W. Toll, Annual Report for Yellowstone National Park, 1931, 2, https://archive.org/details/annualreportsofs31unse.

80. Dixon, field notes, 1931, 177. Today in Yellowstone, it is recommended that visitors stay at least 300 feet away from bears and wolves.

81. United States Department of the Interior, National Park Service, General Information Regarding Yellowstone National Park, Wyoming, Season June to October 15, 1933, 5–6, http://npshistory.com/brochures/yell/1933.pdf.

82. Wright, Dixon, and Thompson, Fauna No. 1, 54.

83. Wright, field notes, 1932, 408.

84. Thompson, field notes, 1932, 284–85.

85. Thompson, field notes, 1932, 287. Thompson was not pleased about killing the grizzly, but she was obviously a problem. After she was shot, her cubs ran into the forest, followed by the other adult grizzlies. Thompson collected the body, then proceeded to perform a complete necropsy over the next few days, measuring every aspect of her body, skinning the body, then eventually roughing out the skeleton for preservation.

86. Thompson, field notes, 1932, 315. According to Victor Cahalane et al., "Bear-proof food caches and garbage cans" were built in Yellowstone in 1934 and replicated in other parks, yet there is no mention of their efficacy. Victor H. Cahalane, Clifford C. Presnall, and Daniel B. Beard, "Wildlife Conservation in Areas Administered by the National Park Service, 1930 to 1939," 357, http://npshistory.com/publications/wildlife/wildlife-status-1940.pdf. In Roger Toll's 1935 annual superintendent's report he mentioned that bear encounters continued, and that they had at least built "garbage disposal facilities" at Fishing Bridge, Old Faithful, and West Thumb— all sites extremely popular with tourists, and bears. Roger Toll, "Annual Report for Yellowstone National Park, 1935," 17, https://archive.org/details/annualreportsofs35unse.

87. Alice Wondrak Biel, Do (Not) Feed the Bears: The Fitful History of Wildlife and Tourists in Yellowstone (Lawrence: University of Kansas Press, 2006), 36.

88. The wildlife biologists ultimately won the bear shows debate. The spectacles didn't all stop at once, but when the United States entered World War II in December 1941—and the nation's attention was focused on the war effort, and visitation numbers plummeted in the national parks—the new director, Newton B. Drury, decided it was the right time to completely stop the shows. Not surprisingly, former director Horace Albright—the principal advocate in favor of the shows—was not pleased. Sellars, 160–61; Wondrak, 40–41; Alfred Runte, Yosemite: The Embattled Wilderness (Lincoln: University of Nebraska Press, 1990), 174; Lary M. Dilsaver and William C. Tweed, Challenge of the Big Trees: A Resource History of Sequoia and Kings Canyon National Parks (Three Rivers, CA: Sequoia Natural History Association, 1990), chap. 6.

89. George Wright to Horace Albright, March 27, 1929, RG 79 NPS, Region IV, Regional Naturalist, Wildlife Files, 1929–1940, accn: 82-001 (FRC 52-0235B), General Program and Pest Control Files, container #1.

90. Ben H. Thompson, interview with the author, Glenwood, New Mexico, October 17, 1987.

91. Harold C. Bryant and Wallace W. Atwood Jr., *Research and Education in the National Parks*, United States Department of the Interior, National Park Service, 1932, 57, https://archive .org/details/researcheducatio00brya.

92. George Wright to Joseph Grinnell, Museum of Vertebrate Zoology Archives, University of California, Berkeley, March 9, 1932.

93. Sellars, 98.

94. Wright, Dixon, and Thompson, 1.

95. Wright, Dixon, and Thompson, 10; Sellars states that efforts to study and understand American Indians' influence on "prepark conditions" did not truly begin until the late twentieth century (23).

96. See Mark David Spence, *Dispossessing the Wilderness: Indian Removal and the Making of the National Parks* (New York: Oxford University Press 1999), 5; Janet A. McDonnell, *Dispossession of the American Indian, 1887–1934* (Bloomington: Indiana University Press, 1991). The author also interviewed Paul F. Starrs, an expert on the cultural and historical geography of the American West, email to the author, July 6, 2020. For Canada, the author interviewed Nadine Spence, an Ahousaht First Nation member and executive director of Indigenous Affairs for Parks Canada, November 12, 2020. See also the Indigenous Circle of Experts, Report and Recommendations, *We Rise Together: Achieving Pathway to Canada Target 1 through the Creation of Indigenous Protected and Conserved Areas in the Spirit and Practice of Reconciliation, March 2018*, Her Majesty the Queen in Right of Canada, 2018, III, 27–28, https://www.changingtheconversa tion.ca/sites/all/images/Biodiversity%20Library/WeRiseTogetherReport.pdf.

97. Wright, field notes, Red Eagle Lake, Glacier National Park, Montana, September 5, 1931, 340.

98. Wright, Dixon, and Thompson, 100.

99. Wright and Thompson, 61. In fact, Horace Albright did have plans at one point to attempt to extend the park's eastern boundary into reservation lands. Theodore Catton, Diane Krahe, and Deirdre K. Shaw, *Protecting the Crown: A Century of Resource Management in Glacier National Park*, Rocky Mountains Cooperative Ecosystem Studies Unit, June 2011, 66, http:// npshistory.com/publications/glac/protecting-the-crown.pdf.

100. Catton, Krahe, and Shaw, 65–66. In late 1934 the reform-minded commissioner of Indian Affairs, John Collier, wrote then director of the Park Service Arno B. Cammerer that they believed it was not the proper time, yet, to start new bison herds on any reservation. The ongoing drought had devastated forage, and their "grazing lands were taxed to the capacity" by the reservations' existing cattle and sheep. John Collier to Arno B. Cammerer, September 28, 1934, RG79, National Park Service, Region IV, Regional Naturalist, 1929–1940, accn: 82-001 (FRC 52-0235B), Wildlife Files, container #4. In 2016, after years of work and preparation, the four tribes that comprise the Blackfoot Confederacy reintroduced eighty-eight bison back onto their land; https://blackfeetnation.com/iinnii-buffalo-spirit-center/.

101. Wright, Dixon, and Thompson, 2, 5.

102. Wright, Dixon, and Thompson, 6.

103. Wright, Dixon, and Thompson, *Fauna No. 1*, 148.

104. George Wright to Harold Bryant, May 8, 1933, RG 79 NPS, Region IV, Regional Naturalist,

Wildlife Files, 1929–1940, accn: 82-001 (FRC 52-0235B), General Program and Pest Control Files, container #1.

105. *Fauna No. 1* was approved "in principle" as official Park Service policy in 1933, but it wasn't until early in 1934 that it was fully approved. "If you think it would be helpful," Bryant wrote to Wright in early 1934, "to set a definite policy through a statement we shall be glad to issue it. Would it not be well for you to prepare this statement so that it will include everything that is necessary to say?" Harold Bryant to George Wright, March 5, 1934, RG 79 NPS, Region IV, Regional Naturalist, Wildlife Files, 1929–1940, accn: 82-001 (FRC 52-0235B), General Program and Pest Control Files, container #1.

106. United States Department of the Interior, Office of National Parks, Buildings and Reservations, Washington, DC, "Memorandum for Field Offices," August 25, 1933. Document held by Pamela Meléndez Wright Lloyd.

107. Lowell Sumner, "Biological Research and Management in the National Park Service: A History," *George Wright Forum* 3, no. 4 (1983): 10.

108. Wright, Dixon, and Thompson, *Fauna No. 1*, 38.

109. It is interesting to note that the previous day was when Wright sent the director his four-page memo about the status and potential recovery of the trumpeter swan. He was busy in Belton, Montana.

110. George Wright to Horace Albright, August 26, 1931, RG 79 NPS, Region IV, Regional Naturalist, Wildlife Files, 1929–1940, accn: 82-001 (FRC 52-0235B), General Program and Pest Control Files, container #1.

111. Wright to Albright, August 26, 1931.

112. Wright to Albright, August 26, 1931.

113. George Wright to Harold Bryant, September 7, 1931, RG 79 NPS, Region IV, Regional Naturalist, Wildlife Files, 1929–1940, accn: 82-001 (FRC 52-0235B), General Program and Pest Control Files, container #1.

114. Wright to Bryant, September 7, 1931.

115. Ben H. Thompson to the director, December 19, 1931, RG 79 NPS, Region IV, Regional Naturalist, Wildlife Files, 1929–1940, accn: 82-001 (FRC 52-0235B), General Program and Pest Control Files, container #1.

116. Horace M. Albright to Wild Life Survey, January 16, 1932, RG 79 NPS, Region IV, Regional Naturalist, Wildlife Files, 1929–1940, accn: 82-001 (FRC 52-0235B), General Program and Pest Control Files, container #1.

117. Harold Bryant to George Wright, September 14, 1931, RG 79 NPS, Region IV, Regional Naturalist, Wildlife Files, 1929–1940, accn: 82-001 (FRC 52-0235B), General Program and Pest Control Files, container #1.

118. Wright's new salary is roughly equivalent to $63,000 in today's dollars. And it's important to note that Wright wasn't a "former employee." He'd kept a position in the service the entire time. Also, in a Department of the Interior "Status Change" form filled out by Albright, the director states that Wright had donated $25,000 of his own money during the previous three years, or well over $400,000 in today's dollars. Documents held by Pamela Meléndez Wright Lloyd.

119. David Burner, *Herbert Hoover: A Public Life* (New York: Alfred A. Knopf, 1979), 249–58.

120. Historian James N. Gregory, in his book *American Exodus: The Dust Bowl Migration and Okie Culture in California*, details the out-migration of the "Dust Bowlers," most of whom moved west. "In no other instance was there greater or more sustained damage to the American land," wrote historian Donald Worster, *Dust Bowl* (New York: Oxford University Press, 2004),

24. The *Yearbook of Agriculture* reported that 1934 was the worst year of the drought as it extended over 75 percent of the United States. Some 35 million acres of farmland had been lost to erosion, and the topsoil of an area four times larger had been blown away by intense winds. Dust storms were so massive they traveled to New York City where they darkened the sky and then continued on out over the Atlantic. It was a time, and an unforgettable tragedy, memorably recorded in American literature, photography, and cinematography. United States Department of Agriculture, *Yearbook of Agriculture 1935* (Washington, DC: US Government Printing Office, 1935), 15, 72, https://archive.org/details/in.ernet.dli.2015.212208.

121. President Franklin D. Roosevelt's inauguration was the last to be held on March 4. The Twentieth Amendment was passed in January of 1933, moving inauguration dates up to January 20, as well as shifting the day when Congress was to begin work every year to January 4; https://blogs.loc.gov/law/2013/01/the-20th-amendment-to-the-u-s-constitution/.

122. John Meacham, "FDR and the Great Depression," Hope through History Podcast, https://podcasts.apple.com/us/podcast/hope-through-history/id1507276251?i=1000472150226.

123. The author has chosen to use CCC throughout. FDR's May 2, 1933 radio address, his second Fireside Chat, introduced the CCC. "In creating this civilian conservation corps we are killing two birds with one stone." It is a fascinating address to both read and listen to; both print and audio are here: https://millercenter.org/the-presidency/presidential-speeches/may-7 -1933-fireside-chat-2-progress-during-first-two-months.

124. Donald C. Swain, "Harold Ickes, Horace Albright, and the Hundred Days," *Pacific Historical Review* 34 (1965): 462, https://www.jstor.org/stable/3636355.

125. Donald C. Swain, "The National Park Service and the New Deal, 1933–1940," *Pacific Historical Review* 41, no. 3 (1972): 325, https://www.jstor.org/stable/3637861. Swain details how the Park Service was given more responsibility during this period and therefore more financial support. In addition to funds made available from the CCC, Park Service also received funds from the Works Progress Administration and the Public Works Administration. The service was also asked (and Albright pushed to make this happen) to take on the management of Civil War battlefields, national monuments, and the national capital parks and buildings. The Park Service's formal name was changed to "National Parks, Buildings and Reservations," which appeared on its letterhead for a short period before reverting to its original name.

126. John C. Paige, *Civilian Conservation Corps and National Park Service, 1933–1942: An Administrative History* (National Park Service, 1985), 16, https://archive.org/details/civiliancon serva00paig. By the end of the CCC program in 1942, the effort built or improved an amazing 405 state parks across the country; Ney C. Landrum, *The State Park Movement: A Critical Review* (Columbia: University of Missouri Press, 2004), 132–35. See also Anthony J. Badger, *FDR: The First Hundred Days* (New York: Hill and Wang, 2008).

127. Although it was a complicated and contentious relationship, the Park Service worked closely with the military to create the CCC camps; Paige, 6, and John A. Salmond, *The Civilian Conservation Corps, 1933–1942: A New Deal Case Study* (Durham, NC: Duke University Press, 1967), 81–86, https://archive.org/details/civilianconserva0000unse_h3g1.

128. George Wright to Mr. and Mrs. George F. Baggley, May 27, 1933, RG 79 NPS, Region IV, Regional Wildlife Technician, Wildlife Reports, 1929–1941, accn: 82-001 (FRC 51-0102B), National parks & monuments: Yellowstone to Yosemite, container #5.

129. Dixon, field notes, Sequoia National Park, June 21, 1933, 3062. Catalog #4852, held at Sequoia Kings Canyon National Parks Museum Facility, Ash Mountain, California.

130. Thompson, field notes, 1933, 368.

131. Paige, 17, 38, 41.

132. Sellars, 100.

133. Wright, field notes, 1933, 541.

134. Wright, field notes, 1932, 541.

Chapter Eight

1. In Ickes's 1943 autobiography, he wrote, "The dictionary says that a curmudgeon is 'an avaricious, grasping fellow; a churl.' I am that—and more. Besides, I am a *self-made* one"; Harold L. Ickes, *Autobiography of a Curmudgeon* (New York: Rynal & Hitchcock, 1943), 2, 4. Albright wrote that Ickes "never appreciated" Cammerer, while the new director "failed to state his views strongly"; Horace M. Albright, *The Birth of the National Park Service: The Founding Years, 1913–1933* (Salt Lake City: Howe Brothers, 1985), 315, https://archive.org/details /birthofnationalp0000albr. Donald C. Swain takes it a step further by stating that Ickes, widely recognized as acerbic, verbally abused Cammerer in front of Park Service employees on a routine basis; Donald C. Swain, *Wilderness Defender, Horace M. Albright and Conservation* (Chicago: University of Chicago Press, 1970), 250, https://archive.org/details/wildernessdefend 0000swai.

2. United States Department of the Interior, *Annual Report of the Secretary of the Interior, for the Fiscal Year Ended June 30, 1933* (Washington, DC: United States Government Printing Office, 1933), 186–87, https://archive.org/details/annualreportofse00unit_4.

3. Swain details that, due to the influx of new funds, the Park Service was "on the threshold of an unprecedented expansion of its jurisdiction and bureaucratic structure"; Swain, "The National Park Service and the New Deal, 1933–1940," *Pacific Historical Review* 41, no. 3 (1972): 314; Albright, *Birth of the National Park Service*, 298–303. The only pushback from Albright after these new responsibilities were approved was a desire to return active cemeteries, such as Arlington National Cemetery, and the Capitol Park buildings, to their previous managers. He succeeded. Swain, *Wilderness Defender*, 230.

4. For a brief but concise online history of Hyde Park, see https://www.nps.gov/articles /springwood-timeline.htm; Anna Eleanor Roosevelt, FDR's famous wife, was also a distant cousin. She was the niece of Theodore Roosevelt; see https://www.fdrlibrary.org/fdr-biography. Although FDR contracted polio in 1921 (at the age of thirty-nine) and lost the use of his legs, he remained very active and loved visiting national parks and the CCC camps when he could.

5. Douglas Brinkley, *Rightful Heritage: Franklin D. Roosevelt and the Land of America* (New York: Harper Collins, 2016), 227.

6. T. H. Watkins, *The Great Depression: America in the 1930s* (Boston, MA: Little, Brown, 1993), 309, https://archive.org/details/thegreatdepressi00watk. The Fish and Wildlife Coordination Act was also passed during this period. It authorized the secretaries of Agriculture and Commerce to collaborate with other federal agencies and states to increase the populations of mostly game species, fur-bearing animals, and fish.

7. Additionally, the president created the "Shelterbelt" project across the Great Plains to help mitigate the continuing, disastrous impacts of the Dust Bowl. Shelterbelt was a success: over 200 million trees and shrubs were planted on thirty thousand farms between 1935 and 1942; see Gerald W. Williams, *The USDA Forest Service—The First Century* (FS-650; Washington, DC: USDA Forest Service, Office of Communications, 2005), 72–73, https://www.fs.fed.us/sites/de fault/files/media/2015/06/The_USDA_Forest_Service_TheFirstCentury.pdf.

8. T. H. Beck, J. N. Darling, and A. Leopold, *Report of the President's Committee on Wild Life* (Washington, DC, Government Printing Office, 1934), v, https://archive.org/details/CAT31126980.

9. Brinkley, 227–29; "Thomas H. Beck, 70, Retired Publisher," *New York Times*, October 17, 1951, 31, https://timesmachine.nytimes.com/timesmachine/1951/10/17/issue.html.

10. United States Geological Survey, National Water Summary on Wetland Resources, US Geological Survey Water Supply Paper 2425, 1997, https://water.usgs.gov/nwsum/WSP2425/history.html.

11. Aldo Leopold, *Report on a Game Survey of the North Central States*, Sporting Arms and Ammunition Manufacturer's Institute, 1931, 5, https://archive.org/details/reportongamesurv00leoprich.

12. "'Duck for Every Puddle' Goal in Game Restoration," *New York Times*, January 7, 1934, sec. 2.2, https://timesmachine.nytimes.com/timesmachine/1934/01/07/issue.html?zoom=15.16.

13. Beck, Darling, and Leopold, 1–2, 13. Bolder yet, the committee requested the president issue an executive order to create a new position of Restoration Commissioner, to be installed directly beneath the Interior, Agriculture, and Commerce secretaries, to oversee five active directors (including of the Park Service), as well as creating a new director-level position for wildlife. FDR did not agree with their vision and this new organizational chart never became a reality. For additional reading on this dynamic time and actions on behalf of wildlife, see Theodore W. Cart, "'New Deal' for Wildlife: A Perspective on Federal Conservation Policy, 1933–40," *Pacific Northwest Quarterly* 63, no. 3 (1972): 113–20, http://www.jstor.org/stable/40489013.

14. David Leonard Lendt, "Ding: The Life of Jay Norwood Darling," Retrospective Theses and Dissertations, Iowa State Digital Repository, 6464, 1978, 132–33, https://lib.dr.iastate.edu/rtd/6464.

15. Brinkley, 279–80.

16. Arnold G. van der Valk, "Assisting Nature: Ducks, 'Ding' and DU," *Ecology, Evolution and Organismal Biology Publications*, 35 (2018): 64, https://lib.dr.iastate.edu/eeob_ag_pubs/301. Darling started his new job on March 10, just a few days after FDR approved another important waterfowl-and-habitat-related program: the Migratory Bird Hunting and Conservation Stamp Act, commonly known as the Duck Stamp program. Every hunter needed to purchase one of these stamps in order to hunt. Proceeds went to improve and purchase waterfowl habitat, mostly in or adjacent to national wildlife refuges. Darling's art adorned the first stamp. Since the program's creation, it has generated hundreds of millions of dollars and saved over six million acres of habitat: see https://www.fws.gov/program/federal-duck-stamp.

17. George Wright to the director, March 6, 1934, RG 79 NPS, Region IV, Regional Naturalist, Wildlife Files, 1929–1940, accn: 82-001 (FRC 52-0235B), General Program and Pest Control Files, container #1.

18. Wright to the director, March 6, 1934.

19. Wright to the director, March 6, 1934.

20. Wright to the director, March 6, 1934.

21. Wright to the director, March 6, 1934.

22. George Wright, letter and attached memorandum to director, National Park Service, Washington, DC, March 28, 1934, RG 79 NPS, Region IV, Regional Naturalist, Wildlife Files, 1929–1940, accn: 82-001 (FRC 52-0235B), General Program and Pest Control Files, container #1.

23. Wright, letter and attached memorandum to the director, National Park Service, March 28, 1934. When Wright wrote Cammerer and Bryant about his plans to start out the field season in the eastern parks, there was also an impetus generated by the committee's report: "In this way I

feel that we will keep abreast of the wild life restoration program with plans so comprehensive and forward-looking that those in charge of the federal program will recognize our ability to continue to handle from within the Service our own wild life administration." George Wright to the director, March 13, 1934, RG 79 NPS, Region IV, Regional Naturalist, Wildlife Files, 1929–1940, accn: 82-001 (FRC 52-0235B), General Program and Pest Control Files, container #1.

24. George Wright to the director, December 11, 1933, RG 79 NPS, Region IV, Regional Wildlife Technician, Wildlife Reports, 1929–1941, accn: 82-001 (FRC 51-0102B), National parks & monuments: Yosemite National Park, 1929–1934, container #6.

25. George Wright to the director, March 8, 1934, RG 79 NPS, Region IV, Regional Wildlife Technician, Wildlife Reports, 1929–1941, accn: 82-001 (FRC 51-0102B), National parks & monuments: Yosemite to Wind Cave, container #6.

26. Wright to the director, March 8, 1934.

27. Wright to the director, March 8, 1934.

28. Wright to the director, March 8, 1934.

29. John R. White to George Wright, March 9, 1934, RG 79 NPS, Region IV, Regional Wildlife Technician, Wildlife Reports, 1929–1941, accn: 82-001 (FRC 51-0102B), National parks & monuments: Yellowstone to Yosemite, container #5.

30. George Wright to C. A. Harwell, April 14, 1934, RG 79 NPS, Region IV, Regional Wildlife Technician, Wildlife Reports, 1929–1941, accn: 82-001 (FRC 51-0102B), National parks & monuments: Yosemite to Wind Cave, container #6.

31. FDR's daily itinerary can be viewed online at http://www.fdrlibrary.marist.edu/daybyday /resource/july-1934-2/.

32. FDR radio address at Two Medicine Chalet, Glacier National Park, https://www.nps.gov /glac/learn/historyculture/fdr-radio-address.htm.

33. National Park Service, "Park Service Bulletin" 4, no. 4 (1934): 40–43, http://npshistory .com/newsletters/courier/bulletin/v4n4.

34. National Park Service, "Park Service Bulletin," 43.

35. National Park Service, "Park Service Bulletin." 4, no. 5 (August–September): 34.

36. A. E. Demaray, Office Order No. 279, United States Department of the Interior, Washington. Document held by Pamela Meléndez Wright Lloyd; Wright and his team were responsible for two chapters in the Land Planning Committee section. The overall effort was chaired by Secretary of the Interior Ickes; other participants included Frederic A. Delano (vice chairman and FDR's uncle), most of the secretaries of FDR's cabinet, and numerous other luminaries.

37. Franklin D. Roosevelt, "The National Resources Board Is Established. Executive Order No. 6777. June 30, 1934," in *The Public Papers and Addresses of Franklin D. Roosevelt, with a Special Introduction and Explanatory Notes by President Roosevelt*, vol. 3, *The Advance of Recovery and Reform, 1934* (New York, Random House, 1938), 335, https://archive.org/details/4925383.1934.001 .umich.edu.

38. Roosevelt, "National Resources Board," 336.

39. Natural Resources Board, *A Report on National Planning and Public Works in Relation to Natural Resources and Including Land Use and Water Resources with Findings and Recommendations*, December 1, 1934, Submitted to the President in Accordance with Executive Order No. 6777, June 30, 1934 (Washington, DC: United States Government Printing Office, 1934), 144, 217, https://archive.org/details/reportonnational1934unitrich.

40. George Wright to Alden Miller, September 15, 1934, Museum of Vertebrate Zoology Archives, University of California, Berkeley.

41. Joseph Grinnell to George Wright, August 18, 1934, Museum of Vertebrate Zoology Archives, University of California, Berkeley.

42. Robert Marshall, "George M. Wright and Roger W. Toll," *Indians at Work*, Office of Indian Affairs, March 15, 1936, 5–6. For more on Bob Marshall, see https://www.wilderness.org /robert-marshall#.

43. National Conference on City Planning and the American Civic Association, *Planning Problems of City, Region, State and Nation, Twenty-Sixth National Conference* on City Planning, St. Louis, Missouri, October 22–24, 1934, 67–71, https://archive.org/details/planningproblems00natirich.

44. National Conference on City Planning, 146.

45. Conference program held by Pamela Meléndez Wright Lloyd.

46. Although many of the early national parks—designated before the Park Service itself was created in 1916—had the term wilderness in the enabling legislation, the Park Service had no official policy to manage wilderness areas. Directors Mather, Albright, and Cammerer stated, in one way or another, that what wasn't developed was essentially wilderness, and that building roads and visitor centers actually enabled other nondeveloped areas to maintain their primitive state.

47. The classic treatment of the conceptual history of American wilderness, its definition, major proponents, and eventually the efforts to save it, can be found in Roderick Frazier Nash, *Wilderness and the American Mind*, 5th ed. (New Haven, CT: Yale University Press, 2014).

48. Both Thoreau and Muir, although deceased, were popular and celebrated individuals in Wright's time, and they would be exhaustively analyzed and profiled as well. Robert Sterling Yard (1861–1945), wilderness and National Park Service advocate, writer, and cofounder of the Wilderness Society, was probably also read by Wright.

49. For an excellent primer on *Walden* and the unique person that was Thoreau, author Bill McKibben's introduction and annotations to this edition are a must: Henry David Thoreau, *Walden*, introduction and annotations by Bill McKibben (Boston: Beacon Press, 2004).

50. Henry David Thoreau, "Walking," *Atlantic Monthly* 9, no. 56 (June 1862): 662, 665–66, https://www.walden.org/wp-content/uploads/2016/03/Walking-1.pdf.

51. Dennis C. Williams, *God's Wilds: John Muir's Vision of Nature* (College Station: Texas A&M University Press, 2002).

52. Sierra Club, "Chronology (Timeline) of the Life and Legacy of John Muir," John Muir Exhibit, https://vault.sierraclub.org/john_muir_exhibit/life/chronology.aspx.

53. John Muir, *John of the Mountains*, ed. Linnie Marsh Wolfe (Boston: Houghton Mifflin, 1938), 317. The current reassessment relative to Muir's racist views on African Americans, and particularly American Indians, has been a painful but elucidating process for countless Muir devotees and the Sierra Club. As many have commented, the wilderness Muir celebrated erased the influence of American Indians. The club's executive director, Michael Brune, wrote an excellent essay in July 2020 addressing this very issue: https://www.sierraclub.org /michael-brune/2020/07/john-muir-early-history-sierra-club.

54. Joseph Grinnell and Tracy I. Storer, "Animal Life as an Asset of National Parks," *Science* 44, no. 1133 (September 15, 1916): 377, 379, http://www.jstor.org/stable/1643783. The authors also extolled the restorative virtues of wilderness that harkened back to many arguments from previous decades pertaining to physical health; time spent in wilderness "reawakened dormant faculties," "reset physical tone," and "readjusted physiological interrelations."

55. Charles Adams, "Administration of Wild Life in State and National Parks," in *Naturalist's Guide to the Americas*, ed. Victor E. Shelford, Committee on the Preservation of Natural Conditions of the Ecological Society of America (Baltimore: Williams & Wilkins, 1926), 49.

56. Nash refers to Aldo Leopold as a "prophet," as have many others. He is commonly mentioned as the "father" of wildlife management (particularly game management) and the principal advocate for wilderness, among many other accolades. There is no questioning Leopold's greatness, leadership, and longevity. However, Professor Dale McCullough of UC Berkeley, who fully acknowledges Leopold's greatness, wrote "Regrettably, fostering of legends and dogmas has come to pass." McCullough's point (and those of several other observers and environmental historians) is that there were many others during the early decades of the twentieth century who were researching, writing, and advocating for the very same things Leopold is famous for—often before or concurrently with Leopold. McCullough lists many names to fill this roster, including Joseph Grinnell, "but most of those contemporaries," states McCullough, "suffer from the lack of their own biographers. They remain obscure in the shadow cast by Leopold as illuminated by his biographers." Dale McCullough, "Of Paradigms and Philosophies: Aldo Leopold and the Search for a Sustainable Future: Growth of the Aldo Leopold Legend," presentation, Ideas Matter 1998: The Ethical Legacy of Aldo Leopold, Oregon State University, 1998, https://liberalarts.oregonstate .edu/school-history-philosophy-and-religion/ideas-matter/1998-ethical-legacy-aldo-leopold.

57. Aldo Leopold, "Last Stand of the Wilderness," *American Forests and Forest Life* 31, no. 382 (October 1925), https://www.americanforests.org/magazine/article/aldo-leopolds-the-last-stand -of-the-wilderness/.

58. American Forestry Association and the National Parks Association, *Recreation Resources of Federal Lands, Joint Committee on Recreational* Survey of Federal Lands, National Conference on Outdoor Recreation (Washington, DC, 1928), 93–97, https://hdl.handle.net/2027/mdp .39015063999166.

59. Robert Marshall, "Problem of the Wilderness," *Scientific Monthly* 30, no. 2 (February 1930): 141–48, https://www.jstor.org/stable/14646.

60. National Conference on City Planning, 70.

61. National Resources Board, 144, 217.

62. John C. Paige, *Civilian Conservation Corps and National Park Service, 1933–1942: An Administrative History* (National Park Service, 1985), 39.

63. George Wright, draft memo regarding wildlife technicians, April 1934, RG 79 NPS, Region IV, Regional Naturalist, Wildlife Files, 1929–1940, accn: 82-001 (FRC 52-0235B), General Program and Pest Control Files, container #1.

64. Wright, draft memo regarding wildlife technicians, April 1934.

65. For bureaucratic, organizational, and likely funding reasons, Wright kept to the title of "naturalist assistant" in planning documents. However, the titles "park naturalist" and "naturalist assistant" appeared to be used interchangeably over the next few years in day-to-day correspondence. George Wright to Ben Thompson, May 18, 1934, RG 79 NPS, Region IV, Regional Naturalist, Wildlife Files, 1929–1940, accn: 82-001 (FRC 52-0235B), General Program and Pest Control Files, container #1; Ben H. Thompson to the director, May 25, 1934, RG 79 NPS, Region IV, Regional Naturalist, Wildlife Files, 1929–1940, accn: 82-001 (FRC 52-0235B), General Program and Pest Control Files, container #1.

66. George Wright to the director, April 18, 1934, RG 79 NPS, Region IV, Regional Naturalist, Wildlife Files, 1929–1940, accn: 82-001 (FRC 52-0235B), General Program and Pest Control Files, container #1.

67. George Wright to Ben Thompson, July 3, 1934, RG 79 NPS, Region IV, Regional Wildlife Technician, Wildlife Reports, 1929–1941, accn: 82-001 (FRC 51-0102B), National parks & monuments: Grand Canyon to Kings Canyon, container #2.

68. Wright to Thompson, July 3, 1934.

69. Wright to Thompson, July 3, 1934.

70. Emphasis added by author. George Wright to Ben Thompson, July 18, 1934, RG 79 NPS, Region IV, Regional Naturalist, Wildlife Files, 1929–1940, accn: 82-001 (FRC 51-0102B), General Program and Pest Control Files, container #1.

71. George Wright to the director, August 8, 1934, RG 79 NPS, Region IV, Regional Wildlife Technician, Wildlife Reports, 1929–1941, accn: 82-001 (FRC 51-0102B), National parks & monuments: Grand Canyon to Kings Canyon, container #2.

72. H. C. Bryant, memorandum for George Wright, September 19, 1934, RG 79 NPS, Region IV, Regional Naturalist, Wildlife Files, 1929–1940, accn: 82-001 (FRC 51-0102B), General Program and Pest Control Files, container #1.

73. George Wright, Wildlife Division, Memorandum for Wildlife Technicians: Through the Superintendent, April 27, 1935, RG 79 NPS, Region IV, Regional Naturalist, Wildlife Files, 1929–1940, accn: 82-001 (FRC 51-0102B), Program—General, January 1, 1935–December 31, 1938, container #1; to be thorough, Wright also produced a document listing his staff, with the corresponding staff from the planning division they needed to pair with for that on-the-ground work.

74. George Wright, Wildlife Division, (Confidential) Memorandum to the Wildlife Division, June 27, 1935, RG 79 NPS, Region IV, Regional Naturalist, Wildlife Files, 1929–1940, accn: 82-001 (FRC 51-0102B), Program—General, January 1, 1935–December 31, 1938, container #1.

75. Everglades National Park was not finalized until June 20, 1947. Robert W. Blythe, *Wilderness on the Edge: A History of Everglades National Park* (Chicago: National Park Service/Organization of American Historians, 2017), 113, 130.

76. Blythe, 67.

77. Robert W. Blythe's history of the Everglades contains detailed information about Ernest Coe, as does the PhD dissertation of Chris Wilhelm, which focused on Coe and his role in saving the Everglades: *Prophet of the Glades: Ernest Coe and the Fight for Everglades National Park* (Florida State University College of Arts and Sciences, 2010). Marjory Stoneman Douglas always championed the creation of the park. She became widely known and associated with the Everglades after the publication of her classic book *The Everglades: River of Grass* (New York: Rinehart, 1947).

78. Ernest Coe to George Wright, December 1, 1935, RG 79 NPS, Region IV, Regional Wildlife Technician, Wildlife Reports, 1929–1941, accn: 82-001 (FRC 51-0102B), Proposed parks: General to White Mountain, container #8.

79. Roger Toll, "Photographs of Proposed Everglades Park," Everglades National Park Superintendent's Records, EVER 22965, series 1, subseries B, file unit 001.

80. Harold C. Bryant, "Committee Boundary Line Report," 1935, Everglades National Park Superintendent's Records, EVER 22965, series 1, subseries B, file unit 002.

81. Bryant, "Committee Boundary Line Report," 1935.

82. Jessie Crawford worked for Mr. and Mrs. Ray in Southern California. When Bee married George Wright and had her first daughter, Jessie came to live with the Wrights in Berkeley, then moved with them to Washington, DC.

83. "Wright Indorses Park Plan to Protect 'Glades Wild Life," *Miami Tribune*, January 10, 1935, 2. Article citation provided courtesy of Karen Bodding.

84. George Wright to Ernest F. Coe, January 20, 1933, RG 79 NPS, Region IV, Regional Wildlife Technician, Wildlife Reports, 1929–1941, accn: 82-001 (FRC 51-0102B), Proposed parks: General to White Mountain, container #8.

85. Anna Ickes was a Republican politician, author, and she studied American Indians in the Southwest, which led to her becoming a central and early figure for Indian rights. T. H. Watkins, *Righteous Pilgrim: The Life and Times of Harold L. Ickes, 1874–1952* (New York: Henry Holt, 1990), 203–4, 408, 530–48; for specific information on John Collier, see 530–48.

86. Park Service Bulletin, United States Department of the Interior, National Park Service, Washington, DC, vol. 5, no. 3 (April 1935): 1–2. Document held by Pamela Meléndez Wright Lloyd.

87. George Wright to Ernest Coe, April 2, 1935, RG 79 NPS, Region IV, Regional Wildlife Technician, Wildlife Reports, 1929–1941, accn: 82-001 (FRC 51-0102B), Proposed parks: General to White Mountain, container #8.

Chapter Nine

1. George Wright, memorandum for Miss Story, March 13, 1935, RG 79 NPS, Region IV, Regional Naturalist, Wildlife Files, 1929–1940, accn: 82-001 (FRC 52-0235B), Program—General, January 1, 1935–December 31, 1938, container #1. Isabelle Story is also listed as chief of the Division of Public Relations in Harlan D. Unrau and G. Frank Williss, *Administrative History: Expansion of the National Park Service in the 1930s*, prepared and published by the Denver Service Center, National Park Service, September 1983, 242, http://npshistory.com/publications/adhi-1930s-expansion.pdf.

2. "He made the offer, and the opportunities in conservation and protection of the national parks so attractive, that I immediately went to work with the National Park Service and did not finish my Ph.D. work." Lowell Sumner, Oral History Interview of Lowell and Marietta Sumner, interviewed by Herbert Evison, February 16, 1973, NPS Oral History Collection, HFCA 1817, 5. NPS Oral History Collection, HFCA 1817.

3. E. A. Kitchin, "Distributional Check-List of the Birds of Mt. Rainier National Park," *The Murrelet* 20, no. 2 (1939): 27–37, https://hdl.handle.net/2027/coo.31924062782663. More on Kitchin's life is included in his *Birds of the Olympic Peninsula: A Scientific and Popular Description of 261 Species of Birds Recorded on the Olympic Peninsula, Either as Resident, Summer Resident or in Migration, Together with Description of Their Nests and Eggs* (Port Angeles, WA: Olympic Stationers, 1949), 252–56, https://hdl.handle.net/2027/coo.31924022536266.

4. Ben Thompson to Harold Bryant, June 25, 1934, RG 79 NPS, Region IV, Regional Wildlife Technician, Wildlife Reports, 1929–1941, accn: 82-001 (FRC 51-0102B), National parks & monuments: Mt. Rainier National Park, container #4.

5. Verne E. Chatelain to Edward A. Kitchin, July 17, 1934, RG 79 NPS, Region IV, Regional Wildlife Technician, Wildlife Reports, 1929–1941, accn: 82-001 (FRC 51-0102B), National parks & monuments: Mt. Rainier National Park, container #4.

6. George Wright to Edward A. Kitchin, February 26, 1935, RG 79 NPS, Region IV, Regional Wildlife Technician, Wildlife Reports, 1929–1941, accn: 82-001 (FRC 51-0102B), National parks & monuments: Mt. Rainier National Park, container #4. Kitchin stayed at Rainier for seven years and wrote "A Distributional Check-List of the Birds of Mt. Rainier National Park." He then transferred to Olympic National Park in 1941, retiring from the Park Service in 1945 at the age of sixty-nine. Among numerous other publications, he also authored *Birds of the Olympic Peninsula*, 1949.

7. Supplies for E. A. Kitchin, Naturalist Assistant, Mt. Rainier National Park, Longmore, Washington, January 28, 1935, RG 79 NPS, Region IV, Regional Wildlife Technician, Wildlife

Reports, 1929–1941, accn: 82-001 (FRC 51-0102B), National parks & monuments: Mt. Rainier National Park, container #4; it is not clear if all field staff received similar supplies.

8. John C. Paige, *Civilian Conservation Corps and National Park Service, 1933–1942: An Administrative History* (National Park Service, 1985), 21; Unrau and Williss, 239.

9. In 1983, Lowell Sumner wrote of the division's work in 1935. "About half the time of the biological staff was spent on ecological reviews of proposed development projects; the other half was divided between wildlife management and research." Lowell Sumner, "Biological Research and Management in the National Park Service: A History," *George Wright Forum* 3, no. 4 (1983): 10.

10. As cited in Richard West Sellars, *Preserving Nature in the National Parks: A History* (New Haven, CT: Yale University Press, 1997), 103.

11. Adolph Murie to George Wright, March 26, 1935, RG 79 NPS, Region IV, Regional Wildlife Technician, Wildlife Reports, 1929–1941, accn: 82-001 (FRC 51-0102B), National parks & monuments: Grand Canyon to Kings Canyon, container #2.

12. George Wright to Charles W. Quaintance, June 15, 1935, RG 79 NPS, Region IV, Regional Wildlife Technician, Wildlife Reports, 1929–1941, accn: 82-001 (FRC 51-0102B), National parks & monuments: Lassen to Platt, container #3.

13. Adolph Murie to George Wright, July 13, 1935, RG 79 NPS, Region IV, Regional Wildlife Technician, Wildlife Reports, 1929–1941, accn: 82-001 (FRC 51-0102B), National parks & monuments: Lassen to Platt, container #3. Emphasis added by author.

14. Emphasis added. Adolph Murie, assistant wildlife supervisor, Memorandum for Mr. Thompson, acting chief, Wildlife Division, August, 1935, RG 79 NPS, Region IV, Regional Wildlife Technician, Wildlife Reports, 1929–1941, accn: 82-001 (FRC 51-0102B), National parks & monuments: General to Glacier, container #1.

15. Lowell Sumner to Ben Thompson, July 5, 1935, RG 79 NPS, Region IV, Regional Wildlife Technician, Wildlife Reports, 1929–1941, accn: 82-001 (FRC 51-0102B), National parks & monuments: Lassen to Platt, container #3.

16. Sumner to Thompson, July 5, 1935.

17. Guy D. Edwards to the director, May 7, 1934, RG 79 NPS, Region IV, Regional Wildlife Technician, Wildlife Reports, 1929–1941, accn: 82-001 (FRC 51-0102B), National parks & monuments: Yellowstone to Yosemite, container #5. The author was not able to determine the outcome of these two projects, even though the correspondence has an attached handwritten note by Wright to Thompson stating "Approved by Bryant, Wright, Johnston & we hope by Coffman." If the islands were built, then, according to trumpeter swan expert Ruth Shea, this is the first proof of artificial nesting islands constructed to help save the trumpeter swans; Shea, email to the author, February 21, 2022. It is known that at nearby Red Rock Lakes Wildlife Refuge, established in 1935, the first refuge manager, Archie V. Hull, built twenty-four artificial nesting islands there because the natural base of swan nests—partially submerged muskrat nests—was reduced due to trappers killing off the muskrat population. Hull stopped the trapping and the muskrats eventually returned. Winston E. Banko, *"The Trumpeter Swan, Its History, Habits, and Population in the United States," North American Fauna*, no. 63 (1960): 177. Ira N. Gabrielson, *Report of Chief of Bureau of Biological Survey*, United Stated Department of Agriculture, Bureau of Biological Survey, Washington, DC, June 30, 1936, 37.

18. George Wright and Ansel Hall (a Berkeley Forestry graduate) went back years to their work together in Yosemite. Hall was chief naturalist of the National Park Service from 1923 to 1930, senior naturalist and chief forester from 1930 to 1933, and chief of the Field Division from 1933 to 1937. William H. Sontag, ed., *National Park Service: The First 75 Years* (Eastern National Park &

Monument Association, produced in cooperation with the George Wright Society, 1990), 21. Wright and Thompson worked with Coffman to build out the Wildlife Division with CCC funds.

19. Joseph Grinnell and Tracy I. Storer, "Animal Life as an Asset of National Parks," *Science* 44, no. 1133 (September 15, 1916): 377–78, http://www.jstor.org/stable/1643783.

20. George M. Wright, Joseph S. Dixon, and Ben H. Thompson, *Fauna of the National Parks of the United States: A Preliminary Survey of Faunal Relations in National Parks*, Contribution of Wild Life Survey, Fauna Series No. 1 (Washington, DC: Government Printing Office, May 1933) [*Fauna No. 1*], 33. George M. Wright, "Men and Birds in Joint Occupation of National Parks," *The Condor* 35, no. 6 (1933): 217.

21. Thompson, Ben H., Memorandum for Messrs. Vint, Coffman, and Wright, August 7, 1934, RG 79 NPS, Region IV, Regional Naturalist, Wildlife Files, 1929–1940, accn: 82-001 (FRC 52-0235B), General Program and Pest Control Files, container #1.

22. Thompson, Memorandum for Messrs. Vint, Coffman, and Wright.

23. Thompson, Memorandum for Messrs. Vint, Coffman, and Wright.

24. Thompson, Memorandum for Messrs. Vint, Coffman, and Wright. Two other major projects that all divisions of the Park Service fought were the Sierra Nevada National Parks Highway, or Sierra Way, and the Colorado-Big Thompson Project. The Sierra Way road was to be built between Sequoia and Yosemite, high up on the western slope, with one version continuing to Lassen and Shasta. It was denied by the secretary of the interior after input from Wright and the service. The Colorado-Big Thompson Project proposed to transfer water from the western slopes of the Rocky Mountains, through Rocky Mountain National Park via a tunnel, to the eastern slope. The Park Service eventually lost this battle and the project was completed in the 1940s. Sierra Way: http://npshistory.com/publications/proposed-parks/ca-sierra-way.pdf; Colorado-Big Thompson Project: https://www.nps.gov/parkhistory/online_books/romo/adhi8.htm.

25. George Wright to E. Raymond Hall Museum of Vertebrate Zoology, Berkeley, April 19, 1934. Museum of Vertebrate Zoology Archives, University of California, Berkeley.

26. George Wright, memorandum for Miss Story, March 13, 1935, RG 79 NPS, Region IV, Regional Naturalist, Wildlife Files, 1929–1940, accn: 82-001 (FRC 52-0235B), Program—General, January 1, 1935–December 31, 1938, container #1.

27. *Fauna No. 1* cost $1,182 to produce and one thousand copies were printed.

28. Dixon was occupied in Sequoia, seasonally managing the Yosemite Field School of Natural History and concentrating on his own writing projects. *Fauna No. 2* was printed in the same format and style as *Fauna No. 1*, with 127 photographs spread out over 142 pages. Its cover was graced by a beautiful etching of a trumpeter swan.

29. They also thanked Grinnell and the Museum of Vertebrate Zoology, Bryant, and Toll for their continued assistance and support of the Wildlife Division's work.

30. George M. Wright and Ben H. Thompson, *Fauna of the National Parks of the United States, Wildlife Management in the National Parks*, Contribution of Wildlife Division, Fauna Series No. 2 (Washington, DC: Government Printing Office, July 1935) [*Fauna No. 2*], 3.

31. Wright and Thompson, 3.

32. George Wright, in Wright and Thompson, 25.

33. Wright and Thompson, 27.

34. Wright and Thompson, 39.

35. Wright and Thompson, 72, 85.

36. In the winter of 1934–35, "this reduction was accomplished through live shipments of 375 head, hunters kills amounting to 2,567 head, slaughtering of 223 head within the park, and 100

miscellaneous deaths." Roger W. Toll, *Annual Report for Yellowstone National Park*, 1935, 13–14. https://archive.org/details/annualreportsofs35unse. The numbers for 1935–36 can be found in the superintendent's report for fiscal year 1936, 18–19, https://archive.org/details/annualreportsof s36unse.

37. Kendeigh provides background information on research reserves and lists them by park with brief descriptions. Sellars gives an overview of the reserves, why they were problematic, and their ultimate status. Sumner states that the reserve concept continued until approximately 1940, but interest waned due to World War II. S. Charles Kendeigh, "Research Areas in the National Parks, January 1942," *Ecology* 23, no. 2 (1942): 236–38, https://www.jstor.org/stable/1931092; Lowell Sumner, "Biological Research and Management in the National Park Service: A History," *George Wright Forum* 3, no. 4 (1983): 10–11; Sellars, 109–12.

38. A more toned-down version of the lecture was presented at the Interior Department in Washington, DC, on December 19, 1935. Original presentations and citation are held by Pamela Meléndez Wright Lloyd.

39. George Wright, "Some Proposed National Parks in Relation to Conservation of Local Mammals." A program from the meeting and Wright's original presentation are held by Pamela Meléndez Wright Lloyd. Not all of Wright's biologists were able to make to the trip to Pittsburgh, so Wright or Victor Cahalane read many of the papers. "Seventeenth Annual Meeting of the American Society of Mammalogists," *Journal of Mammalogy* 16, no. 3 (1935): 234–41, http://www .jstor.org/stable/1374454.

40. George M. Wright, "Bootstraps of Wildlife Conservation," delivered before the National Association of Audubon Societies, New York City, October 29, 1925. Wright's original presentation text and a convention program are held by Pamela Meléndez Wright Lloyd.

41. John Swansburg, "The Self-Made Man, The Story of America's Most Pliable, Pernicious, Irrepressible Myth," *Slate*, September 29, 2014.

42. Wright, "Bootstraps of Wildlife Conservation."

43. Grinnell and Storer, 377.

44. Wright, "Bootstraps of Wildlife Conservation."

45. The Wilderness Society was created in January 1935 by Robert Marshall, Harold C. Anderson, Harvey Broome, Bernard Frank, Aldo Leopold, Benton MacKaye, Ernest Oberholtzer, and Robert Sterling Yard; see http://www.wilderness.org. William Cronon, foreword to Paul S. Sutter, *Driven Wild: How the Fight against Automobiles Launched the Modern Wilderness Movement* (Seattle: University of Washington Press, 2002), xi–xii.

46. George Greenfield, "Wood, Field, and Stream," *New York Times*, October 26, 1935, 21, https://nyti.ms/3aMUcEp.

47. FDR's inaugural address: https://www.archives.gov/education/lessons/fdr-inaugural; FDR's Good Neighbor Policy: Franklin D. Roosevelt, *The Public Papers and Addresses of Franklin D. Roosevelt*, vol. 5, *The People Approve, 1936* (New York: Random House, 1938), 287, https:// archive.org/details/4925988.1936.001.umich.edu; William E. Leuchtenburg, "Franklin D. Roosevelt: Foreign Affairs," Miller Center, University of Virginia, https://millercenter.org/president /fdroosevelt/foreign-affairs; Richard D. Heideman, "Legalizing Hate: The Significance of the Nuremberg Laws and the Post-War Nuremberg Trials," *International and Comparative Law Review*, Loyola Law School, 2017, http://digitalcommons.lmu.edu/ilr/vol39/iss1/2; Neutrality Act, war and peace: Franklin D. Roosevelt, *Public Papers and Addresses*, vol. 4, *The Court Disapproves, 1935* (New York: Random House, 1938), 345–46, https://archive.org/details/publicpa persaddr0004unse; Roosevelt, *Public Papers and Addresses*, vol. 5, *The People Approve*, 285–92.

48. Arno Cammerer to Jay Darling, February 19, 1935, RG 79 NPS, Region IV, Regional Naturalist, Wildlife Files, 1929–1940, accn: 82-001 (FRC 52-0235B), General Program and Pest Control Files, container #1. Relations did improve between the two services, but Wright bristled when he learned of a Biological Survey employee trapping near Wind Cave National Park and killing a cross-section of wildlife (nearby Biological Survey lands were being transferred to Park Service at the time). He lodged a complaint to Darling. "The advisability of this generalized type of control in such an area seems to me to be mighty questionable. It would appear to be not only unnecessary, but actually unwise." Wright to Darling, June 15, 1935, RG 79 NPS, Region IV, Regional Naturalist, Wildlife Files, 1929–1940, accn: 82-001 (FRC 52-0235B), General Program and Pest Control Files, container #1.

49. Ben H. Thompson, interview with the author, Glenwood, New Mexico, October 17, 1987.

50. George Wright to acting superintendent, Yellowstone National Park, April 2, 1935. Museum of Vertebrate Zoology Archives, University of California, Berkeley. By 1940 an estimated 212 swans thrived across Yellowstone National Park, Red Rock Lakes Wildlife Refuge, and a few in Oregon. Department of the Interior, Information Service, "Rare Trumpeter Swan Increases," September 23, 1940, https://www.fws.gov/sites/default/files/documents/historic-news -releases/1940/19400923.PDF. Trumpeter swan expert Ruth Shea estimates, based on the latest census data and extrapolation, that the 2022 population of swans in North America (adults and cygnets) could have totaled some 125,000 birds; email to the author, February 21, 2022.

51. "The National Parks Program!" May 4, 1935, 3:15 to 3:45 p.m., National Broadcasting Company hook-up, Washington, DC. Transcript held by Pamela Meléndez Wright Lloyd.

52. George Wright to Joseph Grinnell, May 13, 1935, Museum of Vertebrate Zoology Archives, University of California, Berkeley. The Red Rock Lakes Migratory Waterfowl Refuge, as it is called today, consists of 51,386 acres, with an additional 23,806 acres of adjoining conservation easements; US Fish and Wildlife Service, https://fws.gov/refuge/red-rock-lakes. In the fall of 1935, Ding Darling resigned from the Biological Survey.

53. George Wright to Harold Bryant, March 17, 1933, RG 79 NPS, Region IV, Regional Wildlife Technician, Wildlife Reports, 1929–1941, accn: 82-001 (FRC 51-0102B), National parks & monuments: Yellowstone to Yosemite, container #5.

54. Thomson had been in charge of Yosemite since 1929, and White cared for Sequoia since 1920. They had both been through the battle for Kings Canyon many times.

55. C. G. Thomson to the director, June 13, 1935, RG 79 NPS, Region IV, Regional Wildlife Technician, Wildlife Reports, 1929–1941, accn: 82-001 (FRC 51-0102B), National parks & monuments: Grand Canyon to Kings Canyon, container #2.

56. Arno Cammerer to Francis P. Farquhar, June 3, 1935, RG 79 NPS, Region IV, Regional Wildlife Technician, Wildlife Reports, 1929–1941, accn: 82-001 (FRC 51-0102B), National parks & monuments: Grand Canyon to Kings Canyon, container #2. George and Bee Wright, their girls, and Jessie had all moved back into their Berkeley house after the "year's assignment" referred to by Cammerer.

57. Wright, Dixon, and Thompson, *Fauna No. 1*, 131.

58. Robert L. Lipman, "The 1935 Outing," *Sierra Club Bulletin* 21, no. 1 (February 1936): 35. Article provided by Therese Dunn, librarian, William E. Colby Memorial Library, Sierra Club, Oakland, California.

59. George Wright to the director, July 26, 1935, RG 79 NPS, Region IV, Regional Wildlife Technician, Wildlife Reports, 1929–1941, accn: 82-001 (FRC 51-0102B), National parks & monuments: Grand Canyon to Kings Canyon, container #2.

60. Personnel Management Documents, April 22, 1935, Demaray memo for the secretary, Department of Interior, Change of Headquarters Notification. Document held by Pamela Meléndez Wright Lloyd.

61. George Wright to Joseph Grinnell, September 25, 1935, Museum of Vertebrate Zoology Archives, University of California, Berkeley.

62. George M. Wright to Ansel Adams, September 10, 1935, RG 79 NPS, Region IV, Regional Wildlife Technician, Wildlife Reports, 1929–1941, accn: 82-001 (FRC 51-0102B), National parks & monuments: Grand Canyon to Kings Canyon, container #2.

63. George Wright to John H. White, December 19, 1935, RG 79 NPS, Region IV, Regional Wildlife Technician, Wildlife Reports, 1929–1941, accn: 82-001 (FRC 51-0102B), National parks & monuments: Grand Canyon to Kings Canyon, container #2.

Chapter Ten

1. Lowell Sumner, "Biological Research and Management in the National Park Service: A History," *George Wright Forum* 3, no. 4 (1983): 9.

2. Beatrice Newcomer to Mrs. N. L. Ackley (Jane Ray), January 22, 1936. Document held by Pamela Meléndez Wright Lloyd.

3. Oliver Thompson, conversation with the author, November 27, 2021; Jane Ray's license, #7591, was issued on August 31, 1930, and she became a charter member of the prestigious Ninety-Nines, an organization formed in 1929 comprised of the first ninety-nine women in the United States to earn their wings, which included Amelia Earhart.

4. Newcomer to Ackley, January 22, 1936.

5. Conrad L. Wirth, *Parks, Politics, and the People* (Norman: University of Oklahoma Press, 1980), 118; John C. Paige, *Civilian Conservation Corps and National Park Service, 1933–1942: An Administrative History* (National Park Service, 1985), 48.

6. Newcomer to Ackley, January 22, 1936.

7. Harlan D. Unrau and G. Frank Williss, *Administrative History: Expansion of the National Park Service in the 1930s*, prepared and published by the Denver Service Center, National Park Service, September 1983, 254–56.

8. Horace M. Albright, Memorandum for Director Cammerer, "National Park Service Regionalization," February 19, 1936, NARA College Park, RG79, Expansion of the National Park System in the 1930s, box 1, folder 99. A copy of this memo was provided to the author by NPS historian Richard West Sellars, January 31, 2001. By August 1937, the Park Service had settled on four regions, roughly East, Central (but including Montana, Wyoming, and Colorado), Southwest (including Oklahoma and Arkansas), and West; Unrau and Williss, 260.

9. Newcomer to Ackley, January 22, 1936.

10. An original program for this conference is held by Pamela Meléndez Wright Lloyd. The proceedings from this conference were printed in late 1936: Harlean James, ed., *American Planning and Civic Annual* (1936), 13–20, https://archive.org/details/americanplanning07amerrich.

11. The original title to Wright's lecture was "Standards of a National Park System." Document held by Pamela Meléndez Wright Lloyd. James apparently expanded the title in the published proceedings in order, perhaps, to fit more precisely into the session's title; James, 21–25.

12. George M. Wright, "The Philosophy of Standards of a National Park System," in James, *American Planning and Civic Annual*, 24.

13. George M. Wright, "The Philosophy of Standards for National Parks," in James, *American Planning and Civic Annual*, 24.

14. Ben H. Thompson, "Wilderness," in James, *American Planning and Civic Annual*, 72–75.

15. Thompson, "Wilderness," in James, *American Planning and Civic Annual*, 75.

16. Roger W. Toll, "Wilderness and Wildlife Administration in Yellowstone," in James, *American Planning and Civic Annual*, 65–72; C. G. Thomson, "Kings River National Park—A Good Business Project," in James, *American Planning and Civic Annual*, 85–87; John R. White, "Wilderness Policies," in James, *American Planning and Civic Annual*, 34–38.

17. George M. Wright, "Wildlife in National Parks," in James, *American Planning and Civic Annual*, 58–62.

18. Wright, "Wildlife in National Parks," 58.

19. Mary Street Alinder and Andreas Gray Stillman, eds., *Ansel Adams: Letters and Images, 1916–1984* (Boston: Little, Brown, 1988), 80–81.

20. Ansel Adams to Virginia Adams, January 19, 1936, Center for Creative Photography, University of Arizona, Ansel Adams Archive.

21. James, 76–85; a small 12″ × 8″ print of *Peak above Woods Lake* was given to Wright by Adams and is held by Pamela Meléndez Wright Lloyd. On the back of the print, in Adams's distinctive writing, is "Kings River Canyon Proposal, National Park. Sierra Club, Woods Lake, 1935." This photograph was also printed by the Sierra Club: Robert L. Lipman, "The 1935 Outing," *Sierra Club Bulletin* 21, no. 1 (February 1936): plate 15.

22. Ansel Adams, letter to Virginia Adams, January 24, 1936, Center for Creative Photography, University of Arizona: Ansel Adams Archive; Senator Johnson was from California. Eugene Meyer was the owner of the *Washington Post* newspaper. The 1936 Kings River Canyon National Park bill failed, but Adams went on to published the Kings Canyon images as part of his book, *Sierra Nevada: The John Muir Trail*, in 1938. Copies were sent to FDR, Ickes, and Cammerer, among others, and the books proved to be effective lobbying tools (something the club would do with great effect in future park battles).

23. North American Wildlife Conference, *Wildlife Restoration and Conservation*, proceedings of the North American Wildlife Conference called by President Franklin D. Roosevelt, Mayflower Hotel, Washington, DC, February 3–7, 1936, 5, https://archive.org/details/wildliferestorat00nortrich.

24. North American Wildlife Conference, 16.

25. A unique feature of the meeting, borne out in the proceedings, is that all presentations and extensive discussions were recorded and transcribed. This includes disagreements as well as some questionable humor.

26. North American Wildlife Conference, 236–39.

27. George Wright, "The National Parks System in Relation to National Wildlife Restoration," *Wildlife Restoration and Conservation*, Proceedings of the North American Wildlife Conference, called by President Franklin D. Roosevelt, Mayflower Hotel, Washington, DC, February 3–7, 1936, 238, https://archive.org/details/wildliferestorat00nortrich. Wright's original presentation held by Pamela Meléndez Wright Lloyd.

28. *New York Times*, "Wild Life Groups Unite in One Body," February 6, 1936, 4, https://nyti.ms/3tVAfEa; George Greenfield, "Wood, Field and Stream," *New York Times*, February 10, 1936, 24, https://nyti.ms/2ZgLkl8.

Chapter Eleven

1. Many books have been written about the history and ecology of the Big Bend region. The impressively thorough NPS administrative history of the region is a key source: Michael Welsh, *Landscape of Ghosts, River of Dreams: An Administrative History of Big Bend National Park* (National Park Service, 2002), http://npshistory.com/publications/bibe/adhi-2008.pdf. Another excellent read is John Jameson, *The Story of Big Bend National Park* (Austin: University of Texas Press, 1996), and Big Bend National Park's website is rich with information: https://www.nps.gov/bibe/index.htm.

2. Welsh, 20; the NPS has an informative profile of E. E. Townsend on its Big Bend website, https://www.nps.gov/bibe/learn/historyculture/eetownsend.htm.

3. Roger Toll, cited in Welsh, 24.

4. George M. Wright, Memorandum for Cammerer, Demaray, Wirth, April 10, 1935, RG 79 NPS, Region IV, Regional Wildlife Technician, Wildlife Reports, 1929–1941, accn: 82-001 (FRC 51-0102B), National parks & monuments: General to Glacier, container #1. Cammerer wrote back that concerning "the idea of naming the new Texas park project the Rio Grande National Park. . . . I am not willing, at this late date, to make any changes."

5. Ben Thompson to the director, April 18, 1934, RG79 NPS Region IV, Regional Wildlife Technician, Wildlife Reports, 1929–1941, accn: 82-001 (FRC 51-0102B), National parks & monuments: General to Glacier, container #1; Welsh, 29.

6. Conrad Wirth, telegram to Roger Toll, June 29, 1936, RG 79, Records of Roger W. Toll, 1928–1936, box 9, folder: Texas, Big Bend.

7. Arno B. Cammerer, memorandum for the secretary, December 31, 1935. Document held by Pamela Meléndez Wright Lloyd.

8. Carroll H. Wegemann, "Diary of a Trip from Alpine, Texas, to the Big Bend and Old Mexico with the International Park Commission," RG79 NPS CCF 1933–49, Big Bend 207, box 826, file: Report, Carroll H. Wegemann, 1.

9. See Wegemann.

10. To learn more about the amazing but not well-known career of George Grant, and to view many of his beautiful photographs, see Ren Davis and Helen Davis, *Landscapes for the People: George Alexander Grant, First Chief Photographer of the National Park Service* (Athens: University of Georgia Press, 2015).

11. Welsh, 15; Big Bend National Park, "Johnson's Ranch," https://www.nps.gov/bibe/learn/historyculture/johnsonsranch.htm.

12. Big Bend National Park, "Chata Sada," https://www.nps.gov/bibe/learn/historyculture/chatasada.htm; Wegemann, 15; Roger W. Toll, Itinerary, NARA Archives II, Central Classified Files 1907–1949, file 0-32, part 3, box 822, entry 10, RG 79, 4.

13. Toll, Itinerary, 5; Wegemann was referring to what is known today as the Sierra Del Carmen, or Maderas del Carmen, now a biosphere reserve (dedicated in 2006). He also uses an older name, the Fronteriza Range.

14. Wegemann, 22.

15. Wegemann, 26.

16. Today San Carlos, Chihuahua, is known as Manuel Benavides.

17. Toll, Itinerary, 5.

18. A few years later, McDougall recalled that Wright was very excited about the excursions along the border because "he expected to get a liberal education concerning the desert vegetation."

Proceedings of the Second Park Naturalists Conference held at Grand Canyon National Park, November 13–17, 1940, 303, http://npshistory.com/series/symposia/pn/2/park_naturalists.pdf.

19. Marguerite Toll, letter to Ben Thompson, March 13, 1936. "Chapo" (not "Chappo") does mean "shorty," and it is often used in Mexican culture as an endearment for a short, and often tough, person. The nickname was given to Wright by his Mexican colleagues. Document held by Pamela Meléndez Wright Lloyd.

20. Oral History Interview of Walter B. McDougall, interviewed by S. Herbert Evison, March 11, 1936, tape no. 169, series 2: S. Herbert Evison's National Park Service Oral History project, 1952–99 (bulk dates: 1962–1978), subseries B: Interview Transcripts, 1958–78.

21. Arno B. Cammerer, Memorandum to the Service Friends of Roger Toll and George Wright, February 26, 1936, Museum of Vertebrate Zoology Archives, University of California, Berkeley.

22. Harold L. Ickes, Secretary of the Interior. Document held by Pamela Meléndez Wright Lloyd.

23. Joseph Dixon to Jay Darling, March 12, 1936, Museum of Vertebrate Zoology Archives, University of California, Berkeley.

24. Harold Bryant to Joseph Grinnell, February 29, 1936, Museum of Vertebrate Zoology Archives, University of California, Berkeley.

25. Carl P. Russell to Joseph Grinnell, February 29, 1936, Museum of Vertebrate Zoology Archives, University of California, Berkeley.

26. Bee Wright to Marguerite Toll, n.d., Roger W. Toll Papers, CONS220 Conservation Collection, Denver Public Library, FF68: Toll, Marguerite, Correspondence received.

27. Ansel Adams to Ben Thompson. Document held by Pamela Meléndez Wright Lloyd.

28. Margaret Sabin (NPS stenographer, Washington, DC) letter to Marguerite Toll, Roger W. Toll Papers, CONS220 Conservation Collection, Denver Public Library, FF68: Toll, Marguerite Correspondence received; W. F. Ray, letter to Ben H. Thompson, March 24, 1936. Document held by Pamela Meléndez Wright Lloyd.

29. Roger W. Toll Papers, CONS220 Conservation Collection, Denver Public Library. FF68; Toll, Marguerite, Correspondence received.

30. George M. Wright to Dr. MacFarland, n.d. Document held by Pamela Meléndez Wright Lloyd.

31. Ben H. Thompson to Dr. F. M. MacFarland, March 21, 1936. Document held by Pamela Meléndez Wright Lloyd.

32. Robert Marshall, "George M. Wright and Roger W. Toll," *Indians At Work*, Office of Indian Affairs, March 15, 1936, 5–6.

Chapter Twelve

1. Lowell Sumner, Oral History Interview of Lowell and Marietta Sumner, interviewed by Herbert Evison, February 16, 1973, NPS Oral History Collection, HFCA 1817, 7.

2. Lowell Sumner, "Biological Research and Management in the National Park Service: A History," *George Wright Forum* 3, no. 4 (1983): 14.

3. Richard West Sellars, *Preserving Nature in the National Parks: A History* (New Haven, CT: Yale University Press, 1997), 148.

4. Victor H. Cahalane, Clifford C. Presnall, and Daniel B. Beard, "Wildlife Conservation in Areas Administered by the National Park Service, 1930 to 1939," 357, http://npshistory.com/publications/wildlife/wildlife-status-1940.pdf.

5. Sumner, "Biological Research and Management," 16.

6. Marietta Sumner, George Collins, George Sprugel, O. L. Wallis, and R. Linn. "Remembering Lowell Sumner, 7 December 1907–1 October 1989," *George Wright Forum* 6, no. 4 (1990): 36–37.

7. A. Starker Leopold, Aldo Leopold's son, chaired the committee. A. Starker Leopold et al., *Wildlife Management in the National Parks* (Washington, DC: National Park Service, 1963), http://npshistory.com/publications/leopold_report.pdf.

8. William J. Robbins et al., *A Report by the Advisory Committee to the National Park Service on Research*, National Academy of Sciences—National Research Council (Washington, DC, 1963), http://npshistory.com/publications/robbins.pdf.

9. See, for example, *Predator and Rodent Control in the United States* (1964), also by Leopold and colleagues, and *Predator Control* (1971), by noted botanist and ecologist Stanley A. Cain and collaborators (Cain served on several of the committees that produced reports).

10. *George Wright Forum* 1, no. 1 (1981): 1.

11. National Park Service, press release, "Young Scholars Help National Park Service Tackle Climate Change: George Meléndez Wright Programs Premiere This Summer," July 1, 2010, https://www.legistorm.com/stormfeed/view_rss/277568/organization/82250/title/young-scholars-help-national-park-service-tackle-climate-change-george-melendez-wright-programs-premiere-this-summer.html.

12. G. W. Schuurman, C. Hawkins Hoffman, D. N. Cole, D. J. Lawrence, J. M. Morton, D. R. Magness, A. E. Cravens, S. Covington, R. O'Malley, and N. A. Fisichelli, *Resist-Accept-Direct (RAD)—A Framework for the 21st-Century Natural Resource Manager*, Natural Resource Report NPS/NRSS/CCRP/NRR—2020/ 2213, National Park Service, Fort Collins, Colorado, 2020, https://doi.org/10.36967/nrr-2283597.

13. Jerry Emory and Nancy J. Russell, "A Visionary's Lens on Wildlife and Parks Revealed: George Meléndez Wright and the National Park Service's Wildlife Division Photographs," *Parks Stewardship Forum* 37, no. 3 (2021), http://dx.doi.org/10.5070/P537354742.

14. Keep Big Bend Wild, https://keepbigbendwild.wordpress.com.

15. George Wright to the director, August 8, 1934, RG 79 NPS, Region IV, Regional Wildlife Technician, Wildlife Reports, 1929–1941, accn: 82-001 (FRC 51-0102B), National parks & monuments: Grand Canyon to Kings Canyon, container #2.

16. George Wright, field notes, Carlsbad, New Mexico, April 26, 1931, 226.

Epilogue

1. Ben H. Thompson, interview with the author, Glenwood, New Mexico, October 17, 1987; all quotes within this epilogue are from this interview.

Index

Page numbers in italics refer to images.

fauna: and predator control, 87–88; primitive, 118; pristine, 44, 46, 115, 134, 139, 158, 211n4, 213n19; protection of, 134; restoration of in national parks, 44, 134; as spectacle for park tourists, xiii. *See also* wildlife

Fauna No. 1 wildlife survey (Wright, Dixon, and Thompson), 63, 117–19, 123, 148, 155–56, 165, 168, 171, 208n4, 211n4, 214n21, 221n48, 235n20, 235n27; approved as official NPS policy (1933/1934), 225n105; authorship of, 114–15; on bears, 112; on boundary issues, 106; challenges and questions posed in, 156; concerns and recommendations in, 191; and fauna protection, 134; as first wildlife survey of its kind, ix; as landmark document that proposed truly radical departure from earlier practices, 91, 117; as manual regarding park wildlife and its management, 114; out of print, 191; as pioneering publication, ix; policies provided/suggested, 118, 124, 131–33; praise of, 123; on restoration and perpetuation, 134; suggested policies approved, 118, 225n105; on trees as bird habitats, 155; and wildlife restoration policies, 131–33; as working bible for all park biologists, 114–19, 191. *See also* Wildlife Survey (1930–33)

Fauna No. 2 wildlife survey (Wright and Thompson), 156–59, 168, 171, 191–92, 212n1, 219n28, 220n44, 235n28, 235n30. *See also* Wildlife Survey (1930–33)

Fauna of the National Parks of the United States, Wildlife Management in the National Parks, Fauna Series No. 2, 1935. See *Fauna No. 2* wildlife survey (Wright and Thompson)

Fauna of the National Parks of the United States: A Preliminary Survey of Faunal Relations in National Parks, Fauna Series No. 1, 1933. See *Fauna No. 1* wildlife survey (Wright, Dixon, and Thompson)

FDR. *See* Roosevelt, Franklin D.

Fechner, Robert, 122, 152

field notes, xiii–xv, 28–29, 43, 50–51, 58, 69–70, 125; Grinnellian System, xiv, 16–17, 151, 168; and photography, 18

field studies, fieldwork, trips, 3, 8–9, 11, 20–30, 51–55, 60, 62, 91, 196, 207n17; principal sites (1926–36), xvi

Finman, Marshall, 89

Fish and Wildlife Coordination Act, 129, 227n6

Fish and Wildlife Service, 191

Flynn, Joe, 27

Forest History Society, 12, 203n6

forestry: and conservation, 12–13, 203n6; and logging industry, 13–14; scientific, 13

forests. *See* national forests

Forest Service. *See* United States Forest Service

Fort Jefferson National Monument (Fla.), 146

Fox, George, 18

Frank, Bernard, 236n45

FWCA. *See* Fish and Wildlife Coordination Act

FWS. *See* Fish and Wildlife Service

Gabrielson, Ira N., 175

game birds, 78, 130

game management, 104, 107, 120, 135, 227n6, 231n56

Game Management (Leopold), 130

game preserves and refuges, 34, 63–64, 81, 83, 216n75

General Grant National Park (Calif.), 34, 77, 208n5. *See also* Sequoia & Kings Canyon National Parks (Calif.)

General Wildlife Federation, 176

George Meléndez Wright Wilderness Area (Big Bend, proposed), 193

George M. Wright Hall (Schoodic Institute), 192–93

George Wright Society, x, 192, 197

Glacier National Park (Mont.), 23–24, 72, 91, 94–96, 98, 108, 110, 116–17, 119–20, 134–35, 153, 170, 224n99; Swan Lake, 95–96

global warming. *See* climate change

Godfrey, William (Bill), 37, 39, 40, 80–81, 89–90

golden eagles, 40–42

Golden Gate Audubon Society (Berkeley, Calif.), 201n3

Golden Gate Park (San Francisco, Calif.), 8

Goldman, E. A., 64, 88

gophers, 108

Grand Canyon National Monument (Ariz.), 8, 61–62, 213n13

Grand Canyon National Park (Ariz.), xvi, 25, 36, 60–65, 81–86, 89–90, 99, 107–8, 123, 143–44, 150, 158, 213n7, 213n13; Kaibab Plateau forests, 60–61, 82; overgrazing in, 60–61, 84, 100; pronghorn antelope, Indian Garden, 82–84, 83

Grand Teton National Park (Wyo.), xvi, 91, 100, 105, 152–53, 221n54

Grant, George A., 179, 240n10

Graves, Henry S., 13

Great Depression (1929–1939), 24, 55, 79, 121, 131, 134–35, 141–42

Great Dismal Swamp (Va.-N.C.), 141

great horned owls, 95

Great Sand Dunes National Monument (Colo.), 221n54

Greeley, William B., 13–14

Green Mountains (Vt.), 141

Gregory, James N., 225n120

Grinnell, Joseph, xiv, 2–3, 30–31, 33, 37, 45–48, 51, 98, 108–9, 136, 150, 160, 163, 207–8n31, 222n72, 230n54, 231n56; academic lineage, 16; Alaska fieldwork, 21, 26; and conservation biology, 17; and MVZ, 31, 115, 204n22; PhD dissertation,